The Complete Idiot's Refer...

Tips for Getting Starte...

1. Inform the staff at your hospital or birth cent... ...y... ...e chosen to breastfeed.

2. Keep your use of pain medication during childbirth at a minimum.

3. Put your baby to your breast within the first hour after birth. If your baby doesn't show an interest, use skin-to-skin contact and try about a half an hour later.

4. Holding your breast, touch your nipple to your baby's lips. When its mouth is open wide, pull your baby in close to allow a latch-on.

5. Your baby's lips should flare outward and cover most of your areola. You will feel the tongue stroke or massage the milk sinuses of your breast along with a good tug. Colostrum is the first milk available with first feedings. Its small quantity amounts to big nourishment!

6. Let your baby suckle your breast until it is released or your baby falls asleep.

7. Burp your baby after a feeding and try to offer your other breast. If baby declines, it's okay. Offer this breast next feeding.

8. Frequent feedings are typical. A breastfeeding baby suckles at least 8 to 12 feedings each day for the first couple of weeks.

Positive Posture and Positions

The proper position of your baby while suckling helps reduce soreness and uncomfortable breastfeeding. Use several pillows and a supportive chair or couch. Raise up your lap with a stool or floor pillow. Try several of these positions:

- ➤ Cradle hold
- ➤ Football hold
- ➤ Side-lying hold
- ➤ Cross-cradle hold

Please return to:
Breastfeeding Support Group
Salisbury City Children's Centre
24 St Edmunds Church Street
SALISBURY SP1 1EF
01722 323208

Breastfeeding S.O.S.

➤ You don't experience any breast changes during your pregnancy.

➤ Your milk volume has not increased by your fifth day after delivery.

➤ You can't hear swallowing while your baby suckles at your breast.

➤ After your milk volume increases, your baby wets fewer than three diapers or passes fewer than two bowel movements each day.

➤ Nipple soreness or breast pain persists and becomes worse.

➤ After the fifth day, your baby is very sleepy and will not awaken on its own.

➤ Maternal instinct tells you that something is not right.

Breast Milk Storage

Freshly Expressed		
Room temperature	6–10 hours	65°–72°F (18°–22°C)
Refrigerator	5–7 days	32°–39°F (0°–4°C)
Frozen		
Freezer	3–4 months	Variable temperature
Deep freezer	6+ months	Variable temperature
Thawed		
Refrigerator	24 hours	32°–39°F (0°–4°C)

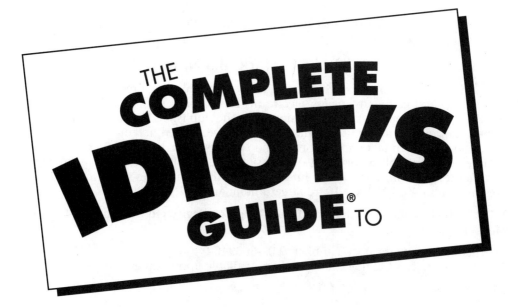

THE

COMPLETE
IDIOT'S
GUIDE® TO

Breastfeeding

by Anne P. Mark, B.S.N., R.N., I.B.C.L.C.

alpha
books

Macmillan USA, Inc.
201 West 103rd Street
Indianapolis, IN 46290

A Pearson Education Company

I dedicate this book to my daughters, Sonja and Sophie, who really taught me how to breastfeed.

Copyright © 2001 by Anne P. Mark, B.S.N, R.N., I.B.C.L.C.

International Standard Book Number: 0-02-863948-0
Library of Congress Catalog Card Number: Available upon request.

03 02 01   8 7 6 5 4 3 2 1

Interpretation of the printing code: The rightmost number of the first series of numbers is the year of the book's printing; the rightmost number of the second series of numbers is the number of the book's printing. For example, a printing code of 01-1 shows that the first printing occurred in 2001.

Printed in the United States of America

Publisher
Marie Butler-Knight

Product Manager
Phil Kitchel

Managing Editor
Cari Luna

Acquisitions Editors
Susan Zingraf
Mike Sanders

Development Editor
Joan D. Paterson

Production Editor
JoAnna Kremer

Copy Editor
Jan Zunkel

Illustrator
Jody P. Schaeffer

Cover Designers
Mike Freeland
Kevin Spear

Book Designers
Scott Cook and Amy Adams of DesignLab

Indexer
Angie Bess

Layout/Proofreading
Svetlana Dominguez
Mary Hunt
Ayanna Lacey
Heather Hiatt Miller
Stacey Richwine-DeRome
Mark Walchle

Contents at a Glance

Contents

Foreword

Anne Mark's *The Complete Idiot's Guide to Breastfeeding* does breastfeeding mothers everywhere a huge service. As a pediatrician and former breastfeeding mother, I wish that this book had been available years ago. Whether embarking on breastfeeding for the first time or returning for your second or fifth child, this book reminds us of the most important message of all: Breastfeeding can be successful with the right information and resources.

Despite the fact that breastmilk is nature's perfect food and that, as mammals, we are built for the task, breastfeeding may not come naturally to all of us. Some of us may feel, truly, like idiots. Ms. Mark's book goes a long way in simultaneously demystifying the potential trouble spots and congratulating new and returning mothers on their breastfeeding accomplishments.

The Complete Idiot's Guide to Breastfeeding takes the breastfeeding manual to an entirely new level of thoroughness. The book begins with a section devoted to the "science" of breastfeeding: the natural benefits to both mother and infant. As a pediatrician and long-time advocate of breastfeeding, this section is near and dear to my heart. Our scientific understanding of the myriad benefits of human milk and breastfeeding have come a long way in the past several decades: the anti-bacterial, anti-viral, and anti-inflammatory properties of breast milk are well documented; the benefits to the breastfeeding mother in terms of calcium balance and the potential for cancer prevention are beginning to be more thoroughly researched. This historical and scientific section can be read and reread as an affirmation of the woman's choice to breastfeed. The sections that follow deal with the nuts and bolts of breastfeeding and constitute the real meat of *The Complete Idiot's Guide to Breastfeeding*.

Through her 17 years of experience as an obstetrics nurse, childbirth educator, and board-certified lactation consultant, Ms. Mark has negotiated all the possible roadblocks that the breastfeeding mother might face. It is in her attention to the potential problems of and barriers to breastfeeding that Ms. Mark's book achieves its unique degree of completeness. From the chapters dedicated to the professional and support systems available to the chapters that get you started and keep you breastfeeding, there is literally no stone left unturned. Breastfeeding mothers and their partners will want to return to these sections again and again.

Unlike several other excellent texts devoted to breastfeeding, this book is universally accessible to breastfeeding parents. It is designed for that frenzied time in the midst of a pregnancy when parents are weighing their choices and for the postpartum weeks and months when parents frankly do not have the luxury of time for digesting encyclopedic material.

The Compete Idiot's Guide to Breastfeeding promises to become a well-worn friend for every pregnant and breastfeeding parent. It was too long in coming, but I am so glad that it now exists.

—Jane A. Oski, M.D.
Tuba City, AZ

Introduction

Breastfeeding, You Idiot!

Congratulations, you're preparing to be a new parent!

You've probably discovered by now there are many considerations and decisions you must make concerning your new baby. It can definitely become a bit overwhelming to make so many decisions about so many things. One of those decisions will have to be about feeding your baby. The very reason that you picked up this book may have been for more information about your feeding choices—namely breastfeeding.

Whether you have already chosen to breastfeed or if you are undecided, this book can help give you some practical information and understanding of what breastfeeding is all about. It should help guide you in your decision-making to help you make an informed choice.

Your first impression of breastfeeding may be met with anxiety and concerns. Someone may have given you an earful about the trials and tribulations of breastfeeding. I wish I could be readily available to answer your questions and alleviate your anxiety about this feeding choice. Truth is, though, I can't. So I wrote this book to be the next best thing. I want to help lead and guide you before and throughout your breastfeeding experience. I want it very much to be your number one choice.

I couldn't have asked for a larger audience when the opportunity to write this book came up. Just the opportunity to print the word "breastfeeding" on the front cover was something I couldn't pass up, either. With so many parents today making an infant-feeding choice without all the information at hand, I wanted to share all the information I could offer about breastfeeding. Every day I live, eat, and breathe breastfeeding as a practicing board-certified lactation consultant. It is my responsibility to act as a breastfeeding informant and health care practitioner to better the health of mothers, fathers, and babies.

Yes, it's a personal choice to breastfeed. And to help you with your choice and to keep you from feeling like a "complete idiot," you can read on to gain a wealth of knowledge and resource. This guide was written to give you some basic education and a practical understanding of what breastfeeding is, of its benefits, of how it works, and of the tools necessary for you to be successful.

Part 1, "A Human Resource," takes a look at the human nature and mammalian behavior of breastfeeding. You'll take a look back through history and find out how long this contact sport has been practiced. It will give you information about what has influenced parents away from breastfeeding. You'll read about the numerous benefits available that you'll definitely want to reap. Find out the differences between fake and real milk for babies, including a cost comparison.

Part 2, "Secrets to Your Success," lets you in on all the people, places, and things that contribute to your success. Find out about making preparations well in advance of your baby's arrival. Get ready, there's some homework and phone work for you!

Part 3, "Breastfeeding 101," lets you in on a little bit of science. It's helpful to read the manual before your breastfeeding experience. You'll need to know how to put things together to get you up and running. Read and reread this part before, during, and after!

Part 4, "Supply and Demand," tells you how to manage your milk supply, how to collect it, and even how to store it. Once you've established your breastfeeding, you want to use it and not lose it! There's also information on troubleshooting any highs and lows with your supply.

Part 5, "It's Back to Work," explains about working and offering breast milk to your baby. From childcare to work options, you'll learn about the challenges of the wonderful world of work.

Part 6, "The Unexpected," reminds you that sometimes things don't go as planned. No matter how prepared you are, obstacles to breastfeeding can pop up. This part will cover simple and complex breastfeeding problems and how to handle them.

Part 7, "Glad You Asked!" tells you things about breastfeeding that you really want to know. You'll have every reason to breastfeed anywhere and any time you wish.

The More, the Merrier

Additional information is presented alongside the text. You'll find sidebars in each chapter containing four types of informational inserts.

Breast Beware

Here's information to keep you out of trouble, as well as things you should avoid.

Nursing Mom's Notes

Mothers' tips and consultants' bits of information are offered to you in this box.

Lactation Lingo

This box offers definitions of words that you may not know. Appendix A, "Glossary," also includes these words.

LactFact

This box contains interesting and factual information for your breastfeeding pleasure. Use it accordingly!

Acknowledgments

Writing this book has been an exhilarating yet humbling experience. Book writing and breastfeeding have a lot in common—late nights, little sleep, as well as the unexpected. Reflecting on the challenges, I'll look back on it all and be glad that I did it—just as you will with breastfeeding. This book would not have been written without the patience and encouragement from my husband, Bruce. Thank you for being my partner in life. For my mother, Evelyn M. Wellman, who wasn't informed nor had the support to breastfeed back in 1958. And for my father, Dr. Henry N. Wellman, who had no formal training in lactation during medical school and residency. You both knew there is an art and a science to breastfeeding.

Tremendous thanks are also in order for a special sister-in-law, Beth Mark, and brother-in-law, Daniel D. Mark. Besides your endless emotional support, you have both helped me make my dreams a reality. Your words of wisdom have truly been a source of inspiration. I would also like to thank a professional mentor, Cheri Hull, who told me that I could successfully combine business and health care. You were right! Thanks to Fran Klene and the doctors of Beacon OB/GYN who advocate breastfeeding education for all parents. May their advocacy for prenatal breastfeeding instruction be a source of inspiration for all practicing obstetricians. And lastly, thanks to my five sisters for the friendship, companionship, and laughter that we have shared.

Special Thanks to the Technical Reviewer

More than just thanks are due to Elizabeth Kashin for reviewing *The Complete Idiot's Guide to Breastfeeding.* Your professional, technical, and maternal competence is greatly appreciated. You have taught me what I helped to teach you.

Trademarks

All terms mentioned in this book that are known to be or are suspected of being trademarks or service marks have been appropriately capitalized. Alpha Books and Macmillan USA, Inc., cannot attest to the accuracy of this information. Use of a term in this book should not be regarded as affecting the validity of any trademark or service mark.

Part 1

A Human Resource

Somewhere during your pregnancy, you'll realize that your responsibility as a parent includes making a choice about what to feed your baby. Once the umbilical cord is cut and your baby disconnects from your ongoing food supply, you'll still be responsible for provisions.

You'll discover what's unique about being human, and about the built-in provisions available. Humans have survived throughout the years because of human milk. The medicinal and nutritional aspects of human milk have been responsible for the sheer existence of the human race. And you'll find out that people in every part of the globe breastfeed their babies.

Every attempt has been made to replicate human milk. Not one baby formula comes close to matching human milk. You'll find out why it will never happen. And you'll also find out the risks that you'll take by trying to substitute for Mother Nature.

Chapter 1

Nature's Resource

> **In This Chapter**
>
> ➤ The behavior of mammals
>
> ➤ Components of human milk
>
> ➤ Breastfeeding through history
>
> ➤ Our global breastfeeding practice

Have you ever stopped to marvel at just how long man and womankind have inhabited this planet? So many years that I find it difficult to comprehend. Day after day, life has gone on. What's so incredible is the fact that men and women have survived on the resources available to them. They've learned what is necessary for survival.

Mothers' milk has nourished infants since men and women have been on this earth. Mothers' milk is one of the valuable resources available that has enabled infants to thrive and survive. The fact that our species has survived until now has been due in part to women's ability to breastfeed. Let's look at the nutritional and medicinal components of human breast milk to help you understand its contribution to our continued existence.

Mammalian Behavior

Carolus Linnaeus, a Swedish physician and botanist, coined the term "mammal." It comes from the Latin *mammae* meaning "milk-secreting organ." He used this term to distinguish animals that suckle their young from those that do not. The class of Mammalia consists of animals whose characteristics include the following:

➤ Milk-producing teats

➤ Hair

➤ Three ear bones

➤ A four-chambered heart

So, you're asking yourself now, "Am I a mammal?" If you can answer "yes" to three of the characteristics listed, then you are a mammal. Men and women have teats, but only women have milk-producing teats. (I'll cover this anatomical difference in Chapter 9, "Key Components.")

Consider this point: Mammals produce milk for their young in response to suckling. Every mammal that reproduces can provide milk for its young. No need to hunt and forage for a meal. No need to find, fix, refrigerate, or store food in order to feed your young.

Nursing Mom's Notes

Mammals carry with them an accessible food supply for their young at all times. It's a reliable fast-food location open day and night, holidays, and weekends.

LactFact

Breastfeeding is a basic act of human nature. It helps meet the infant's needs for food and water, sleep, and protection.

If you've been to the zoo lately, you'll notice that the lions, tigers, monkeys, whales, llamas, and sea lions all suckle their young. It's a basic act of mammalian behavior. Mammals use their instincts to nourish and protect their young. Maybe a big cub is picking on a smaller one. The little guy runs to mom for protection and grabs a snack in the meantime. Or a new spring filly stops in the middle of a green pasture to take milk from its mother. And then there's that new litter of puppies, enjoying breakfast, lunch, snacks, and dinner from mom! It's so natural.

Human Behavior

The human species, *Homo sapiens,* is undeniably of the mammalian class. Humans possess hair, a heart, ears, and breasts. But do we suckle our young as other mammals do? Do we provide the basic instinctual nourishment for our young that our forefathers and foremothers used for us? Just what are the basic needs of every mammal? And what are the needs of every human?

The human body must be nourished on a continual basis in order to survive. We require food and water to provide us with the basic energy needed for survival. The body is a machine that needs fuel to function properly. Your newborn baby requires food and water after its birth in order to survive. Inside the womb, the fetus receives food and water through the umbilical cord. After it is born, an infant continues to depend on its mother for food and water. A basic responsibility of any mother is to provide nourishment for her infant.

Every human being needs sleep. It's another basic human need. Sleep provides us time to rest our machine. You would undoubtedly admit that you don't function well with too little sleep. Following your childbirth, breastfeeding will help you get your sleep and rest needed to recover. The hormones released while breastfeeding cause you to relax and drift off into slumber. These sleep-inducing hormones are present in your breast milk, so breastfeeding helps your baby get its sleep, too!

The last of our basic human needs is protection. Through breastfeeding, a mother can offer her baby comfort, security, and shelter, which all provide protection. We are more apt to eat well when we're comfortable. We are more apt to sleep well, too, with proper shelter. And the sense of security helps pull everything together.

Breastfeeding meets all of these basic human needs for food and water, sleep, and protection. Our species would not have survived without the essentials that breastfeeding provides.

Liquid Gold

The fact is that the human breast produces milk for its young. It's the *teat* that a human infant suckles. The human breast is the milk-secreting organ that Linnaeus identified as unique to mammals. Without the mother's milk, our species would not have survived. Breastfeeding has gotten us this far—even if we weren't breastfed ourselves!

Scientifically, breastfeeding is referred to as *lactation*. Lactation is the time period during which a mother secretes milk for her infant. It's also a continuation of the reproductive cycle; the duration of the reproductive cycle is from the start of pregnancy through the completion of lactation. Lactation can last two to three years or longer if stimulation of the mammary gland and milk release are continued.

Lactation Lingo

The term nipple commonly refers to the protuberance in the center of the breast from which milk is released during lactation. A **teat** can be the nipple of any mammal that lactates and releases milk. Nipple and teat are also used in reference to the artificial mouthpiece of a feeding bottle.

Lactation Lingo

Lactation, the time period when a mother secretes milk for her infant, occurs after the third trimester of pregnancy. It begins in what could be considered the "fourth trimester." Once established, lactation can continue for two to three years or longer when stimulation to the mammary gland and milk secretion occur.

A unique feature of human milk is that it is species-specific. What do I mean? Well, its components are specific to the species for which it was designed. In other words, human milk is meant for human babies. The quality and quantities of human milk components are exactly what a human baby needs.

The significant components of human milk are as follows:

➤ Water
➤ Protein
➤ Carbohydrates
➤ Fat
➤ Minerals

➤ Vitamins
➤ Antibodies
➤ White blood cells
➤ Enzymes
➤ Hormones

Water makes up the largest constituent of breast milk. The other components of breast milk are suspended or dissolved in water. If you are concerned about your infant being thirsty in hot, humid weather, remember that breast milk is mostly water. Water is an essential element for every cell in the body. Water also helps to regulate a baby's temperature. Heat loss occurs as water evaporates from a baby's skin and lungs.

Protein, carbohydrates, and fat are essential nutrients also contained in breast milk.

Lactation Lingo

Lactose is the predominant carbohydrate in breast milk. It is the combination of glucose and galactose.

➤ **Protein.** Immunoglobulins are proteins unique to human milk that provide a protection against bacteria and viruses.

➤ **Carbohydrate.** The predominant carbohydrate in breast milk is *lactose*. It is highly concentrated and is the combination of two simple sugars: glucose and galactose. A carbohydrate provides quick energy and is easily digested.

➤ **Fat.** The fat component is essential for a baby's growth and development. Fat contributes about 50 percent of the calories and is the second largest constituent in breast milk. Fat contributes to overall nervous system development, including the brain. Your appetite is satisfied when fat is present in your meal.

Minerals and vitamins are essential elements necessary for the cellular functions in your body.

➤ **Minerals.** Calcium and phosphorus help with bone growth in your baby. Sodium and potassium move freely in and out of the cells in your body. Iron is essential for red blood cells that carry oxygen throughout your body.

➤ **Vitamins.** Vitamins, important to many systems in your body, are also in human milk. Vitamin A helps with new cell growth and keeps tissues healthy. Vitamin B helps convert many nutrients into energy. Vitamin C helps with tissue repair and the synthesis of enzymes and hormones. Vitamin E is necessary for the production of red blood cells as well as maintaining the integrity of muscles. Vitamin K is essential for blood clotting.

Antibodies and white blood cells are essential components for preventing infection and maintaining good health in your baby.

➤ **Antibodies.** Each mother passes her immunity to her baby through her breast milk. A transfer of antibodies through the placenta as well as through breast milk is considered passive immunity. When a baby develops antibodies in response to an antigen, it's known as active immunity.

➤ **White blood cells.** An abundant source of white blood cells protects against infection that viruses and bacteria can cause. White blood cells line the baby's digestive tract and the lungs to fight off ingested and airborne contaminants. Phagocytes and lymphocytes are the main types of white cells in human milk.

➤ **Enzymes.** Enzymes present in breast milk can help with a baby's digestive activity and are necessary for growth and development.

➤ **Hormones.** Hormones such as thyroxine, cortisol, and estrogen are present in breast milk. They help stimulate the activity of certain organs within a baby's body.

There are many, many more components of human milk that you may read about in some of the titles listed in Appendix B, "Further Readings." These components in breast milk are in exactly the right quantities and proportions needed. And these quantities and proportions change according to your baby's milestone in growth and development. No need for you to worry about what's needed and when it's needed. It's all been programmed for you. Research continues to identify and study new components found exclusively in human milk.

LactFact

Studies have shown that babies fed human milk score better on tests of their intelligence than those fed baby formula.

A Look Through History

Roman goddesses of fertility and love were thought to aid the lactating woman. Worshipping them in return for an abundant milk supply was common practice. It was known that the lactating woman needed good health and lots of breast milk with which to nourish and nurture her baby. Spartan women were required to nurse their eldest sons. Ancient laws required citizens to respect breastfeeding women. Roman doctors wrote the standards for infant care that included suckling from the breast until three years of age. And Hippocrates wrote that only the milk of an infant's own mother was beneficial, not the milk of others.

LactFact

The Book of Genesis tells of Sarah, who bore Abraham a son and "gave suck" to him. The Talmud instructed Jewish women to breastfeed for 24 months before weaning. French medical expert Ambroise Paré wrote of breastfeeding in his sixteenth-century publication *Oeuvres Complètes*. He believed that a mother's breastfeeding was healthier for her infant than the suckling of a wet nurse. Wet nurses who had suckled for months and years, he believed, lacked the "first milk" that contained maternal antibodies. George H. Napheys, M.D. wrote in his 1869 book, *The Physical Life of Woman: Advice to the Maiden, Wife, and Mother*, about the early secretion in the breast which was "desirable" and advised mothers to begin breastfeeding immediately after birth.

The Bible contains several references to suckling and breast milk feeding, including passages that promise blessings of goodness and kindness for mothers who breastfeed their young. We find that baby Moses was suckled by a wet nurse. It just so happens this wet nurse was his own mother! The people of that time knew that a woman's milk had nutritional and medicinal effects that nonhuman milk could not provide.

The Talmud specifies a time period of 24 months for breastfeeding. It was common for the ancient Hebrews to wean their infants at about three years of age. "And Abraham made a great feast on the day that Isaac was weaned." (Genesis 21:8) The Koran also specifies that an infant be suckled up to two years of age. And an ancient Indian text specifies that weaning from the breast can begin after a child's second birthday.

Along with all the good about breastfeeding came the not-so-good. Some physicians and scholars began concluding that breastfeeding was problematic, based on the common concerns that many women voiced and questioned about their babies. This resulted in mixed messages and rules about breastfeeding that convinced mothers it wasn't good for them to do. A Roman doctor, Soranus (early second century C.E.), wrote exactly when and when not to feed a baby. He wrote that crying before being put to breast was good for the respiratory organs. Writings by M. Ettmüller in the late 1600s wrote that suckling too often "disordered" the child and that large milk quantities "stagnated" in the stomach. Many women followed the advice of these experts of their time. Breastfeeding was not encouraged during the sixteenth and seventeenth centuries in upper-class families throughout Europe because of its contraceptive effect. French doctor Pierre Budin, an advocate of breastfeeding, wrote in 1900 that it was better to give "too little, than too much". Many mothers were convinced that they didn't have "good" milk. Physicians instructed mothers to schedule a baby's feeding because "irregular feedings were harmful." Mothers were told to let their babies cry rather than to feed them in between scheduled feedings. They got a scolding for feeding their babies at night, because nighttime milk was considered "spoiled." Mothers were taught that overfeeding caused their babies stomach problems. Some of the experts wrote that breastfeeding would give mothers a "nervous disease, become emaciated, and even cause blindness"!

Whence Wet Nurses?

When breastfeeding gets tough, find someone else to do it, right? Well, that's exactly what happened. A woman for hire to breastfeed your baby was called a *wet nurse*. The term nurse means to tend and to suckle. Combine it with lactation and you get a wet nurse. There is reference to wet nursing during the Greek and Roman times, but the common practice of hiring a wet nurse began in England and Europe in the 1600s and 1700s. Wealthy and middle-income families could afford to employ wet nurses. Breastfeeding was not considered appropriate for the lifestyle of the wealthy. It was thought to make your breasts sag, to interfere with your social life, and to keep you from bearing a fruitful amount of offspring to carry on your name. Corsets, worn by girls as early as three to four years of age, may have impaired the breasts for proper feeding and milk production.

The Victorian era helped bring about an obsession with cleanliness and purity. Since breast milk is a bodily fluid, it was associated with being "unclean" and was left to the underlings to carry out. Infants were sent away with a wet nurse and returned to the parents after weaning, around the child's second or third birthday. French and British laws governed the practice of wet nursing. Breastfeeding in public, especially for women of social status, was also considered unacceptable. The act of breastfeeding could expose the breast, which was forbidden at that time.

Lactation Lingo

A **wet nurse** is a woman hired to suckle one or several infants with her breast milk. Wet nursing was very popular during the 1600s and 1700s in England and Europe. A wet nurse could suckle her own baby but her primary purpose was breastfeeding the infant she was hired to suckle!

The practice of wet nursing fell by the wayside when the public became concerned about the moral character of wet nurses. Philosophers and physicians wrote about the harm that wet nursing caused. The infant might acquire some of the unwanted moral character traits of its wet nurse. If you were rich and famous, why risk having the traits of poverty passed on to your heirs? Diseases of the wet nurse could be spread through her breast milk. Physicians demanded a return to a "mother feeding." The majority of people at the time understood that a mother's own milk helped her baby to survive.

Formulas: Chemically Correct?

Physicians then sought an alternative to wet nursing for mothers. The mid-nineteenth century saw the introduction of substitutes for a mother's own milk. Chemists began mixing concoctions that supposedly resembled breast milk, and then marketed it to mothers and physicians. Advertising claimed that their formula was exactly like mother's milk. Physicians agreed that it was better than wet nursing, and chemists assured the public that the mixture was scientifically sound.

Breast Beware

In the mid-nineteenth century, the fact was overlooked that formulas concocted by chemists had to be mixed with water that was often contaminated.

In the early twentieth century we saw a change in the childbearing practice of the time. Home births and the use of midwives took a nosedive as childbirth increasingly took place in hospital institutions. General anesthesia relieved the pain of childbirth. Newborns were taken from their mothers, bundled, and sent to the nursery. The hospital required gloves and masks for most procedures. Hospitals had routines that included feeding schedules. Babies were fed baby formula rather than breast milk, while their mothers recovered from the birth, often for two weeks. The hospitals and medical personnel helped to determine the infant feeding practice of the time. Science, hospital routines, and breast milk substitutes all contributed to the disappearance of maternal breastfeeding trends.

The industrial era and world wars also contributed to a decline in breastfeeding. The growth of industry offered increased work opportunity to women. The workplace did not offer women the opportunity to bring their suckling babies with them. Babies and small children were cared for away from their mothers. The long and exhausting workday did not allow for a mother to breastfeed. Physicians and baby formula manufacturers assured mothers that milk substitutes were just as good as their own breast milk. The world wars demanded that both women and men work to help support the cause. The focus at the time did not support the best interest of mother and baby.

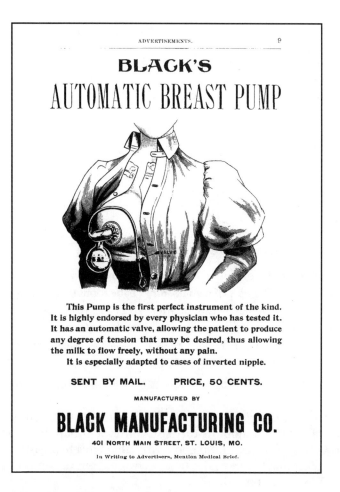

We've come a long way, breastfeeding mama!

Global Perspective

Over the years we've seen several trends and practices that have contributed to the decline of breastfeeding. But let's not get too worried. Society determines "normal" practices based on what the majority chooses to do. When breastfeeding rates were at an all-time low in the United States and Canada, scientists busied themselves researching what made human milk unique. Their scientific results are helping to reestablish the normalcy of maternal breastfeeding again today.

Cultural practices are also helping to increase the rates of breastfeeding. The skills of breastfeeding are taught from woman to woman within a cultural setting. Growing up with family and friends who breastfeed helps determine its normalcy for you. It's also learned through observation. Several countries have heeded the advice of the World Health Organization that human milk feeding is essential for infant survival. More and more data offer conclusive results that mothers' milk reduces the rate of infant mortality worldwide.

The effects of natural disasters, acts of war, and environmental accidents have helped to confirm that breastfeeding is essential. Victims of war and disasters have learned why they mustn't depend on breast milk substitutes. Fresh water and formula supplies are scarce, if not absent, under these circumstances. The ability to buy, prepare, and store milk for one's baby can be almost nonexistent. A mother's own milk resolves this dilemma.

Breast Beware

Let's also consider the monetary resources around the world. If you rely on a baby formula, you have to be able to afford it. The cost of manufactured baby formula on a global scale is unbelievably high. Many people simply cannot afford to buy it. Why buy formula when you can produce breast milk yourself? Most brands of baby formula must be reconstituted with water. And fresh, clean water may not be readily available in many areas of the world.

Slowly but surely the return to breastfeeding continues. The same factors that have determined trends and practices throughout history still continue for all of us today. Scientists, health care providers, cultures, and parents who all advocate breastfeeding will help to reestablish this feeding choice as the norm. The chapters ahead point out what you really need to know about breastfeeding.

The Least You Need to Know

➤ Breastfeeding is unique to mammals.

➤ Human breast milk is specific to humans.

➤ Breastfeeding provides a baby with food and water, sleep, and shelter.

➤ Wet nursing has been used as an alternative to maternal breastfeeding.

➤ Modern childbirth practices and manufactured baby milk helped to decrease breastfeeding rates.

➤ Breastfeeding is practiced globally.

I'll tell you the benefit. I'm hungry. If you feed me, I won't scream until 2 am. That's a benefit.

Chapter 2

Your Benefits Package

In This Chapter

➤ Breastfeeding benefits for mother and baby

➤ Cost savings associated with breastfeeding

➤ Benefits for everyone

➤ Benefits of breastfeeding duration

It's hard to believe that a product like breast milk has so many great benefits. Some of these are benefits you can actually see. Other benefits happen behind the scenes, and you may never actually realize their value. The fact is that the benefits from breast-feeding are numerous. Why not take advantage of its great benefits package?

Benefits to Mom

There is much hidden protection against female cancers when you begin and con-tinue with the breastfeeding of your baby. And your uterus will shrink back to the size it was before your pregnancy. Also, any additional weight that you've gained during pregnancy will be shed rather quickly, just from the energy demands of breast milk production.

Healthy Moms

Among 35- to 55-year-old women, breast cancer is the most common and primary cause of death. It was estimated in 1999 that 43,300 women would die from this disease. Although men are at low risk for developing breast cancer, according to the American Cancer Society, 1,300 cases and 400 deaths were also expected in 1999.

To start with, breastfeeding makes you less likely to develop breast cancer. Long-term studies are showing that the babies who are breastfed, namely female babies, also are less likely to develop breast cancer. Breast cancer claims the lives of so many women today. And researchers are busy looking for a cure. It seems that breastfeeding may be a key link to the cure for this deadly disease.

Breast Beware

Remember that the reproductive cycle includes the time allotted for lactation. It's wise not to fool with Mother Nature. If you don't allow your body to do what's natural, it may have an adverse effect on you.

Lactation Lingo

Anemia is the deficiency of red blood cells or hemoglobin in the blood. During breastfeeding, the hormone oxytocin is released, which helps the uterus contract after childbirth. Frequent uterine contractions significantly reduce your chance of blood loss, which may result in anemia.

The reduced incidence of breast, cervical, and ovarian cancers occurs when a mother breastfeeds exclusively for at least four to six months. This breastfeeding may include expressing milk from her breasts, for example through pumping. A mother also has a reduced incidence of ovarian and cervical cancer when she breastfeeds. Keep in mind that the hormones released with breastfeeding may play a key role in cancer prevention. The production and excretion of breast milk also reduces the possibility of calcification of breast milk within the milk ducts and sinuses. These calcifications are thought to cause the dimpling or lumps found with some breast cancers.

The cost of cancer is considerable: monetary costs as well as mental and physical costs. You won't know the mental costs associated with cancer unless you've been there. Ask any family who has experienced this dreadful disease. If you can help reduce your chances of experiencing this, I strongly recommend it.

Did you know that breastfeeding helps control blood loss associated with childbirth? This seems to be a built-in benefit. One of the dangers of childbirth is blood loss. After delivery of the placenta, your uterus must squeeze hard on all of its many blood vessels, which were connected to the placenta. With the start of breastfeeding, one of the key hormones released causes your uterus to contract. And each time you breastfeed, your uterus squeezes again and again. All that squeezing controls blood loss and will eventually shrink your uterus back to its pre-pregnant size.

Control of blood loss also means the prevention of anemia. *Anemia* is a condition that results from loss of too much blood. Red blood cells, containing hemoglobin, carry oxygen to all the key places in your body. When blood loss depletes your oxygen supply, your body doesn't work as well. You become tired, out of breath, and without energy. Now imagine trying to take care of your new baby this way. You can keep this from happening, all through breastfeeding!

A big concern for most women is getting rid of their pregnancy weight. Breastfeeding burns up a lot of calories, and in return, it helps you to lose this weight. With your baby dependent on you for breast milk, you'll naturally eat a healthy assortment of foods. Eating well and keeping up with the care of your new baby, in addition to breastfeeding, will help to shed more than a few pounds.

Other Benefits

Okay, I've got a few more points about the benefits package. Breastfeeding keeps your bills for doctor visits at a minimum. I used to get comments in my classes stating that if you have insurance, you really don't pay doctor bills. To the contrary, there's a co-pay, and frequent doctor visits eventually drive up the cost of everyone's insurance premiums. If your employer offers health insurance, it will cost you someway, somehow. Complications and long-term illnesses cause us all to pay more in health care premiums in the long run.

So breastfeeding helps to keep health care costs at a minimum. This includes tests associated with illness and disease. You have less chance of hospitalization when you're in good health. Breastfeeding reminds you to stay healthy because your baby depends on you for its nourishment and well-being.

The healthier you are, the less likely you'll need drugs to cure an illness. Pharmaceutical costs can be enormous, especially when an illness requires expensive medications. Big problems we face today are drug-resistant bacteria. These are bacteria that resist any and all medications available to cure an infection. Let's do what we can to keep this from happening.

Breastfeeding helps delay your return of fertility. That means a practical source of family planning for you and a break for your uterus! The hormones associated with breastfeeding help to keep your ovaries from releasing an egg. That means no egg, and no pregnancy. But you have to remember that

LactFact

A lactating mother should consume between 200 and 500 additional calories each day for adequate milk production. In the first six months after delivery, mothers who breastfeed more frequently tend to lose weight more rapidly than those who don't.

Breast Beware

The length of natural infertility is dependent on the frequency, duration, length of feeding, and time interval between breastfeeding. A small percentage of women can conceive while breastfeeding.

15

it's the actual act of a baby breastfeeding that causes hormone release. Your return of fertility depends on how long and how often your baby actually breastfeeds.

Nursing Mom's Notes

As your baby grows, your body produces the nutrients in your milk specific to your baby's developmental age. This means that the correct proportions of protein, carbohydrate, minerals, vitamins, and fat are produced according to the age and nutritional needs of your baby. So sit back, relax, and just breastfeed!

The cost to you for breast milk itself is absolutely free. That's right, all you have to do is make it. The costs associated with a breast milk substitute are downright expensive. Saving money is a benefit all of us appreciate. The benefits of not having to shop, fix, prepare, store, and run out are a blessing.

Healthy Babies

Your baby benefits from breast milk and breastfeeding in plenty of ways. First and foremost is the product itself. We've learned about the components of breast milk in the preceding chapter that classify it as liquid gold. It contains the perfect balance of vital nutrients all at the right time. Yes, breast milk adjusts its content and quantities at the age-appropriate levels. That means if your baby is born prematurely, the breast milk you produce is specific to your baby's developmental age. The milk you produce in the first weeks will differ from the milk you produce at two or three months. No need for you to mix or measure its consistency. It's automatic.

Protection Collection

Your breast milk protects your baby against viruses and bacteria. There are two ways for a virus or bacteria to enter your baby's body:

➤ **Eating.** What babies eat winds up in their digestive systems. Breast milk provides white blood cells that line your baby's digestive system like a great army to fight off any virus and bacteria.

➤ **Breathing.** The other opportunity for infection comes from airborne particles. The air your baby breathes can bring unwanted viruses and bacteria into its lungs. Again, an army of white blood cells lines the lung tissue and destroys any invaders. Babies also receive antibodies from their moms that help protect against additional illness and disease.

You may not see these effects directly, but having a healthy baby is a result no one can dispute. Your breast milk helps to ensure protection in the way that *immunizations* protect your baby. Immunizations are often a weakened strain of a virus or bacteria. By introducing a very small amount into your baby's body, the body responds with its "army" of defense. Breastfed babies have a boosted defense system that offers a great deal of protection against life-threatening diseases.

Smart Babies

A baby's brain doubles its size in the first year of life. Wow, I hear you exclaim! When you consider that in one year a baby can crawl, walk, and practically feed itself, it's truly amazing. Studies show us that a baby fed breast milk gets essential fatty acids that help develop its brain and nervous system. Breast milk helps develop bright, smart babies. Breastfeeding babies makes them smarter when compared to those babies fed breast milk substitutes. Breastfeeding improves your baby's learning and developmental skills.

Breastfeeding helps your baby to bond with you. The value of mother-to-infant bonding is immeasurable. Parent bonding provides love and security that builds a lasting relationship from your baby's start in life. Your baby learns to trust you. Your baby identifies you as the source of its existence. Getting all this from breastfeeding is pretty amazing.

Lactation Lingo

Immunization means to introduce a viral strain or substance into the body that stimulates it to form antibodies. Antibodies, in turn, help counteract the growth and action of harmful bacteria. A mother passes her antibodies to her baby during pregnancy as well as breastfeeding.

Benefits to Everyone

Breastfeeding has many direct benefits for all of us. An enormous amount of our taxpayer dollars is spent to supplement food and health care for low-income recipients. I'm speaking about the Women, Infant, and Children (WIC) program. You'll learn more about it in Chapter 8, "Health Insurance." For now you should know that the U.S. government is the largest purchaser of breast milk substitutes from their manufacturers. Yes, that's right: artificial formula. The recipients of these breast milk substitutes are low-income mothers, who in turn, feed them to their babies. They receive vouchers for artificial formula as well as low-cost or free health care.

A 1995 Colorado Department of Public Health study of its WIC and Medicaid recipients showed that $112 for each recipient could be saved annually if these mothers breastfed their babies for six months. This could result in reduced long term health care costs. Monies would be saved from not purchasing baby formula. Dr. Miriam Labbok at Georgetown University in Washington, D.C., has published studies showing annual cost savings of $2.16 billion in health care expenditures for infections and disease. That would result in a savings of billions of taxpayers' dollars. Think about those numbers!

Breastfeeding also benefits employers by providing them healthy employees. Employees who breastfeed are healthier and thereby reduce an employer's health care costs.

Healthy employees show up for work. A healthy breastfed baby means you'll take fewer sick days from work caring for a sick baby. You'll be more productive in the work that you do. When you're back to work and pumping your breast milk, your baby can continue to benefit from breastfeeding. Your breastfeeding efforts at work should not go unnoticed. It sets an example and raises awareness about the many benefits of breastfeeding.

The amount of glass, aluminum, and paper used in the manufacture of baby formula is phenomenal. A reduction in the amounts used for packaging would help conserve our natural resources. Glass, aluminum, plastics, and paper also add to the waste that results from their use.

The bottom line is that every mother, father, and baby benefits some way, somehow, from breastfeeding.

> **LactFact**
>
> The United States government spends over $600 million each year on the purchase of artificial formula. The formula recipients are babies of low-income mothers, who exchange food vouchers for these breast milk substitutes.

The Benefits of Time

There are several organizations that advocate and recommend a time frame for breastfeeding. Perhaps the most compelling statement is from the *American Academy of Pediatrics*. The AAP is a collective group of physicians who specialize in the medical care of infants and children. The AAP recommends breastfeeding a baby through its first year of life. It recommends longer than a year if a mother and her baby so desire.

> **Lactation Lingo**
>
> The **American Academy of Pediatrics** is a collective group of physicians who specialize in the medical care of infants and children. It was founded in Detroit in 1930 by 35 pediatricians. The organization was formed to address issues surrounding the health, safety, and well-being of infants and children. Immunizations and regular health exams are examples of preventative health practices the AAP helped to establish. It operates as a not-for-profit corporation headquartered in Illinois. It publishes a monthly scientific journal, *Pediatrics*.

Other organizations have also made recommendations for the duration of breastfeeding. The World Health Organization (WHO) recommends that infants be exclusively breastfed for at least the first six months of their life. The U.S. Department of Health and Human Services coordinates the Healthy People 2010 Campaign. The Healthy People 2010 objectives include goals for increased breastfeeding rates. Increasing our breastfeeding rates here in the United States is an important public health goal. The target goals for breastfeeding rates in 2010 are as follows:

➤ 75 percent of women breastfeeding in early postpartum

➤ 50 percent of women breastfeeding at six months

➤ 25 percent of women breastfeeding at one year

Realistically, the benefits of breastfeeding are seen over time. It's not something that you will see with one day or one week of breastfeeding. You'll realize these benefits only with a commitment to breastfeeding. This will be one of the most challenging commitments you make as you experience parenting. It is a commitment, though, that provides rewards above and beyond your greatest expectations.

LactFact

There are hundreds of scientific studies that cite the medicinal, immunological, and economical benefits of human milk and breastfeeding. These publications listed can help provide the evidence and proof about breastfeeding for any doubtful readers.

➤ Churchill R.B. & Pickering L.K. "Breastfeeding: The Pros (many) and Cons (few)," *Contemporary Pediatrics* 15:108–119, Dec 1998.

➤ Goldman A.S. "The Immune System of Human Milk: Antimicrobial, Anti-Inflammatory and Immunomodulating Properties," *Journal of Pediatric Infectious Disease* 12:664–671, 1993.

➤ Hornstra G. "Essential Fatty Acids in Mothers and Their Neonates," *The American Journal of Clinical Nutrition* 71:1262–9, May 2000.

➤ Montgomery D.L. & Splett P.L. "Economic Benefit of Breastfeeding Infants Enrolled in WIC," *Journal of the American Dietetic Association* 97:379, 1997.

➤ Radetsky P. "Got Cancer Killers? Apoptosis Induced by a Human Milk Protein," *Discover* 68:70–75, June 1999.

The Least You Need to Know

➤ Breastfeeding ensures good health for mothers and babies.

➤ Breast milk transmits antibodies and immunity to babies.

➤ Breastfeeding reduces health care costs.

➤ The AAP, WHO, and Healthy People 2010 endorse breastfeeding for most infants.

Chapter 3

Real or Fake?

> **In This Chapter**
>
> ➤ Facts about artificial formula
>
> ➤ Risks of using breast milk substitutes
>
> ➤ Health outcomes
>
> ➤ Costs of formula feeding
>
> ➤ Making an informed choice

The practice of exclusive and extended breastfeeding fell by the wayside when commercial baby formulas saturated the market. Many parents today believe that the difference between breastfed and formula-fed infants is minimal. I usually have a parent comment that they know of a baby who was fed formula and everything seems "just fine." Well, plenty of research and statistical data show that artificial breast milk does increase your baby's risk of illness. Artificial breast milk lacks the immunological and balanced nutrients that human milk contains. Let me give you a few things to consider about substituting breast milk with something artificial.

Reading the Product Label

A manufacturer's advertisement can claim that a breast milk substitute is just like breast milk. But it isn't. The truth is, an infant formula can never duplicate human milk. Despite all attempts, the living cells, hormones, enzymes, and antibodies contained in human milk just cannot be replicated. Period.

Nursing Mom's Notes

Kindly decline any free baby formula samples and the formula company's diaper bag to ensure your breastfeeding success. As the saying goes, "Out of sight, out of mind."

The ingredients contained in baby formulas are based on a cow's milk, soy, or meat-based protein. If you read the label it can be an alarming discovery. You'll find ingredients like whey protein; palm, coconut, and safflower oils; maltodextrin; soy lecithin; inositol; pyridoxine hydrochloride; biotin; and so on. Cow's milk and soybeans are chosen as protein ingredients because of their low cost and abundance when it comes to mass production. Artificial ingredients are usually the culprits when it comes to causing allergies. An allergen is a substance that causes an allergic response. When it comes to babies, the milk protein from cows is a common allergen. You see, the human body knows what's real and what's fake.

Consumers have the hardest time getting the facts about baby formulas. All you have to rely on is what the manufacturer advertises as well as what the medical community endorses. Health care providers unknowingly distribute free formula samples as well as free marketing of merchandise to your doctor's office and hospital. It may appear to be educational material but in fact is direct advertising for the manufacturer. If you sign up for a newsletter or a baby magazine in your childbirth class, a box of formula lands on your doorstep about the time your baby is delivered. Registries at department stores share or sell their list to formula manufacturers. You can't help but think that breast milk and baby formula are somewhat equal.

LactFact

Patented breast milk substitutes were first marketed in Europe and the United States in the 1860s. A Swiss merchant named Henri Nestlé mixed together sugar, flour, and cow's milk for a product he advertised as "scientifically correct." By the 1880s, milk foods and milk modifiers such as Horlick's Malted Milk were very popular. The 1890s saw the modification of cow's milk in an attempt to resemble human milk. The proportions of fat, protein, and sugar in cow's milk were modified to resemble the breast milk produced at each developmental stage. This resulted in chemists constantly changing the formula proportions, sometimes weekly.

Varying Quantities and Content

Many people are under the impression that the U.S. Food and Drug Administration carefully monitors the manufacture of baby formulas. The fact is that the FDA has only minimal standards for the production and sale of these formulas. Manufacturers of baby formulas are required only to list the mandated ingredients on their packaging.

Even though the name reads formula, there really isn't a "formula" for formula. Each brand of this synthetic product varies greatly from one to another. Some brands have more of one nutrient and less of another. Some brands don't provide the proper amounts of vital nutrients. And worse yet, some brands omit vital and essential ingredients altogether.

An ingredient lacking from the formulas manufactured and distributed in the United States is DHA. *Docosahexaenoic acid,* or *DHA*, is the primary fatty acid found in brain matter and in the retina of the eye. It is essential for normal brain and eye development. DHA is naturally found in breast milk. During pregnancy, your baby receives DHA through your placenta and then through your breast milk after birth. Test scores have shown that breastfed babies rate higher for IQ's and visual development than formula-fed babies because of DHA.

In 1981 the World Health Organization approved an International Code for Marketing Breast Milk Substitutes. It passed by a vote of 118 to 1. The one country that voted against the Code was the United States. The Code provides a recommended marketing practice for the sale of artificial formula. The Code forbids the direct advertisement to consumers by formula manufacturers.

Lactation Lingo

Docosahexaenoic acid, or **DHA,** is the primary fatty acid found in brain matter and in the retina of the eye. It is an essential fatty acid necessary for development of the newborn baby's nervous system. Because it is omitted in breast milk substitutes manufactured in the United States, babies can reap its benefits only through their own mother's breast milk.

International Code for Marketing Breast Milk Substitutes

No advertising of these products to the public.

No giving of free samples to mothers.

No promoting of products in health care facilities.

No company mothercraft nurses to advise mothers.

continues

continued

No giving of gifts or personal samples to health workers.

No words or pictures idealizing formula feeding, including pictures of infants, on the products.

Information to health workers should be scientific and factual.

All information on artificial feeding, including the labels, should explain the benefits of breastfeeding, and the costs and hazards associated with formula feeding.

No promotion of unsuitable products for babies, such as condensed milk.

All products should be of a high quality and should take into account the climatic and storage conditions of the country where they are used.

Product Recalls

When it comes to formula production and distribution, consumers rely on the manufacturer for a clean, safe food product. Well, mistakes can happen in the manufacture of baby formula. These mistakes usually surface after-the-fact, and place each consumer at risk. The FDA has made several product recalls due to health and safety problems with infant formula. There have been seven recalls of infant formula in the United States since 1982. Laboratory testing has revealed bacteria and contaminants in infant formula. Salmonella, klebsiella pneumonia, glass particles, and lumped and curdled milk contaminants have all been found in recalled infant formulas. The FDA has classified some of these recalls as "potentially life threatening." In March of 2000, 2.5 million cans of Nestlé formula were recalled because they potentially lacked proper sterilization.

The other problems with the manufacture of artificial breast milk are ingredient proportions. I've already pointed out that formulas in the United States omit DHA. Infant formulas can contain too much of one ingredient and not enough of another. Years ago, the FDA uncovered the sale of counterfeit formula. Thousands of cans were mislabeled and sold to unsuspecting consumers. Infants become the innocent victims. The shelf life and product expiration can also pose a threat to unknowing consumers.

Equipment Needed to Prepare Formula

Keep in mind that formula is packaged several ways. There are ready-to-feed, concentrate, and powder varieties. Ready-to-feed is already prepared and can be costly to purchase. Powder and concentrate require that you add water. Your measurements must be accurate. Your water supply must be clean and fresh, free from bacterial and elemental contaminants. Water should be boiled to ensure hygiene and safety.

You need supplies to prepare, store, and offer infant formula. This means a supply of plastic, disposable, or glass bottles. Most bottles use a rubber or silicone nipple for liquid to flow through. You'll need to buy those, too. There are gadgets and gizmos for cleaning, drying, and storing your supplies. You must refrigerate formula after it's prepared or opened. Formula needs to be carefully handled and stored since any bacterial contaminants can multiply quite rapidly.

Shopping for and preparing the formula for feeding takes time. Prepared formula from powder or concentrate should be used within 24 hours. So, you'll spend money just to boil, cool, store, warm, give, and clean every day. Who wants to do this day in and day out?

Risks of Substitutes

Baby formulas increase the risk of ill health among infants. An artificial food product lacks immunological and other health-promoting factors found in human breast milk. Formula-fed infants are denied the benefit of "autoimmunization" whereby the breast produces antibodies to which the infant has been exposed. Passive immunity, or automatic immunity, passes from the mother to her baby in the breast milk. Formula-fed babies do not reap this benefit. Disorders of the immune system are often associated with formula feeding because of the lack of stimulation.

Baby formulas do not enhance the body's immune response to vaccinations. Vaccinations work better in breastfed infants because the white blood cells from breast milk respond to viral and bacterial exposure. Manufactured formulas do not enhance the body's immune response to vaccinations.

Formula-fed infants are more likely to suffer from gastrointestinal infections and diarrhea. They can suffer from meningitis and are at great risk for respiratory infections. Infants fed cow's milk are more likely to have eczema and other allergies because its protein is often an allergen. It appears that formula feeding increases the risk of *SIDS,* or *Sudden Infant Death Syndrome.* A 1988 epidemiological study by the National Institute of Child Health and Human Development showed that less than 10 percent of SIDS cases were breastfed infants, while approximately 25 percent were non-breastfed control groups.

Lactation Lingo

Sudden Infant Death Syndrome (SIDS), or crib death, is the sudden, unexplained death of a baby that happens while the baby is napping or sleeping.

Beyond infancy, the effects of formula feeding can increase a child's chance of developing insulin-dependent diabetes, lymphoma, and celiac disease.

Adults with diseases of the bowel, such as Crohn's disease or ulcerative colitis, have formula feeding in common.

Formula feeding affects the health of the mother. The risk of osteoporosis, breast cancer, and ovarian cancer are greater for mothers who choose not to breastfeed. A mother also misses out on the contraceptive effects that breastfeeding has to offer.

Costs of Artificial Milk

The costs to each family, the community, and the country as a whole are affected by the consumption of baby formulas. Everyone feels these costs directly or indirectly.

LactFact

For each dollar charged for infant formula, the manufacturer spends about 16 cents on production.

Lactation Lingo

The Special Supplemental Nutrition Program for Women, Infants, and Children is popularly known as **WIC.** It was established in 1974 and is administered by the Food and Nutrition Service of the United States Department of Agriculture.

The average family in the United States feeding its baby a breast milk substitute spends between $1,500 and $2,000 each year. These costs include the purchase of formula, bottles, nipples, and additional supplies for preparation and storage. Families with limited income may eat more poorly because of the cost realized to purchase formula. Working parents must endure the costs of their baby's illnesses. Time off from work, doctor visits, buying and giving medicines, as well as sleepless nights from a sick baby all add up for new parents who don't choose to breastfeed.

Infant illness requires health care, and that alone costs all of us. A study five years ago by Kaiser Permanente's health maintenance organization in the United States found that health care costs for formula-fed infants averaged $1,400 more than breastfed infants. Hospitalizations, doctors' fees, pharmaceuticals, and health care treatments all cost money. Illness eventually drives up the cost of health care and everyone pays more as a result.

The infants and children most likely to receive baby formulas are those from low-income families. The greatest purchaser of baby formula in the United States is a government agency called *WIC*. WIC provides free nutrition counseling and food supplements to low-income mothers and their infants. WIC provides 37 percent of all infants born in the United States with breast milk substitutes. More than $600 million is spent each year on the purchase of this formula. And it's every tax-paying American who ultimately funds this purchase.

The Least You Need to Know

➤ There are hidden risks associated with feeding formula to babies.

➤ The absence of human milk causes illness and disease.

➤ The average family spends almost $2,000 for formula feeding per baby each year.

➤ Health care costs have risen as a result of formula feeding.

➤ Facts and accurate information should be used to make your infant feeding choice.

Part 2
Secrets to Your Success

Breastfeeding is a natural part of motherhood. If it makes you a bit nervous, read on to find out about getting a successful start.

Your second trimester of pregnancy offers you an excellent opportunity for hunting down resources. You'll find out the right time to shop for a nursing bra. Time is of the essence to call on the lactation professionals, ask for information, and formulate your breastfeeding plan. You won't want to go it alone. Others who have been there and have done what you're about to learn can offer you the best support.

The information for you in Part 2 is meant to help make you successful in your breastfeeding pursuit. You'll learn about locating resources, finding support, and meeting professionals, all to empower you for successful breastfeeding.

...You called?

Lactation Consultant

Chapter 4

Find the Pros

In This Chapter

➤ Where and why to locate professional resources

➤ Health care providers for women and children

➤ Professionals to consider for breastfeeding management

➤ Birth facilities that encourage and support breastfeeding

➤ Resources your company may offer

Whenever we need someone with expertise or need help mastering a new skill we are learning, we often turn to a professional. That's right, someone who professes more knowledge and expertise than we have. When it comes to breastfeeding, getting professional help and advice may be crucial to your success. It's also important to get the right professional. Why? you ask. Well, a health care professional may be your best source for help and management because breastfeeding affects the health, nutrition, and well-being of you and your baby.

Keep in mind that not every health care provider today offers expertise in breastfeeding management. Understanding and knowing who's who in the health care system, and who does what, will be helpful in your search for the pros. I will explain to you the different types of health care professionals who may have breastfeeding services available for you.

Also, keep in mind that a professional usually charges a fee for any services rendered. After all, professionals don't work for free! Fees may be included in your prenatal care, hospital bill, or well-baby visit. A professional in private practice, or anyone whom you hire, will bill you for services.

It's best to locate and meet your professional resources well in advance of your expected delivery date. Your second trimester of pregnancy should offer ample time to do this. You'll know how and when to reach them, and feel more comfortable with them if you should need their services.

Lactation Lingo

A **lactation consultant** is an expert who advises and professes an in-depth knowledge about breastfeeding.

Lactation Lingo

An **International Board Certified Lactation Consultant** (**I.B.C.L.C.**) is a lactation consultant who has passed a certifying exam and has been awarded the credential given by the International Board of Lactation Consultant Examiners (IBLCE). I.B.C.L.C.s can be nurses, doctors, dieticians, physical therapists, occupational therapists, social workers, anthropologists, accountants, and even attorneys!

Lactation Consultant

A consultant is one who gives expert advice and professes an in-depth knowledge about a certain topic or field. A *lactation consultant* is one such "expert" in the field of breastfeeding. Maybe you've heard or read about such a consultant. Some parents feel this may be your most valuable professional resource.

The professional lactation consultant evolved within the health care system about 20 years ago, as more and more women chose to breastfeed their babies and needed expert advice and assistance. Several of the first lactation consultants were nurses who already cared for mothers and babies who breastfed. The lactation consultant represents the largest segment of health care professionals whose practice is focused solely on the promotion, protection, and support of breastfeeding. Lactation consultants work in hospitals, clinics, doctor's offices, nutrition programs, and private practice settings. Lactation consultants spend most of their time working with breastfeeding families. They have firsthand knowledge about what families need to be successful at breastfeeding. The number of lactation consultants in practice today continues to increase, to meet the growing demand for this type of professional.

Unfortunately, just about any health care professional can call himself or herself a "lactation consultant." So how do you know when you've got the real thing? Before you deliver, I recommend that you locate a lactation consultant resource and ask if his or her credentials include an *International Board Certified Lactation Consultant (I.B.C.L.C.)*. I.B.C.L.C.s have passed a certifying exam given by the International Board of Lactation Consultant Examiners (IBCLE). That's how they are awarded the credential "I.B.C.L.C." These professionals have worked several thousand hours with breastfeeding families and stay current of research in the field of lactation. I.B.C.L.C.s adhere to practice standards and a code of ethics established by the certifying body. They also maintain their credentials by completing mandatory continuing education, and they must recertify by exam every 10 years.

The following might help you to locate an I.B.C.L.C.:

➤ Yellow Pages

➤ Your physician's office

➤ Your local hospital or birth center

➤ Referral from family or friend

➤ International Lactation Consultant Association (ILCA)

Ask these consultants about their credentials, where they practice, the services they provide, when and how you can secure their services, and the fees for any products purchased and services rendered. Self-employed lactation consultants or those in private practice will often send you a brochure for the asking!

Licensed Health Care Providers

You may have another professional resource in place already. If you receive prenatal care from a licensed health care provider, it should be quite simple to ask about the availability of breastfeeding assistance. Your health care provider may provide the necessary skills and information to assist you with breastfeeding your baby. I need to make you aware, though, that breastfeeding and human lactation are subjects that receive little attention in many medical and nursing school curriculums. Therefore, doctors, nurses, dieticians, and therapists who do possess the skills for proper management of breastfeeding have often learned them only through additional courses of study. They may have had a personal breastfeeding experience, or may have encountered clients, within their practice, in need of breastfeeding assistance.

Licensed health care providers may include evaluation and management for breastfeeding among their professional services. Let's look at the following health care professionals and why they may be sources for breastfeeding management services.

Physicians

A physician is a person skilled in the art of healing—a doctor of medicine. A physician has completed four years of undergraduate study, four years of medical school, and three to seven additional years of training in a medical specialty. Doctors who specialize in the health care of women and infants include the following:

➤ Obstetrician-gynecologist

➤ Family practitioner

➤ Pediatrician

➤ Neonatologist

OB-GYN

Your obstetrician-gynecologist, or OB-GYN, is responsible for your health care during pregnancy, as well as for your female reproductive health when you are not pregnant. Since breastfeeding lowers the risk of breast cancer for mothers and daughters, obstetricians today are recommending that their clients choose to breastfeed. An obstetrician cares for you throughout your pregnancy, your delivery, and the days immediately following your baby's birth. Your obstetrician's office may offer classes about breastfeeding. Be sure to ask about any assistance or follow-up that may be available to you after you deliver your baby.

Family Practitioners

A doctor who's trained in several general areas of medicine and provides primary health care is a family practitioner. He or she wants the optimal health for mother, father, and baby. Breastfeeding impacts the health of the whole family, and family practitioners know this. A family practitioner will care for you and your baby while you're breastfeeding. Some parents find that they prefer this type of care.

Pediatricians

Pediatricians are doctors who specialize in the health care, development, and diseases of babies and children. They want you to give your baby the healthiest choice of nourishment, and are strong advocates of breastfeeding. With the American Academy of Pediatrics' recommendation that breastfeeding continue for at least 12 months, pediatricians are making every effort to support and encourage this outcome. Ask your pediatrician what percentage of his or her patient population is breastfeeding.

Neonatologists

Doctors who specialize in the care and diseases of premature and hospitalized newborns are called neonatologists. They usually practice in an area of the hospital called the Newborn Intensive Care Unit, or NICU. Neonatologists, too, are strong advocates of breastfeeding because of the medicinal and healing properties of human breast milk. Since the breast milk a mother produces is specific to her infant's age of development, neonatologists advise mothers of premature babies to pump and collect their own milk.

Nursing Mom's Notes

Mothers living in a metropolitan area may have an abundance of professionals from which to choose for help in breastfeeding. Mothers living in a remote area or town may not have any of these professionals available. With or without these available resources, you can rest assured that you should be able to breastfeed. Know that it's your choice to seek help from a professional resource. After all, women have been breastfeeding successfully without special health care professionals for centuries.

Nurses

A nurse is trained to care for the sick and the injured. Nurses providing health care today can offer a wealth of education, information, and up-to-date research regarding women's and infants' health. Any nurses out there can count how many times they've been asked a health care question because they are a "nurse"! Nurses spend most of their time with the patient by observing, recording, listening, and providing bedside care.

A *registered nurse (R.N.)* is a member of the health care delivery team with a license to provide care under the directive of a physician. A registered nurse cannot diagnose, order, or prescribe a treatment for you. A registered nurse works jointly with a doctor when a procedure or treatment is necessary for your breastfeeding management. A registered nurse in your doctor's office may help you to locate breastfeeding assistance. It's possible that your childbirth educator may be the R.N. professional you're looking for!

A licensed health care provider educated in nursing as well as in midwifery is a certified nurse-midwife. A midwife offers women skilled

Lactation Lingo

A **registered nurse (R.N.)** completes a two-year, three-year, or four-year course of study at an accredited nursing school or program. When a nursing student passes a state examination, he or she becomes "registered with the certifying body in that state." B.S.N. stands for Bachelor of Science degree in Nursing. M.S.N. stands for Master of Science degree in Nursing. C.N.M. stands for Certified Nurse Midwife. N.P. stands for Nurse Practitioner.

assistance during childbirth as well as offering prenatal care to women with low-risk pregnancies. A physician, hospital, or birth center employs most practicing midwives. Some may attend your birth at home. Because a midwife cares for you during pregnancy and birth, she can help you get breastfeeding off to a great start. A midwife should include information about breastfeeding in your prenatal education, but it won't hurt to ask about classes and follow-up services.

A nurse who holds a master's degree and has additional training in the allied health sciences is a nurse practitioner. Nurse practitioners may specialize in women's health, pediatrics, or family health.

Dieticians and Therapists

A dietician focuses on the science and study of food values and their effects on health. A dietician who is licensed is a *registered dietician*, or R.D. Because human breast milk is the optimal food source and it positively impacts your infant's health, the American Dietetic Association advocates the exclusive feeding of breast milk for 4 to 6 months and breastfeeding with weaning foods for at least 12 months.

Therapeutics is a branch of medicine concerned with the treatment and cure of diseases. Physical and occupational therapists may provide breastfeeding management for women and infants, among their therapeutic services. Check with your clinic to find out if this is available.

You'll want to ask a few questions of any health care professionals as you assemble your resources before your delivery date. Some questions to consider asking include the following:

➤ Do you evaluate and manage the care of a breastfeeding mother and baby?

➤ To whom do you refer if breastfeeding evaluation and management services are not provided?

➤ How do I contact you with a breastfeeding problem or concern?

➤ Is there someone on staff with expertise in breastfeeding?

➤ If my baby won't directly feed at the breast, what kind of nourishment should be given to my baby?

➤ Are breastfeeding follow-up services provided?

➤ What is your fee for these services?

➤ Do you offer a prenatal lactation consultation?

Some physician practices employ a lactation consultant or a registered dietician, so try to schedule a visit with this person well in advance of your baby's delivery. Your certified nurse-midwife will usually prepare and help you get breastfeeding off to a good start, but it's a good idea to ask what kind of breastfeeding management he or she will include with your prenatal and postnatal care.

Breastfeeding Welcome Here!

You'll get not only the royal but also the right treatment for breastfeeding when you choose a hospital or birth center that's designated "Baby Friendly." If you have the opportunity to choose where you deliver, this facility should rank at the top of your list.

The Baby-Friendly Hospital Initiative (BFHI) is a worldwide program sponsored by the World Health Organization (WHO) and the United Nations Children's Fund (UNICEF). Its purpose is to recognize hospitals and birth centers that provide the best environment for breastfeeding. This program helps hospitals and birth centers give mothers the information, confidence, and skills necessary for successful breastfeeding. The review board gives the Baby Friendly Hospital Award after fulfillment of the Ten Steps to Successful Breastfeeding. About 14,000 hospitals worldwide have received this award. Approximately 26 hospitals and birth centers in the United States and one in Canada have been designated as "Baby Friendly."

The Ten Steps to Successful Breastfeeding that birth facilities must implement to be designated "Baby Friendly" are the following:

1. Have a written breastfeeding policy that is routinely communicated to all health care staff.

2. Train all health care staff in skills necessary to implement this policy.

3. Inform all pregnant women about the benefits and management of breast-feeding.

4. Help mothers initiate breastfeeding within an hour of birth.

5. Show mothers how to breastfeed and how to maintain lactation, even if they should be separated from their infants.

6. Give newborn infants no food or drink other than breast milk, unless medically indicated.

7. Practice "rooming in" by allowing mothers and infants to remain together 24 hours a day.

8. Encourage breastfeeding on demand.

9. Give no artificial teats, pacifiers, or soothers to breastfeeding infants.

10. Foster the establishment of breastfeeding support groups and refer mothers to them upon discharge from the hospital or birthing center.

The following facilities have been recognized as "Baby Friendly" in the United States and Canada:

Evergreen Hospital Medical Center
Kirkland, Washington

Alice Peck Day Memorial Hospital
Lebanon, New Hampshire

Cottage Grove Health Care
Community
Cottage Grove, Oregon

Mercy Franciscan Hospital, Mount
Airy Campus
Cincinnati, Ohio

Goleta Valley Cottage Hospital
Santa Barbara, California

Kaiser Permanente Medical Center
Honolulu, Hawaii

MidMichigan Regional Medical
Center
Midland, Michigan

Miles Memorial Hospital
Damariscotta, Maine

PeaceHealth Nurse Midwifery Birth
Center
Eugene, Oregon

Reading Birth and Women's Center
Reading, Pennsylvania

Women's Health and Birth Center
Santa Rosa, California

St. John's Hospital
Springfield, Illinois

Maternity Center of East Tennessee
Knoxville, Tennessee

Blount Memorial Hospital
Maryville, Tennessee

San Luis Obispo General Hospital
San Luis Obispo, California

Weed Army Community
Hospital
Fort Irwin, California

Women's Wellness and
Maternity Center
Madisonville, Tennessee

Inland Midwife Services—
The Birth Center
Redlands, California

Northeastern Vermont
Regional Hospital
St. Johnsbury, Vermont

St. Elizabeth Medical Center
Edgewood, Kentucky

Three Rivers Community
Hospital
Grants Pass, Oregon

Boston Medical Center
Boston, Massachusetts

Kaiser Sunnyside Medical
Center
Clackamas, Oregon

Rochester General Hospital
Rochester, New York

Cape Canaveral Hospital
Cocoa Beach, Florida

Providence Medford Medical
Center
Medford, Oregon

Brome-Missisquoi-Perkins
Hospital
Cowansville, Quebec, Canada

Look in Appendix C, "Resources," for more information or to contact the Baby Friendly Hospital Initiative.

Corporate Wellness Programs

If you are one of the many women who work, you should look into any programs and benefits that your company has to offer. In recent years, businesses have begun to offer on-site wellness programs that include preparing for pregnancy, childbirth, and breastfeeding. Businesses may employ or contract a health care consultant to teach wellness programs, often offered during the lunch hour. Your human resources department may schedule these programs.

Your company may also have contracted for employee discounts with a local provider of health care education or lactation consulting services. Ask if your company offers the services of a lactation consultant, nurse, or dietician, and if it offers instructional classes about breastfeeding. Look for a designated lactation or new mothers' room at your place of business. It should provide information about breastfeeding resources, as well as about your company's participation in a breast pump rental program. Contact your human resources manager to help you locate and identify resources within your place of employment.

Nursing Mom's Notes

Look for or ask about a lactation room or mothers' room at your place of business. They should have information available about lactation consultants, breastfeeding instruction, and company benefits.

The Least You Need to Know

➤ Locate your professional resources well before you deliver.

➤ Meet with your professional before your baby's birth.

➤ Have your professional's name, address, telephone number, and business hours handy.

➤ Try to use a "Baby Friendly" birth facility.

➤ Find out if your company offers professional lactation resources.

Line Up Support

When we look at the meanings of support, we find the following descriptions: to bear the weight of; to hold up; to sustain, to advocate or maintain. Why would you need support when you are breastfeeding? There will be times when you feel like you are the only person in the world taking on this new adventure. There may be times when you question your choice of infant feeding. It's 3:23 A.M. and you're asking yourself, "What am I doing here?" Maybe no one else in your family has ever breastfed, and you feel like you are in this alone. You may get negative and unkind remarks about breastfeeding. Your mother-in-law comments, "That just wasn't the thing we did back when I was having babies."

Just when the thought occurs that you might throw in the towel, you'll really need someone else's help and advice. There's no better resource than the supportive kind.

On the Home Front

Let's first consider what may be right in your very own home. Yes, home, where you feel most comfortable and can really be yourself. How about the baby's father? The

FOB, or "Father-Of-Baby," has a significant role in supporting your decision to breast-feed. He may, in fact, be the one who decided that your baby should be breastfed. After all, he does have say so in this partnership! Maybe he grew up in a home where breastfeeding was the everyday lifestyle of infant feeding. The baby's father has every right to choose human milk feeding, even if he can't actually produce the milk himself.

The baby's father may be your legal spouse, partner, or significant other. I want to be fair in describing the several potential relationships in today's society. As a couple, you should choose the feeding method for your baby that the both of you are most comfortable with. If you have a difference of opinion, then by all means you should seek out additional information and advice to help you make an informed choice. You might turn to one of the professional resources that I addressed in the previous chapter.

Your support at home should be able to listen and offer words of encouragement. He or she should help you seek other resources when necessary. Don't feel you need to bear the weight of this decision by yourself. Discuss with your partner the importance of breastfeeding and what this choice means to you. Decide in advance how much listening and discussion is needed before it's necessary for you or your partner to contact professional resources. Let your partner know who and where your professional resources are in the event that your partner needs to contact them. If possible, have your partner meet with your professional resource beforehand.

Nursing Mom's Notes

When a mother and father choose breastfeeding for their infant, both are making a commitment to provide the best possible choice of nourishment for their baby. When the going gets tough or when tears come to the eyes, you have each other to turn to. You're in this together.

What's important here is to not have to make a decision by yourself. You're in this together with the baby's father, and he should be able to help make some decisions, too. Communication is the key to your success here. Don't be afraid to discuss, share, and voice your thoughts and concerns with your loved one. The person closest to you during this important life-cycle event should be your first choice for support.

I made a comment earlier about this being a commitment. Your spouse or significant other should be prepared to support you for the amount of time that you will be committed to this choice. Remember that the American Academy of Pediatrics advises that an infant be breastfed through the first year of life. Also remember that other sources indicate that we see the health benefits result from at least six months of active breastfeeding. That means that you will commit for a 6- to 12-month period. It's important to discuss and define your breastfeeding goals well in advance of your delivery.

LactFact

In its statement about breastfeeding, the American Academy of Pediatrics says, "Exclusive breastfeeding is ideal nutrition and sufficient to support optimal growth and development for approximately the first six months after birth. Gradual introduction of iron-enriched solid foods in the second half of the first year should complement the breast milk diet. It is recommended that breastfeeding continue for at least 12 months, and thereafter for as long as mutually desired."

Another important point to discuss with your support "on the home front" is the effect that breastfeeding will have on your sex life. Every new mom and dad, regardless of the feeding method, usually finds that the priorities of parenting place sex near the bottom of the list. The hormones involved with milk production and milk release also affect your libido. The resulting effect is a decrease in your sex drive, which also serves as a means of family planning. Add to that your altered sleeping patterns and the time spent on the care of your newborn, and your energy and opportunities for sex become minimized.

Family and Friends

Any people you consider family, whether they are blood relatives or not, should be next in line when considering sources of support. Consider your sister, your mother, or a relative to whom you feel close. Whether they are on the home front or not, you need to be able to communicate with them as often as necessary. This support source may be in addition to that which you receive from your partner.

It's important to consider family who may have had a previous breastfeeding experience, and a positive one at that. The worst-case scenario is a relative who consistently and constantly bombards you with misinformation and negative remarks. A few negative comments about breastfeeding can undermine all the efforts of education and information that you have spent time gathering. And if it comes at a vulnerable time, you begin to second-guess yourself. Then, after hearing it for the fourth time, you cave in to his or her suggestion because you have only a few hours of sleep on board.

Look for family members who have a positive outlook, are open to new information, and have a respect for your decision to breastfeed. Otherwise, kindly thank them and

43

indicate that you have other resources in mind. Saying "no" may be the hardest thing you have to say to a family member. Remember, though, it's in the best interest of supporting your decision to breastfeed your baby.

Friends are another great resource for support, especially if they are just like family. Someone you grew up with, or have remained close with since college, may be just the source of support you're looking for. I think friends can be honest with you when family may be holding back. It may be easier to confide in a friend if your family tends to be a little intimidating. A friend should accept your honest and candid comments and should respect your decisions. That's the beauty of friendship.

Again, find a friend who's had a successful breastfeeding experience. Or maybe someone who hasn't but who'll be there, rain or shine. He or she will have positive and funny comments to make about this lifestyle event. You'll laugh over the "you-won't-believe-how-big-they-get" stories and find comfort in the fact that someone else has "been there" and "done that."

Nursing Mom's Notes

Ask your mother or father if you were breastfed. Ask about other siblings. Find out if your spouse or partner was breastfed. If possible, ask if the grandparents-to-be were breastfed. It makes for some interesting table talk!

What Is a Doula?

An emerging source of support today, during birth and throughout the first days of parenting, is the *doula*. Literally, it means one who supports during birth and parturition. A doula nurtures and protects your birthing choice, as well as your decision to breastfeed.

Doulas work with birthing experiences in homes, hospitals, and birth centers. They provide emotional, physical, and informational support. Doulas often contract their services; that is, you arrange a private agreement to receive childbirth and breastfeeding support from this type of provider.

Insurance may cover the services of a doula as well as the mother-baby care and breastfeeding instruction that they may provide after delivery. A doula usually offers childbirth instruction as well as basic breastfeeding information in preparation of childbirth.

Lactation Lingo

A **doula** is an individual who surrounds, interacts with, and aids the mother at any time within the period that includes pregnancy, birth, and lactation.

More and more mothers are choosing the doula's childbirth services as labor and delivery nurses increasingly are given large patient assignments and cannot offer the specialized attention that you may need. Ask your friends, your childbirth instructor, or your physician for a referral if this childbirth assistant is of interest to you. Third-party payers may cover the cost of labor support and assistance in the first days after delivery.

Mother Support Groups

A grassroots organization formed in the early 1970s in the United States is La Leche League International (LLLI). This international, not-for-profit organization shares a mission of global breastfeeding for every mother and baby. Members provide support, information, and encouragement to women who want to breastfeed. The league is comprised of chapters located throughout the world. Meetings are held in different locations and directed by leaders qualified to help and support a woman's breastfeeding efforts. Mothers who plan to breastfeed are encouraged to attend meetings, where mothers can breastfeed their babies and ask questions on location.

Another support group with a good reputation for helping mothers and their infants with breastfeeding is the Nursing Mothers Counsel. This nonprofit organization also provides essential information and support to breastfeeding mothers. It has affiliate chapters in California and Colorado.

You can find further information about LLLI and Nursing Mothers Counsel in Appendix C. Look in your White Pages for local chapter listings or for leaders and their telephone numbers.

New Mothers Support Group

A good place to look for breastfeeding support is your local hospital or birth center. Ask about a group for new mothers that may focus on breastfeeding support and information. Your local church or synagogue may also have a mothers' group that meets; be sure to inquire at these locations.

It's also possible to host your own breastfeeding support group, gathering friends or family who share this common need and interest. A small number, such as three or four mothers, works best. What's helpful is to include someone who's previously breastfed. A group of mothers once contracted with me to provide counseling and

Nursing Mom's Notes

The lyrics of a song from summer camp come to mind: "Make new friends, but keep the old; one is silver and the other's gold." Find the "gold" friend when it comes to breastfeeding support.

LactFact

The La Leche League mothering support group was established in 1957 in Franklin Park, IL. Its purpose is to provide information, encouragement, and moral support to nursing mothers. Today, over 4,000 active chapters are worldwide, including the United States, Canada, Europe, Australia, and Africa.

information about breastfeeding their toddlers. Hiring a lactation consultant or a health care professional to provide information and instruction in a group setting is a creative alternative for bringing the support to your location.

The Least You Need to Know

➤ Ask for support from your spouse or partner.

➤ Identify family members and friends with a positive attitude about breastfeeding.

➤ Consider hiring a doula for birth and breastfeeding support.

➤ Locate mother-to-mother support groups in your area.

➤ Ask if your hospital or birth center offers support services for new mothers.

Chapter 6

Gather More Information

In This Chapter

➤ Classes available about breastfeeding

➤ Other types of literature and media

➤ Magazines and periodicals for parents

➤ Information on the Internet

The more information that you have at your fingertips, the greater your knowledge and confidence will be about learning the new skill of breastfeeding. As you seek additional sources of information, you will probably meet others who share the same interest. You can start to network with other parents who will breastfeed or may already be breastfeeding.

It's always important to consider the source of any information that you access. Look at the author of any written material. I've had parents tell me that they read about "toughening" the nipples in preparation for breastfeeding. When I looked to find who wrote such a thing, I found that someone had written it over 10 years ago without any knowledge of breastfeeding! Find out who publishes any brochures or flyers that you come across. Your class instructor should have experience and knowledge in the field of human lactation. You should also carefully examine any information found in cyberspace.

Class Time

In addition to reading, it may be very helpful to take a parenting class that focuses on breastfeeding. Consider this if you learn best when someone presents the information to you. Some of us feel more comfortable with new information when a knowledgeable instructor can answer our questions. Reading and class instruction may be a great combination for learning all you can prior to breastfeeding.

Find out about the instructor of the class before you sign up. Ask for the teacher's bio or read a description of the class to help you decide. Remember to find a class whose instructor has credentials or qualifications specific to breastfeeding. Look for a nurse instructor with mother-baby experience. Find a lactation consultant with experience in a hospital, an office, or a private practice environment who teaches this specialty. Perhaps your childbirth educator teaches a class about breastfeeding in addition to childbirth preparation. Don't feel pressured to register for a class until you have the information you need to make a decision.

Ask about the class content and the number of class sessions that meet. Most classes cover the basics and may meet for one or two class sessions. Look for a class for beginners if that's what you are. A class for working mothers or for mothers of multiples might be appropriate if you are planning to return to work or are expecting twins, triplets, or quadruplets. Be sure to ask about the topics covered.

Is your spouse or partner welcome, or is it intended for women only? Most classes welcome you and your spouse or partner. After all, it is a feeding method that both parents should understand. Many men are surprised about what they learn from this type of class. And it makes great conversation in the office the next workday! Grandparents-to-be may be interested in attending, too.

Look for classes offered at your local hospital, birth center, doctor's office, or breastfeeding center. Ask for a flyer about parenting classes in your area. Get some recommendations from friends or family members. Many mothers take a class before they deliver, but I've had some mothers attend with breastfeeding babies in their arms! Be sure to ask if a follow-up class is offered, preferably taught by the same instructor.

Nursing Mom's Notes

Breastfeeding classes are in demand in some areas and fill quickly. You may need to register as early as your fourth or fifth month of pregnancy. Choose a class offered in your seventh or eighth month of pregnancy.

Breast Beware

Don't let anyone tell you that twins, triplets, or quadruplets can't be breastfed. Plenty of parents are proud to say they did. It can be done!

Literature and Videos

You may find additional types of literature of interest to you. Medical textbooks are a fascinating read for those seeking a greater knowledge about breastfeeding. These are the books that health care professionals themselves look to for management and counseling guidelines. The words and content may be on the scientific side, but the content helps you to understand the value of this human resource.

Look for additional literature sources covering the anthropological and cultural aspects of breastfeeding. Many cultures outside the Western world consider breastfeeding a part of their lives. In other words, women in many communities consider breastfeeding to be a given when it comes to infant feeding. It's been handed down from generation to generation. You may gain a whole new perspective on breastfeeding if you consider it a way of life!

There are several videos on the market that show mothers breastfeeding their infants. This can be extremely helpful to you if you have never seen a mother feed her baby from the breast. A video format may ease your concerns and offer you the opportunity to view it several times. Videos can be a safe way to introduce your spouse, partner, or the grandparents-to-be to breastfeeding, especially if they feel uncertain or uncomfortable at the mention of it. Ask about videotapes for loan at your local library, doctor's office, or hospital resource center. You may find videos on breastfeeding for purchase where parenting resources are sold.

Magazines and Periodicals

You may also find information about breastfeeding in magazines and journals. Look for those that feature baby and parenting topics. Journals usually publish research and science-related articles, but it makes great reading material if you want the challenge. You can usually find parenting magazines at your bookstore, shopping mart, and local library; check with your librarian for the availability of professional journals.

LactFact

Some magazines and journals to consider include *Abreast of Our Times, Breastfeeding Abstracts, Breastfeeding Review, Journal of Mammary Gland Biology and Neoplasia, Journal of Human Lactation, Mothering, The Compleat Mother,* and *New Beginnings.*

The World Wide Web

The Internet has a vast array of information available, covering the ABCs of everything. It's important for you to validate the source of breastfeeding information before you use it. Look to those Web sites that represent professional organizations or sources with professional representation. Look to see that an individual or company representative has some professional expertise in the field of lactation. Someone's personal experience is not the same as a professional's perspective, regarding the evaluation and management of breastfeeding.

It may be difficult or challenging to find the author of the information on the Internet. Request more information from the "about us" or "company profile" buttons. Send e-mail and ask if a lactation consultant is on staff and what credentials he or she possesses. Find out if a medical advisory board exists and if it reviews the information posted on the site.

Breast Beware

Breastfeeding information found on the Internet should not replace the health care, advice, and expertise that your health care provider offers.

Most sites post a disclaimer that the information they give should not replace the advice and care that your health care provider may render. Again, you are looking for information to collect for your file in the event that you need to resource everything available. What you'll find as you "network" on the Internet are the supporters and advocates of breastfeeding. Some mothers have told me that their breastfeeding success came from other mothers online who answered their question or calmed their fears.

So, surf the Web as often and as much as you'd like. Be cautious, though, about the breastfeeding information that's available if you can't identify the source. The Internet is a great resource to use in combination with your other sources of information.

The Least You Need to Know

➤ A breastfeeding class can address your concerns and answer additional questions.

➤ Your spouse, partner, or a grandparent-to-be should attend class with you.

➤ Class participants can also be sources of support.

➤ Consider videos, magazines, textbooks, and journals as additional sources of information.

➤ Use the Internet to complement your resource list.

Chapter 7

Tools of the Trade

In This Chapter

➤ A review of breastfeeding products on the market

➤ The best time to buy your breastfeeding supplies

➤ The different types of breast pumps available

➤ Where to look for products and supplies

I grew up hearing my dad say over and over that you've gotta have the right tool for the task at hand. It makes life simpler, and you're satisfied in the long run. When it comes to breastfeeding, you are probably wondering what "tools" there are that makes your life simpler and make you more satisfied. If you've taken a peek in any baby catalogue or store you may already know what's available. And the choice is overwhelming.

I've taken the tools that I feel may be essential to your breastfeeding experience, and will explain them. With our technological advances today, finding the appropriate information to make a choice can be a challenge. It's important to know ahead of time what to choose and what to stay away from. In this day and age, the right product or equipment can make or break your breastfeeding experience.

Your Breast Supporter

I've spoken about the importance of good support during your breastfeeding experience, and your bra should be one of your best supporters! During and after pregnancy your breast size can change considerably. Your breasts enlarge, becoming heavier and more sensitive as hormones influence tissue growth. Your breast sensitivity may have been one of the first signs that you were pregnant. Remember that the mammary gland increases during pregnancy to prepare for milk production. Add to this an increased blood supply and retention of fluid, and you get fuller, bigger, and heavier breasts.

Unsnap your bra cup and you're open for food service.

(Source: Bravado! Designs, Inc.)

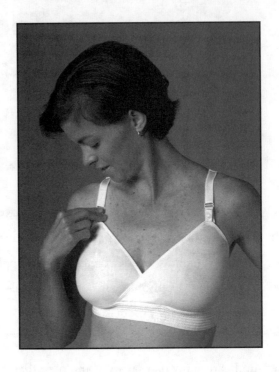

Nursing Mom's Notes

When the bra you're wearing becomes too tight, and your breasts are spilling out the cups, it's time for a new bra. Find a retailer that stocks several sizes and styles of nursing bras, and ask about getting measured and fitted.

What this means in relation to your bra is this: Your band and cup size usually increase, and you will need to shop for a new bra. A combination maternity-nursing bra is different than an everyday bra for women. This kind of bra provides more support, with wider bands, straps, fuller cups, and more fabric. A nursing bra offers you convenient, easy access to your breast and a cup adjustment to allow for breast fullness. A bra that enables you to open the cup with one hand when you're holding your baby and readying to breastfeed is also very helpful.

Look for a bra made of all cotton. The breathable qualities of cotton make it the best fabric to wear against your skin during pregnancy and breastfeeding. Pregnancy hormones affect your body's thermostat, resulting in "surges" that make you hot and sweaty.

Bras made of a synthetic material, like polyester, may keep moisture against your skin. Moisture can contribute to nipple soreness and skin irritation. A cotton knit bra washes and wears better than a woven cotton bra. Stay away from decorative trims that may be scratchy and irritating to your skin.

Any bra with a back closure should have several "hooks" so that you can adjust its fit as needed. Look for wide, cushioned, supportive straps for shoulder comfort. Consider a nursing bra with a sports style, which pulls on over your head. Bravado! Designs, a Canadian manufacturer, makes a comfortable nursing bra in several fabric colors. This style of bra can be quite supportive and provide much-needed back support. Your posture can take any help it can get!

Find and wear a well-designed softcup bra through your last trimester of pregnancy and first three months of breastfeeding. That's right, no wire! An underwire bra is not flexible and doesn't accommodate the changes you experience in your breasts, especially in your cup size. Underwire bras often become quite uncomfortable. The compression from a wire may inhibit adequate emptying of your milk glands and the proper flow of lymph throughout the breast tissue. When milk volume increases, so does your bra cup size. The wire under a bra cup will not expand when the lactating breast fills with milk. A softcup bra can accommodate some increase in breast cup size.

Breast Beware

Take a break from an underwire bra until your third month after delivery. The compression from a wire may inhibit adequate emptying of your milk glands and the proper flow of lymph fluid throughout your breast tissue.

Breastfeeding support is available from the back as well.

(Source: Bravado! Designs, Inc.)

I've been asked many times "when" it's best to shop for a nursing bra. If you experience changes in your breast size early in pregnancy, then shop early for a new bra. Don't suffer throughout your pregnancy because you are waiting until closer to your delivery date to buy a new bra. The important thing is to choose a bra that fits well early in your pregnancy, knowing that you may have to buy a larger size later if needed. The start of your third trimester of pregnancy may be a good time to shop. You might want to be generous in the fit if you're shopping early. Expect to get bigger in your cup size when your milk "comes in."

LactFact

The brassiere, as we know it today, was transformed from a corset and gave lift from above, rather than a push from below. The first patented *soutien-gorge* (brassiere) was designed and sold in Paris, France, in the early 1900s. Mary Phelps Jacobs received the first U.S. brassiere patent in 1914. Her brassiere was designed from two handkerchiefs held together with a pink ribbon. She sold her patent rights to Warner Brothers Corset Company for $1,500, later valued at $15 million!

It's best to be measured correctly for your band and cup size. Seven out of 10 women today do not wear the correct bra size. Ask for an experienced salesperson to measure and fit you for your bra. The common measurements taken give you your band and cup size. The measurement just under your breasts, around your ribcage, helps determine your band size. Band sizes are even numbers; if you get an odd number, you round up. The measurement around the fullest part of your breasts, just at the nipple line, helps determine your cup size. Cup sizes are assigned a letter that corresponds to the difference in the two measurements taken. A one-inch difference is an A cup, a two-inch difference is a B cup, and so forth. Refer to the following illustration and the instructions to help determine your bra size.

To determine your bra size, take these measurements while wearing a good-fitting, unpadded bra: With a measuring tape, measure around your body just under your breasts. Add 3" to this number if your measurement is 32" or more. Add 5" to this number if your measurement is 31" or less. This is your bra band size. Bands are sized as even numbers, so round up if your measurement is an odd number.

Example: 37" + 3" = 40" or 40 band size

Example: 28" + 5" = 33" or 34 band size

Measure around your body over your nipples at the fullest part of your breasts. Subtract your band measurement from this measurement to determine your cup size.

Example: 45" − 40" = 5" or 40E bra size

Example: 36" − 33" = 3" or 34C bra size

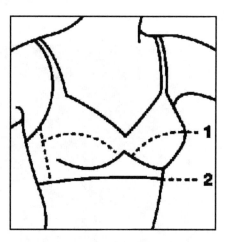

Your cup measurement corresponds to #1; your under-bust measurement corresponds to #2.

Difference	Cup Size
Up to 1"	A
Up to 2"	B
Up to 3"	C
Up to 4"	D
Up to 5"	E (DD)
Up to 6"	F (DDD)
Up to 7"	G
Up to 8"	H
Up to 9"	I
Up to 10"	J

Breast Shells

Also called a breast cup, breast shells have several uses. They can be used to correct inverted nipples, protect sore nipples, relieve engorgement, and collect leaking milk between feedings. The breast shell design is a plastic cup with a hole in its backing that enables the nipple to protrude through the opening. The cup is contoured and the back is concave, to fit against the shape of your breast. The hole fits over an average-sized nipple, and puts pressure on the areola at the base of the nipple. The front and back separate for emptying and cleaning. Holes placed in the shell allow for air circulation and help to equalize pressure.

Breast shells protect and shape the everyday nipple.

(Source: Hollister, Inc.)

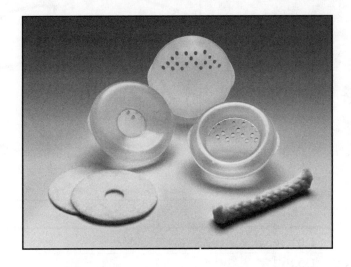

Breast Beware

If you are at risk for preterm labor, are experiencing contractions, or have a high-risk pregnancy, the use of breast shells is contraindicated.

If you have flat or inverted nipples, you can wear a breast shell during your pregnancy to improve nipple elasticity. The shell's circular opening in the back is centered over your breast, enabling your nipple to evert, or protrude, through its center. Your bra holds the breast shell in place. You begin wearing breast shells for a few hours each day and then gradually increase wear to 8 to 10 hours.

Your physician, health care provider, or lactation consultant should help you to evaluate your nipple elasticity and to be certain that there aren't any contraindications for use. If you are at risk for preterm labor, are experiencing uterine contractions, or have a high-risk pregnancy, the use of breast shells is usually contraindicated.

Many mothers who have flat or inverted nipples can often breastfeed successfully without wearing a breast shell prenatally. Your baby's suckling may be strong enough to evert a flat or inverted nipple with repeated breastfeeding. Some mothers feel comfortable using this "wait and see" option.

Breast shells can be lifesavers after delivery to protect nipples that have become sore, tender, or show signs of blistering and cracking. If you experience cracked or blistered nipples, have your baby's latch-on and positioning at your breast evaluated by a trained lactation professional. The evaluation can be a lifesaver, too!

In the first days of breastfeeding when your nipples can be tender, shells help keep clothing from touching your nipples. They also allow for air circulation and enable soothing ointments and salves to remain on your nipples. Some women wear breast shells to collect dripped milk in between feedings and to keep their breast pads in place.

Breast Pads

You may or may not experience leaking of breast milk while breastfeeding. If you do, great. If you don't, that's okay, too. Just because you don't leak milk doesn't mean that you won't make milk. Rest assured that with or without any leaking, you can make breast milk.

Ameda® breast pads for wash and wear.

(Source: Hollister, Inc.)

The purpose of a breast pad is to absorb any milk that may leak from your breast. You may leak milk before delivery, while sleeping long periods during the night, and in between feedings. The types of pads available are washable, reusable, and disposable.

Washable and reusable pads are made of fabric. They are usually several layers thick, with at least one layer of absorbent fabric like cotton, felt, or flannel. Look for an absorbent fabric and try to avoid any pads with plastic layers. A pad with a plastic moisture barrier may add to nipple soreness, especially if the pad is not changed frequently.

Super-absorbent washable breast pads with a stay-dry liner.

(Source: Bravado! Designs, Inc.)

Like a disposable diaper, a disposable breast pad can be discarded after it becomes wet and saturated. Most disposable breast pads are made with cellulose or paper and usually have a plastic moisture barrier.

Before you purchase breast pads, consider the following:

Nursing Mom's Notes

Wash fabric pads with baby's clothing. They will soften up over time and will smell like your baby!

➤ **Size.** Will the diameter of the pad cover your breast?

➤ **Shape.** If it's fabric, has it been sewn flat or with a dart for contour? Women with larger breasts may prefer a flat pad. A contoured pad may fit a smaller-breasted woman better. Some disposable pads are designed to shape around the breast.

➤ **Quantity.** During your first month of breast-feeding, you may use four to six pads a day. This alone may help you decide between reusable and disposable.

Lanolin

Rated the number one ointment of choice for chapped, sore nipples is lanolin. Extracted from sheep's wool, lanolin is an emollient that helps to restore moisture and to heal the skin. Choose a "USP-modified lanolin" that's been purified. It's safe if ingested by your baby, and you do not need to remove it before breastfeeding. Pure lanolin is very sticky and spreads better when "warmed." Take a pea-sized amount and roll it between your fingers to warm it. Spread it all over your nipple(s) and areolar tissue.

Lanolin is safe to use during your pregnancy if the skin around your nipple and areola becomes dry and itchy. Be sure to cleanse your breast with only water if this occurs. Soap can dry your skin and re-move the natural oils that your glands secrete.

Breast Beware

Look for a hypoallergenic lanolin if you are allergic to wool or wool products. Wool allergens are removed during processing and it's considered safe for your baby if ingested.

Breast Pumps

Breast pumps have been used as an aid for breast milk extraction since the 1800s. In the early 1970s women began to return to the workplace. Faced with the need for milk collection while away from their babies, women opened a market for breast pumps that helped them express their breast milk.

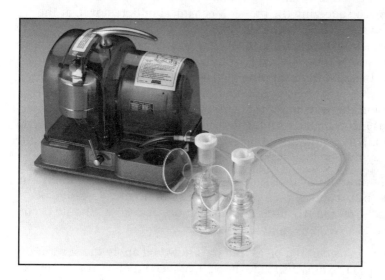

Dr. Einar Egnell's first electric piston breast pump—the SMB.

(Source: Hollister, Inc.)

Let's review the activity involved with a baby's suckling, as this relates directly to the function of a breast pump. When a baby feeds at the breast, it makes a seal around the breast with its lips, and the jaw helps to support the breast inside the mouth. A negative pressure develops inside the mouth when the baby starts a sucking action. The tongue massages or "milks" the breast and creates the stimulation necessary for milk production. In response to this suction and stimulation, the milk begins to flow, and it continues as long as suckling continues. Therefore, the baby determines the amount of milk produced, depending on how well the breast is stimulated and emptied. The frequency of suckling and effective milk removal determines the quantity of milk production.

A breast pump should be able to create suction and massage action much like a baby. The suction from the pump should start the milk flowing and empty the milk ducts. The suction, or negative pressure, created by a breast pump should match the suction a baby uses while feeding from the breast. A baby uses its tongue to massage or pull milk from the breast to help with milk release. The repetitions of the tongue as it massages the breast are known as cycles. A breast pump should apply negative pressure in cycles to the breast for efficient and effective milk collection.

Lactation Lingo

SMB stands for Sister Maja's Broestpump.

The amount of suction or negative pressure a breast pump creates is the next important point to consider. In his landmark research during the 1950s, a Swedish physician, Einar Egnell, studied various methods of emptying milk from the human breast. He knew that a woman could manually or mechanically empty milk from her breast. Manual removal involved squeezing the breast. Mechanical milk removal, at the time, involved continuous suction that often resulted in blood vessel rupture and tissue damage. Dr. Egnell studied the effects of continuous suction and intermittent suction on the human breast. He also studied the amount of "safe" suction that could be applied to the human breast without causing damage or tissue breakdown. The results of his research showed that negative pressure, or vacuum, up to –220 mm Hg could be safely used, and that vacuum must be intermittent, releasing every 1.5 seconds. His research was incorporated into the design of the first piston-driven electric breast pump, the SMB. This piston-driven breast pump continues to be manufactured in Switzerland today by the Ameda Corporation.

The ideal breast pump should provide a suction and cycle pattern that simulates an infant's suckling pattern. Vacuum should provide a range of negative pressure between –50 mm Hg and –220 mm Hg. Intermittent suction, or cycling, should occur between 30 cycles and 60 cycles per minute.

An important feature to consider in a breast pump is how you apply the suction or vacuum to your breast(s). The breast shield, known by several names, is a flange designed to cover the breast, much like a baby does with its mouth and jaw. It supports your breast and seals it against the flange when suction is applied. The center opening for the nipple, the nipple tunnel, fits an average-sized woman. A reducing-insert is available for smaller sizes, to custom fit the breast shield. The breast shield should connect to the suction source with tubing, or be designed with its suction source attached close to the breast shield.

The types of breast pumps available on the market today include the following:

➤ Hospital-grade piston breast pump

➤ Electric breast pump

➤ Battery breast pump

➤ Manual breast pump

Let's take a look at each type and consider which pump is best for your circumstance.

Hospital-Grade Piston Breast Pump

This is the best breast pump available on the market today. The hospital or medical-grade piston breast pump is found where you might expect—in a hospital or medical practice location. This is a breast pump designed after Dr. Egnell's prototype, and in some cases may actually be his piston-driven breast pump, the SMB.

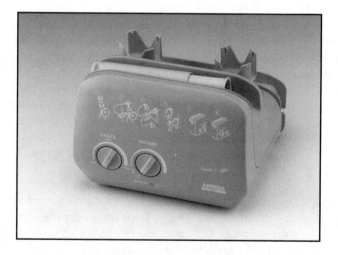

The Elite™ piston breast pump by Ameda®.

(Source: Hollister, Inc.)

The demand for and use of this type of breast pump in a hospital or medical setting means that it is designed for frequent use, and for multiple users. It can be used 24 hours a day, 7 days a week, if necessary. It is therefore classified as Durable Medical Equipment, or DME. An electrical source powers the piston. This means that you plug the attached electric cord into a wall outlet. It is the breast pump of choice for any mother needing to establish, augment, complement, or maintain her breast milk supply. It is the best equipment to remove breast milk from the breast, period. In my practice, whenever the need for frequent milk removal or for effective and efficient breast stimulation arises, I always recommend the use of a hospital- or medical-grade piston breast pump.

LactFact

When you use a hospital-grade piston pump, it is especially important that breast milk and condensation from milk collection do not back up into the piston or motor. The HygieniKit, manufactured by Ameda, is a unique breast milk collection kit that prevents this from happening. Its silicone diaphragm provides a barrier between the breast shield and the vacuum source. Therefore, condensation and breast milk cannot pass through the tubing and into the piston. Many hospitals and birth centers use this milk collection system to ensure patient hygiene and to prevent cross-contamination.

The suction level or vacuum on this pump adjusts to a maximum –220 mm Hg. Remember, this is the safest vacuum level determined by Dr. Egnell. Its cycle or piston repetitions may be preset, or adjustable between 30 and 60 cycles per minute. Each breast pump user must use an individual milk collection kit to access the suction source. The milk collection kit often contains the breast shield, tubing, and piston connector. One of Medela's collection kits contains the piston itself. An individual kit prevents cross-contamination and ensures hygiene between each user. Your hospital or birth center may supply this kit if the need arises for a piston breast pump. The kit is usually available for single or dual collection. Pumping with a dual collection kit means that you can stimulate and empty both breasts at the same time. You can cut your pumping time in half when you pump both breasts simultaneously. It can also raise or improve your prolactin levels, increasing your milk volume. Expect single pumping to last from 15 to 30 minutes, and dual pumping from 10 to 20 minutes. Mothers with premature babies or those unable to nurse directly from the breast are advised to pump both breasts at the same time.

Nursing Mom's Notes

Use a dual milk collection kit to pump both breasts at the same time. It will also increase your amount of hormone, prolactin, that stimulates your milk production.

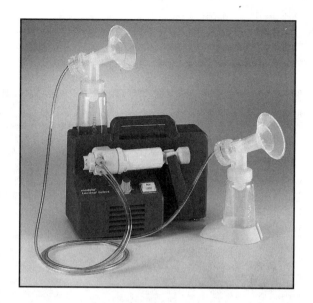

The Lactina® Select Breastpump by Medela®. Just add the piston collection kit and pump away.

(Source: Medela, Inc.)

It may be cost-prohibitive to own one of these breast pumps, and they are usually available for rental from a lactation consultant, hospital, or pharmacy. The average retail price for an electric piston breast pump ranges from $725 to $1,395 depending on the model and features. Rental rates may range from $2.50 to $3.00 (USD) per day, with long-term daily rates as low as $1.25 (USD). Most leases require a monetary deposit when renting a breast pump. Some pumps have a vehicle lighter adapter that draws power from your car battery. Some models have a nickel cadmium (NiCd) battery option available. Refurbished models may be available for purchase. Be sure to ask about service, warranty, and return policy before you purchase.

Electric Breast Pump

This is a purchasable, single-user breast pump that many working mothers use to collect breast milk while separated from their babies. The dual collection kit that comes standard with this pump enables most users to collect breast milk from both breasts at the same time. This type of breast pump is designed with a small piston or balloon diaphragm that creates the suction. An A/C adapter that plugs into an electrical outlet usually powers this type of breast pump. Battery sources as well as a vehicle lighter-adapter are power options for these pumps. The suction, or vacuum, is adjustable to a maximum of –220 mm Hg. The cycling may be preset or can be adjusted between 30 and 60 cycles per minute. Most of these pumps retail between $160 and $290 (USD).

Breast Beware

An electric breast pump is a single-user breast pump. Only the purchaser should use it. It should not be shared or used by more than one person. This may present a risk to your health and to the health of your baby.

This type of pump is ideal for three to four uses per day, five days a week. They can usually perform between 300 to 500 operational hours before the motor needs service. Most working mothers report that their pump "lasted" through two children.

The lightweight and compact electric breast pump by Ameda®—the Purely Yours™ Breast Pump.

(Source: Hollister, Inc.)

This is a single-user breast pump and should not be shared or used by more than one person. The possibility of breast milk overflow into the suction source or of moisture residue in the collection kit may present a health risk to you and your baby. Home-sanitizing, or boiling parts of the pump or the collection kit, does not kill all bacteria and viruses, including HIV and Hepatitis A, B, and C. Only the use of an autoclave can ensure sterilization. Autoclaving can be a costly endeavor and most parts, including the pump, cannot withstand this process.

The first portable personal breast pump for working mothers—the Pump In Style® Breast-pump by Medela®.

(Source: Medela, Inc.)

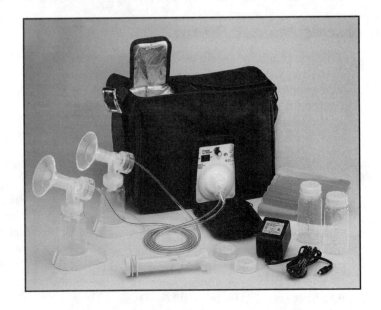

Battery Breast Pump

This type of breast pump generates a continuous suction during operation. It is powered by batteries and may have an optional A/C adapter available, which usually increases the price. By pushing a button release or moving your finger away from a hole on the motor or breast shield, you release or break the suction. This is how you cycle the pump, thus creating a piston-like action. It may take you 6 to 10 seconds, however, to build up to the maximum suction. This can be a major drawback. It means that you can only cycle your suction four to eight times per minute; it doesn't come close to the 60 cycles per minute needed to simulate a baby's suckling pattern. Since you control the suction, your maximum suction could exceed –300 mm Hg, far beyond the recommended safe-suction level. This may result in pain and in nipple damage. This type of pump may retail between $45 and $110 depending on features.

Nursing Mom's Notes

Keep a fresh supply of alkaline batteries on hand for this type of pump. Rechargeable batteries may not power the motor as well.

A portable MiniElectric™ battery-operated breast-pump by Medela®.

(Source: Medela, Inc.)

The small, compact size and the battery operation are the only conveniences that this type of pump has to offer. It is a poor choice in pumps for long-term pumping, or for establishing or maintaining your milk supply. Pumping time may be 10 to 20 minutes for each breast. If you are collecting breast milk only on occasion for your baby, this may be your choice in pumps.

Manual Breast Pump

The last pump to consider is the manual breast pump. Just like it sounds, your operational efforts make you the motor! There are no motorized or electrical components involved. Suction is created as a gasket is drawn through a cylinder, and suction is released when the gasket is returned to the starting point. Your frequency of draw and release is your cycle pattern. Most manual pumps require squeezing a handle, a bulb, or pulling a piston through a cylinder. The suction level with this type of pump may range from –60 mm Hg to –400 mm Hg. Some pumps enable you to cycle as frequently as 60 per minute, while others limit your cycling frequency.

Your pumping time will be about 15 to 20 minutes with each breast. This pump may work well for you if you are patient and can learn the "art of pumping." It also will work well once you have breastfeeding and your milk supply well established. Many mothers choose to pump one breast as baby nurses from the other, to learn their pumping technique. It is not a breast pump recommended for frequent pumping, for establishing your milk supply, or for women with carpal tunnel syndrome. Look for this pump to retail between $35 and $60.

Nursing Mom's Notes

The "bicycle horn" manual breast pump was originally manufactured by Corning Glass in New York in the 1800s.

Operate Ameda's manual breast pump with the squeeze of one hand!

(Source: Hollister, Inc.)

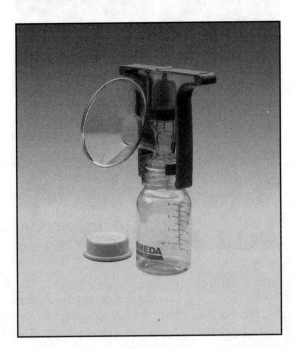

Comparison of Breast Pumps

	Medical-Grade	Personal	Battery	Manual
Daily use	5 to 12/day	2 to 4/day	1 to 2/day	1 to 3/day
Weekly use	4 to 7 d/wk	3 to 5 d/wk	1 to 3 d/wk	3 to 5 d/wk
# of users	Multi	Single only	Single only	Single only
Accessory kit	Dual/Single	Dual/Single	Dual/Single	Dual/Single
Pumping Time				
Dual	10 to 15	10 to 15	10 to 15	
Single	15 to 30	15 to 30	15 to 30	20 to 30
Availability	Hospital LC Pharmacy Med supplier	Hospital LC Pharmacy Med supplier	Hospital LC Pharmacy Mail order	LC Pharmacy Mail order
Brand Names				
Ameda	SMB Lact-e Elite	Purely Yours	One Hand	Breast Pump
Avent				Isis
Medela	Classic Lactina Plus Lactina Select	Pump In Style	Mini Electric DoubleEase™	ManualEase™ SpringExpress

Suppliers

Not every mother needs a breast pump. Getting help from the pros and frequent breastfeeding from the start may not necessitate the use of a breast pump. Sometimes, though, the need may arise.

It's very important to locate breast pump suppliers in your area before you deliver your baby, even if you don't think you'll need one. A medical indication may arise and necessitate pumping your breast milk. I've heard several mothers tell me, "Oh,

I'm not going to need a breast pump; I plan to stay at home." Then, in the first week of breastfeeding, they may experience unexpected engorgement that necessitates milk removal. It's 11:00 P.M. and you're calling everywhere to find one. Your possible suppliers include the following:

➤ Lactation consultant

➤ Hospital or birth center

➤ Pharmacy

➤ Medical supply store

➤ Baby store

Gather information from a supplier that includes rates, terms, business hours, supplies, and additional services. You may ask for a rental contract to have on hand that you can fill out if needed. Find out if your supplier has someone who can explain the different types of breast pumps that they handle.

Breast Beware

Some lactation consultants employed by a hospital corporation or a health care system supplement their incomes by selling breastfeeding supplies and handling breast pump rentals. This presents a conflict of interest when a consultant conducts business on company time. Liability also becomes an issue. Be certain that such a consultant discloses to you any such conflict and that business is conducted outside his or her employer's premises.

The decision to rent or purchase a breast pump depends on your circumstance, budget, and preference. You'll want to wait until your third or fourth week to start pumping extra breast milk. I usually recommend that you hold off making a breast pump purchase before the birth of your baby. Your circumstance may require the use of a hospital-grade piston breast pump in the first weeks. Some retailers offer a discount toward a breast pump purchase if their customer rents from them. Ask yourself what you can afford to spend. Your budget may indicate rental over purchase. Also consider your preference. Do you prefer to own or to rent a breast pump? Compare the advantages that one has over the other.

Last, but certainly not least, is availability. Find out what your supplier keeps readily available. It doesn't help to find out that the shelves are empty when you're in need of something. Ask what breast pumps your supplier stocks on location. It may be possible to place a deposit toward a breast pump rental or a purchase, in order to ensure availability for you.

The Least You Need to Know

➤ Be measured and fitted for a nursing bra in the second or third trimester of your pregnancy.

➤ Choose a cotton softcup bra, and decline on the underwire.

➤ Buy some breastfeeding supplies ahead of time.

➤ Look into the several types of breast pumps that are available.

➤ Consider the type of breast pump that's best for you, based on your circumstance.

➤ Locate breast pump suppliers before your delivery date.

Health Insurance

I've been asked on several occasions, "Will my insurance cover my consultation?" or "Shouldn't my breast pump rental be covered under my insurance?" My answer goes like this: yes, no, and maybe so. It depends on the terms and conditions set forth in one's insurance policy. I never really took a look at my insurance policy until I had a claim denied with my first pregnancy. It turned out that my physician, not my physical therapist, had to order a therapeutic device so that it would be considered for coverage. I resubmitted the claim along with a written explanation and product literature, and received coverage the second time around.

When I became a provider of specialty services and supplies, I found it especially important to make clients aware of their insurance policies and their benefits. Several times someone would tell me "that's not covered" or "insurance won't pay." As a provider, I would get a different answer. So let's take a look at health insurance. Let me explain how medical supplies and health care services for breastfeeding may be covered under insurance plans and policies.

Policy or Plan

First and foremost is to find your insurance policy or to call customer service and ask how to obtain a copy. The policy will indicate the name of the insured person or persons who have coverage. It's important to know who the primary policyholder is and who has coverage. You will need to add your newborn baby to the policy within a certain time period after your baby's birth. Better yet, have your expected delivery date documented on your policy.

Find and read the major medical portion of your policy. It should define some of the following provisions:

➤ Third-party administrator

➤ Health care provider(s)

➤ Coinsurance and deductible

➤ Covered charges and services

➤ Medical necessity

➤ Dependent(s)

It's important that you understand beforehand what your policy provides in order to avoid confusion and frustration after-the-fact.

Let's consider the following scenario. Your baby is admitted to the Newborn Intensive Care Unit (NICU) after a difficult delivery, and cannot take anything by mouth. That means you won't be able to actually initiate breastfeeding. To establish your milk supply, you will need a hospital-grade electric piston breast pump and collection kit to stimulate breastfeeding. You will need to use the pump at least 8 to 12 times each day to stimulate and express your breast milk.

Nursing Mom's Notes

Look for the phone number for customer or member services on your insurance card. Have some paper and a pen handy before you call to jot down any information they provide you.

Look over your policy and see if you can find answers to the following questions:

➤ Which providers does your policy cover for breastfeeding services and supplies?

➤ Do you need prior authorization from your insurance company for these services and supplies?

➤ Does your insurance company have a health care professional or lactation consultant who will locate and authorize these supplies and services for you if needed?

➤ Is your insurance company contracted with a breastfeeding specialist to provide lactation consultation?

➤ Are services rendered in your home or your provider's office?

➤ Are services covered under the mother's policy, baby's policy, or both?

You may find it helpful to call member services or to contact your case manager with these questions. Having answers in advance will ease your circumstance if it becomes necessary to access services and supplies during your breastfeeding experience. Understanding what is covered and how to file a claim is also beneficial.

Policy Administrator, Agent, Manager

The *third-party administrator* is the person or group licensed to perform policy administrative services and to pay claims on behalf of the insurance company. Your insurance company designates its third-party administration. Find out who this is; this person or group decides whether to pay or decline your claim. They consider the provider, the services, and the supplies involved and decide how the benefits of your policy will apply to your claim.

Your insurance agent represents your insurance company and may be able to answer your questions about coverage for breastfeeding services and supplies. Call your agent and ask if he or she can help to explain or clarify any questions that you may have.

Contact the human resources manager at your company or place of business with questions about your policy. One of the benefits of your employment may be health insurance coverage, and your HR manager should be able to help clarify and explain any benefits you are eligible for.

Lactation Lingo

A person or group that administers and pays claims for an insurance company is a **third-party administrator.** Many administrators have a health care professional on staff to help review or determine what's medically necessary. One such person may be a case manager. He or she reviews your policy and authorizes or denies any necessary health care products and services. Jot down any names and contact information in case you have to call someone in a time of need.

Coverage and Deductible

Any charges you incur for *medically necessary* services, supplies, care, and treatment while breastfeeding should be considered for coverage. The key words here are "medically necessary." Breast milk directly affects your baby's nutritional status and overall health and is often defined as medically necessary. Your physician usually determines what is medically necessary, and needs to prescribe, perform, or order these services or supplies for them to be considered as a covered charge.

Keep in mind that a medically necessary service and supply applies to both you and your baby. Breastfeeding involves the two of you, or more with multiples, and anything that happens to one of you directly affects the other. Your physician may order or prescribe a service or supply for you, or your baby, or both of you. You depend on your baby, and vice versa, to initiate and maintain breastfeeding. When one of you cannot breastfeed or an interruption occurs, it becomes medically necessary to utilize a service or supply for breastfeeding.

Your insurance company, however, ultimately determines whether any services and/or supplies are appropriate and necessary for your medical diagnosis and treatment. The fact that your physician prescribes or recommends a service or supply does not necessarily mean it's deemed medically necessary. This is what has everyone up in arms today about "who's practicing medicine?" The end-decision for covered charges lies with your insurance carrier. Yes, you read it right!

An *explanation of benefits,* or *EOB,* indicates which services and supplies are covered or not covered. You'll receive this after you or your provider has filed a claim. You always have an opportunity to appeal for services and supplies not covered that you feel should be covered. Your EOB should include how to proceed with an appeal for any denied charges.

Your *deductible* is the monetary amount that you choose or that has been determined for you to incur before benefits will be paid under your policy. If your deductible is $500 per calendar year and the plan pays

> **Lactation Lingo**
>
> **Medically necessary** means that which is appropriate and necessary for the symptoms, diagnosis, or direct care and treatment of the medical condition. For example, a premature baby may not be able to feed directly from the breast after birth. A medical-grade piston breast pump becomes appropriate and necessary for a mother to stimulate and express breast milk under this condition.

> **Lactation Lingo**
>
> An **EOB**, or **explanation of benefits,** describes the kind of services or supplies covered by your insurance company. Your **deductible** is the dollar amount you pay before your insurance company pays the rest.

80 percent of your charges, then you pay $500 plus 20 percent of the remaining fees for all supplies and services. Be sure to look at the portion of your policy that defines dependent newborn children.

Medical Aids

Your policy should list and define under the benefits section any medical aids that are covered. Medical aids include prosthetic devices, *durable medical equipment,* and orthotic appliances. A prosthetic device is that which replaces a body part or performs a body function. Durable medical equipment is equipment that is appropriate for home use and is manufactured mainly to treat the injured or ill.

Prosthetic devices that may be considered for breastfeeding include the following:

➤ Breastfeeding supplementation device

➤ Nipple shield

➤ Specialty-feeding bottle or cup

➤ Breast milk collection kit

➤ Manual breast pump

Electric piston breast pumps are classified as durable medical equipment (DME). They are manufactured mainly for mothers needing to pump a breast milk supply for an ill or hospitalized infant. A mother's pregnancy or postpartum illness may also warrant the use and application of breast pump DME. These breast pumps are portable, a new mother can handle them, and they are appropriate for use at home. Many insurance companies reimburse the provider, or cover your rental of an electric piston breast pump, if your breastfeeding baby is hospitalized.

The Health Care Financing Administration (HCFA) recently assigned an alphanumeric code for the Ameda Egnell Elite electric piston breast pump. This enables providers of durable medical equipment to file the designated code for rental of electric piston breast pumps when a physician determines it to be medically necessary.

Lactation Lingo

Durable medical equipment is equipment that is appropriate for home use and is manufactured mainly for use in medical circumstances. Many mothers will not need any specialty equipment or feeding devices for their breastfeeding experience. An eager baby and plenty of feeding opportunity may be all that's necessary for successful breastfeeding.

Nursing Mom's Notes

Look in the Yellow Pages directory under breastfeeding information, breast pumps, or pharmacies to locate a provider or supplier of medical aids for breastfeeding.

Governmental and Other Insurance

If you don't have health insurance, you should call your local hospital and ask about any free clinics or charity programs that might be available to you. Eligibility for free services may depend on your income. Be prepared to provide information about the amount of money that you earn and the number of people who depend on your income.

Nutrition and breastfeeding education, as well as access to health services, are provided to low-income women, infants, and children, under the Special Supplementation Nutrition Program for Women, Infants, and Children, popularly known as WIC. The Food and Nutrition Service of the U.S. Department of Agriculture administers the WIC program. WIC provides grants to individual states for supplemental foods, health care referrals, and nutrition education, for eligible participants. Most state WIC offices have breastfeeding education, new mother support groups, breast pump DME, and supplies available for its participants.

Another insurance source to consider may be a secondary policy that you or your spouse or partner carries. The purpose of secondary insurance is to supplement or pick up after the primary source has been fulfilled. Again, read through its contents and call to ask any questions or to clarify your coverage.

LactFact

The WIC program is available in each state, the District of Columbia, 33 Indian tribal organizations, Puerto Rico, the Virgin Islands, American Samoa, and Guam.

Another possibility for reimbursement is a medical savings account. This is an account that some employers offer where pretax monies are set aside to use for medical supplies and services. You file a claim, along with proof of payment for supplies or services, to obtain reimbursement.

Lastly, I must mention that some of you may live in a country or province, for example, Canada, where your government provides health care to you regardless of your income level or work eligibility. It's referred to as socialized medicine. Everyone is eligible. It's best to ask your health care provider where you live about the breastfeeding services and supplies available to you. Remember to do this well in advance of your expected delivery date.

The Least You Need to Know

➤ Find and read through your health insurance policy.

➤ Contact your administrator, benefits manager, or agent for questions and explanations.

➤ Ask your physician about medically necessary services and supplies for breast-feeding.

➤ Locate a provider of medical aids and durable medical equipment for breast-feeding before your delivery date.

➤ Consider a secondary insurance policy or governmental program.

Part 3

Breastfeeding 101

What does it take to breastfeed? What's required and what will you need? A quick and painless review of how your body works will help give you a good understanding of breastfeeding.

Understanding the form and function of breastfeeding helps to reassure you of your progress. A parent's biggest worry about breastfeeding is how much milk she has and whether there's enough. You'll feel more comfortable knowing the signs that tell you that breastfeeding is going fine. Learning how and when your body makes milk is an amazing discovery. Reassurance comes when your baby gives you satisfactory feedback.

This part will offer you an overview of the first day, first week, and first month of your breastfeeding adventure.

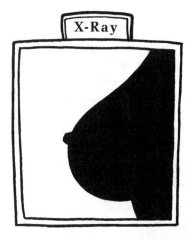

X-Ray

Chapter 9

Key Components

In This Chapter

➤ A scientific look at the human breast

➤ Early breast milk production

➤ Hormones essential for lactation

➤ How you make breast milk

➤ How you release breast milk

In a previous chapter I talked about the classifications of mammals, and that the milk-secreting gland is one of the "features" to be classified in the mammalian category. Any animal with hair, three ear bones, a four-chambered heart, and milk-secreting organs is considered a mammal. The primary function of a mammal's breast is to secrete milk. This is a scientific fact. I will also accept the point that the function of the breast, a woman's breast, is to attract a mate. But let us stick to the scientific facts for right now!

Breastfeeding is not only a skill, but also a science. We need to consider the science of breastfeeding to gain a better understanding of milk production. We'll look at what it takes and how it works, keeping the science part as simple as possible. It's important to understand what the components are and how they work together, to appreciate this amazing feat of mankind—well, womankind!

The Human Breast

If you've figured out by now that one of the key components for breastfeeding is a breast, then you're on the right track. You may also have identified that both women and men have breasts. Right you are! Breasts of men and women come as a pair, usually a matched set. Breasts are located on the front of the chest, just inside and slightly below the armpits. The breasts remain rudimentary, or not fully developed, in men throughout their lifetime. In women, however, development of the breasts begins at *puberty*.

But if men have breasts, then why can't they breastfeed? Well, a woman's breast differs from a man's, more in the function than in the form. Let's take a look at the form of a woman's breast, both inside and out, to better understand this difference.

Lactation Lingo

Puberty is the earliest age at which an individual is capable of reproduction.

LactFact

Mamma is a child's name for mother. It also means milk-secreting gland. The breast in Latin is **mammae**. The mammary gland is really a modified sweat gland. It will secrete a substance given the right stimulation and circumstance.

Woman's Breast

The mammary gland is the milk-secreting gland in females. It comes from the Latin word *mammae*, which means "the breast." A gland is an organ of the human body. It can be a collection of cells that secrete and abstract certain substances from the blood and turn them into new compounds. The mammary gland is an organ that abstracts substances from the blood and turns them into milk.

Taking a look from the outside, you'll find these features on a woman's breast:

➤ Nipple

➤ Areola

➤ Skin

The nipple is in the center of the areola. Your nipple contains about 15 to 25 milk ducts that open onto the skin surface. These ducts are for secreting milk. Your nipple and the surrounding skin appear darker in color than the overall skin of your breast. The nipple usually everts, or stands out, from the base of the breast tissue. I'll address nipples that appear as flat or inverted in Chapter 24, "Unique Nipples." The nipple contains many muscle fibers and a whole lot of nerve endings. This is an important feature because transmitting a sensory signal through your nervous system to your brain is essential for breastfeeding. The nipple is a very sensitive area of the woman's breast. It is extremely elastic. The nipple has an abundance of oil and sweat glands, too.

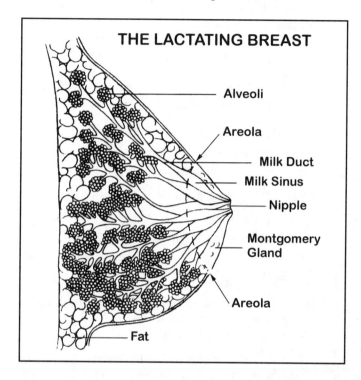

THE LACTATING BREAST

- Alveoli
- Areola
- Milk Duct
- Milk Sinus
- Nipple
- Montgomery Gland
- Areola
- Fat

Underneath it all, the lactating breast.

(Source: Hollister, Inc.)

The areola is a circular, pigmented area that surrounds your nipple. Before your pregnancy it is faintly darker than the surrounding skin. During pregnancy it becomes darker in color, and usually stays darker thereafter. The darker color may be so that your newborn closes its mouth on your areola, not on just the nipple. It may also appear as a target to your baby, showing where to latch on. Its average diameter measures about three to four inches across. This range can enlarge greatly during pregnancy. The areola contains *Montgomery glands,* which look like small pimples during pregnancy and lactation. The Montgomery gland is a kind of oil gland that secretes a lubricant, which protects your nipples and areola during pregnancy and lactation. Don't be tempted to squeeze these pimple-like bumps. They will release oil naturally. They also secrete a scent that helps your newborn locate its food source!

Lactation Lingo

Montgomery glands are small oil glands in the areola of the breast. They become more prominent during pregnancy. They secrete a fluid that lubricates the nipple and they may number between 20 and 24.

Breast Beware

Don't squeeze the oily substances from your Montgomery glands. They will secrete this lubricant naturally.

Nursing Mom's Notes

During pregnancy and breast-feeding cleanse your breasts with just water during your daily bath or shower. Soap may irritate or dry out your skin, making it itch or flake around your nipple and areola.

Lactation Lingo

Acini are the milk-producing cells of the mammary gland.

Your breast skin is a thin, almost elastic cover over your breast. Your breasts are the color of your skin in general. Breast skin contains hair, sweat glands, and oil glands. The skin hairs may be very fine and barely visible, or they may be coarse and dark in appearance. During pregnancy you may see dark blue veins in the breast through your transparent skin. This is the much-needed blood supply for your breast tissue. Stretch marks may also appear on your breasts.

If we take a look from the inside, we see these features:

➤ Mammary fat

➤ Connective tissue

➤ Milk-duct system

➤ Blood supply

➤ Lymphatic system

I'll bet you never thought that a woman's breast had fat, but the truth is, it makes up a majority of the breast's size. Fat, or adipose tissue, surrounds the glandular part of the breast. The "pecs," or pectoral muscles, lie under this fat layer.

Connective tissue, known as ligaments of Cooper, fixes the mammary ductal system to the overlying skin and the underlying pectoral muscle. These ligaments help provide the framework for the interior of the breast.

The ductal system itself is your production and distribution center for breast milk. Think of it as a large cluster of grapes, with each grape representing a milk lobule. A lobule is further subdivided into alveoli where thousands of milk-producing cells, called *acini*, actually make the milk. A lobule empties into a milk duct. Milk ducts empty into sinuses of the nipple. Milk sinuses then empty through the nipple openings onto the surface of the nipple itself.

The blood supply throughout the breast is rather extensive. This is because the blood supplies all the nutrients necessary for breast milk production and for the removal of cellular waste products. The increase in breast size during pregnancy is in part due to the amount of blood contained in the blood vessels of the breast. Blood supply to the nipple is abundant at the surface, which contributes to its color. The veins and arteries run side by side in the breast tissue.

Lymph is a watery, alkaline fluid contained in the tissues and organs of the body. It carries waste products and toxins excreted by cells. The lymphatic drainage of the breast runs through the skin, the areola, and the glandular tissue. Lymphatic fluid drains into the lymph nodes, with a major amount of lymph drainage from the breast emptying into nodes of the axilla, or armpit.

Man's Breast

If you've picked up on the point that certain features on the inside of the breast contribute to its size, then you're well on your way to understanding the difference between the breast of a man and a woman. In other words, men are missing many features that won't allow them to produce milk.

From the outside we see that a man has a nipple, an areola, and general breast skin just like a woman. The nipple and areola are darker in pigmentation, similar to a woman's. The size of the nipple and areola, however, are significantly smaller. The man's breast doesn't protrude from the base of the chest. A man won't fit into the cup of a bra!

On the inside we see that a milk-duct system doesn't proliferate throughout the male breast. There aren't any grape clusters present. No lobules, milk ducts, milk sinuses, and nothing opening onto the surface of the nipple. And we also see that the fat layer is missing to a certain extent. A man's breast size comes from the pectoral muscles, not from the fat and connective tissue like a woman's.

LactFact

Many mammals increase their mammary glandular tissue's surface area by 10,000-fold during pregnancy. The increases in blood supply, in glandular tissue, and in actual breast milk in a woman's breast, help it to weigh in between one and two pounds!

LactFact

A man has a nipple, an areola, and general breast skin just like a woman. A milk-duct system doesn't proliferate throughout the man's breast.

So now you know the structural difference between male and female breasts. I'm sorry if some of the men reading this guide are a bit disappointed. But just like with pregnancy and childbirth, perhaps your time to experience this will come!

Form Meets Function

We've taken a look at form, so now let's look at function. How do these structural features actually work? The unique thing about pregnancy is that it starts to prepare the breast for feeding and milk production well ahead of your delivery date. Behind the scene, food prep has already started. When the celebration begins, there will be food for baby to eat, too!

In the first months of pregnancy, the breasts become tender and start to enlarge in response to hormones. One of the unique things about women is the particular *hormones* they possess. The hormones circulating in your bloodstream cause growth in the milk ducts, lobules, and alveoli.

By your second trimester and as early as 16 weeks of your pregnancy, the production of colostrum in the mammary glands begins. Colostrum is considered the early or "first" milk. This is the food that's being prepped within your breasts. The cells of the acini secrete this substance, and it collects in the alveoli, or milk sacs. Once colostrum fills up the milk sacs, it collects in the milk ducts. The milk ducts drain into the milk sinuses, and eventually colostrum secretes through the openings in the nipple.

Colostrum is a yellow, sticky fluid that provides your baby with essential nutrition and protection against infectious disease. The amount of fluid is small, maybe just a few drops. The quantity may be small, but the quality of nutrients is remarkable. Colostrum contains protein, sugar, fat, vitamins, minerals, hormones, enzymes, and an army of white blood cells that fight off bacteria and viruses. No synthetic substance can replace this remarkable human fluid.

So, it's very important that your baby consumes this first milk to help get the best start in life. We'll look at how colostrum changes into mature breast milk in a later chapter. You may experience some leaking of this colostrum during your pregnancy. It's okay. Some women don't leak this fluid prior to the birth of their baby; that's okay, too. If you do have some leaking, just rub the fluid around your nipple and areola. It's a great moisturizer and lubricant, especially if you have experienced some skin dryness. Leaking some colostrum will reassure you that you are already producing milk for your baby.

Lactation Lingo

A **hormone** is a substance, secreted by certain glands, which passes into the blood and stimulates the actions of various organs.

Breast Beware

Oral or manual stimulation of the nipple and breast can cause colostrum to leak from your breasts. Inform your doctor if you experience leaking together with uterine contractions.

Prolactin: An Important Hormone

Keep in mind that many important hormones play a role throughout lactation. To keep things simple for you, I will only tell you about two hormones that are critical for the production and release of your breast milk. One of these hormones is prolactin.

Remember that a hormone is a substance that is secreted by a gland into your bloodstream to stimulate the activity of one or several organs. Prolactin is primarily a "milk-making" hormone. It plays a part in other bodily functions, but is essential for milk production. Prolactin stimulates and prepares the alveoli during pregnancy to secrete milk. With breastfeeding, prolactin always signals milk production and secretion.

Your pituitary gland, located in your brain, secretes prolactin into the blood. Another hormone controls the amount of prolactin that circulates in your blood during your pregnancy. The placenta releases a certain hormone that suppresses the quantity of prolactin present in your blood. This keeps you from producing large quantities of milk until after your baby is born. When the placenta is expelled after delivery, the hormone that suppressed your prolactin production is gone. By the second or third day after you deliver, your levels of prolactin rise sharply and start to produce abundant quantities of breast milk.

The essential stimulus for the production and secretion of prolactin is your baby's *suckling*. Suckling describes what a baby does when it feeds at the breast. Your baby not only creates suction, but also pulls the milk from your breast with its lips, jaws, and tongue at the same time. Stimulation of your breast, especially through your baby's suckling, causes a reflex between your breast and your brain. As a result, the pituitary gland releases prolactin. If milk is not removed from your breast, prolactin secretion stops within a few days, and the milk secretion in the breast returns to a colostrum-like fluid.

Lactation Lingo

Suckling is the act of pulling milk from the mother's breast using the lips, jaws, and tongue.

LactFact

Prolactin is primarily a hormone that stimulates the mammary gland to produce and secrete milk. The term describes its action, meaning to support or stimulate lactation. Both males and females have this hormone. Prolactin is involved in more than 80 different processes in the human body. Prolactin release in the new mother enhances sleep, helps to lower the blood pressure, and decreases the heart rate. Prolactin levels are usually higher at night than during the day.

Oxytocin: Another Important Hormone

The other hormone that plays a key role in lactation is *oxytocin*. This hormone is also secreted by the pituitary gland in your brain. Stimulation of the breast, either by your baby's suckling or by manual stimulation, triggers its release.

Lactation Lingo

Oxytocin is a hormone secreted from your brain that stimulates the release of breast milk.

Nursing Mom's Notes

MER stands for milk-ejection reflex. It's also called letdown because of the release of milk.

Nursing Mom's Notes

Feeling a cramping or contraction of your uterus means that you have released oxytocin.

Oxytocin stimulates the alveoli to release the milk that's been produced. It does this by stimulating certain muscle cells to contract, which causes a squeeze around the milk sac. This contraction, or squeeze, pushes the milk out of the sac and into the milk duct. More muscle cells that line your milk ducts contract and push the milk along the path toward the exit. This activity of milk release occurs in every "cluster" of the mammary gland where milk is produced.

The action of oxytocin on these muscle cells is a reflex known as the milk-ejection reflex, or MER. Both your milk production and milk-release reflex occur at about the same time. It may take about one to two minutes from the time your baby starts to suckle for the result of these reflexes to take place.

You'll know when milk release takes place if you feel a tingle or pulsation from the milk passing down and out into your milk ducts. The common term for this sensation is "letdown." If you don't feel this sensation, it's okay. I always instruct mothers to look for other signs of milk release when they don't feel anything. We'll discuss these other signs of milk release in a later chapter.

The hormone oxytocin also plays an important role in controlling blood loss after your delivery. Oxytocin causes contractions of your uterus during labor. After the baby is pushed from the uterus and the placenta is expelled, thousands of uterine blood vessels need to be squeezed to control the loss of blood. Oxytocin also stimulates the muscles of your uterus to contract and thus helps control blood loss. Every time your breasts are stimulated, oxytocin causes milk release and uterine contractions. What a package deal!

So when you feel uterine contractions or cramping, rest assured that milk release should occur, too. And each time your baby suckles the breast, the uterus contracts again and again. These frequent contractions help to return your uterus to its pre-pregnant size and shape.

There are other ways that you can stimulate oxytocin release. Seeing, touching, hearing, and smelling your baby can trigger a release of this hormone. This is why you may leak milk in between feedings or while you're asleep. Activities like washing a load of baby's clothes, looking at pictures, or writing to a friend about your new addition can all trigger a release of oxytocin.

Other hormones play a role in milk production and milk release, but I've told you only the ones that are essential. Research in the field of human lactation continues to identify additional functions of hormones. There may be other components for lactation that have yet to be identified. If I've sparked your interest for more anatomy and physiology, resource one of the medical textbooks listed in Appendix B, "Further Readings."

LactFact

Oxytocin and prolactin are released by stimulation of the nipple. Sight, touch, smell, and hearing sensations can also stimulate oxytocin release. Pain, stress, exercise, cold, and heat also cause oxytocin release but not during lactation. Only nipple stimulation can cause prolactin release.

The Least You Need to Know

➤ A woman provides milk for her infant from her breasts.

➤ A man is not capable of breast milk production.

➤ Colostrum is baby's first milk.

➤ Prolactin is your milk-making hormone.

➤ Oxytocin is your milk-releasing hormone.

Chapter 10

D-Day

In This Chapter

➤ Getting started

➤ Breastfeeding positions and holds

➤ How long, how much, how often

➤ Feeding cues

➤ The pitfalls

Well, it's time to put all the pieces together to make this thing happen. It's time to start what you've readied and prepared for up to now. I've titled this chapter "D-Day" because the day you deliver is a historic event. It's a day that you'll celebrate for a lifetime.

What I'm going to cover in this chapter will be crucial for getting breastfeeding off to a great start. After you read this chapter, have your spouse or labor partner read it, too. Reread it again when your labor begins. It will help refresh your memory and remind you of the essential steps to take, on Delivery Day.

The First Hour

When you first check in to the facility where you will deliver, one or several health care professionals will ask how you plan to feed your baby. You should respond with a solid answer, like: "I'm breastfeeding my baby." This emphasizes a commitment to your choice and empowers you for what lies ahead.

Following delivery, you'll want your baby placed in your arms for you to see, feel, hold, and marvel over! This starts the bond you'll develop with your baby. The labor pains, transition, all the pushing, and the apprehension of delivery are behind you. You've just finished an incredible aerobic workout. Guess who wants to eat?

The first hour after birth offers the best time for your baby to start breastfeeding. Your baby is usually awake, very alert, and eager to nuzzle up close to your breast. Babies often show a readiness to suckle at your breast with a "rooting reflex." Rooting is the action of opening and closing their mouths in search of something to put in their mouths. This is the ideal time to introduce your baby to breastfeeding.

LactFact

Try to use minimal or no medications during your labor. Medications and anesthetics used for relief of labor pains can make babies sleepy and lethargic for several days after delivery. A sleepy baby may not stimulate and suckle your breasts effectively.

Nursing Mom's Notes

Begin breastfeeding soon after delivery, preferably within the first hour. Inform any health care providers or medical staff that you wish to begin breastfeeding at this time. If breastfeeding within this first hour is not possible, it's okay to begin when circumstances do permit and you feel ready.

Let's give it a go! Ask your nurse, doula, spouse, or partner to help you get in a comfortable position with plenty of pillows and some good support behind your back. If you have a bed with an adjustable back, put it in a chair-like position. Open your top, or drop your sleeve down around your arm, to expose your breast. Babies love to be held against your bare skin. You may pull a blanket around your back to the front and swaddle your baby in your arms.

If you've had a Cesarean section, ask your nurse in the recovery room to help you into a sitting up or side lying position. Use several pillows for comfort and positioning. You may find additional information in Chapter 19, "Surgical Delivery," about breastfeeding following Cesarean surgery.

Many moms choose a "cradle hold" to first bring their babies to the breast. We'll look at some other positions for breastfeeding in this chapter. The most important thing is bringing your baby to the level of your chest so it can easily reach your breast. Avoid hunching over or reaching toward your baby. You should always pull your baby up close to you. Position its face and its tummy toward your face and your tummy. Cradle its head in your elbow and hold its bottom in the palm of your hand. You should be able to hold your baby in one arm. Use pillows under your arm and elbow for support.

Using your free hand, hold one of your breasts and touch the nipple to baby's lower lip. If baby isn't actively rooting, this should stimulate your baby to open its mouth. If the response isn't automatic, be patient. It should happen with a few more tries. When your baby's mouth is open wide like a yawn, quickly pull your baby close to your breast. You want baby's mouth to close around most of your breast. This means the nipple and most of the areola are being suckled. You want baby's gums positioned over the sinuses where milk is readily available. Remember that the milk sinuses are positioned under the dark circular skin of your areola.

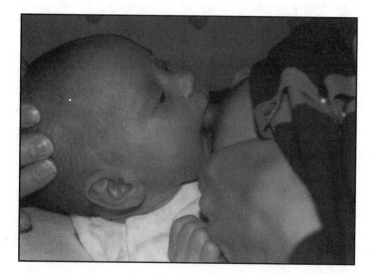

Pull baby onto your breast when its mouth is wide open.

(Source: Anne P. Mark)

Baby should start to suckle the breast soon after it latches on. Latch-on means baby should be fastened well to your breast! The frequency of suckling is about once every second to stimulate and release breast milk. You should feel a good tug and suction on your breast. If you close your eyes, focus on the feel of your baby's tongue cupping around your breast and pulling milk from it. It's a lot like using your tongue to pull ice cream from a cone into your mouth. Your baby will pull your breast in toward the back of its mouth. Your baby will get small amounts of clear-yellow colostrum with its first feedings.

Your baby is latched on to your breast when you see, hear, or feel the following:

➤ Baby's lips should flare outward around your breast like "fish lips."

➤ Baby's mouth covers most of your areola.

➤ You feel a strong pull on your breast.

➤ Baby's earlobes move as its jaw compresses the milk sinuses.

➤ You'll hear baby pause to swallow milk.

It's possible that you may feel some initial pain with your baby's first feedings. It may last one or

Nursing Mom's Notes

Touching your baby's lip with your nipple helps stimulate your baby to open its mouth.

two minutes from the start of suckling. Once your baby has pulled enough of your breast into its mouth, any pain felt should lessen. If it persists during the feeding, reattempt a better latch-on to your breast.

The best latch in town! Note the position of baby's lips and nose.

(Source: Anne P. Mark)

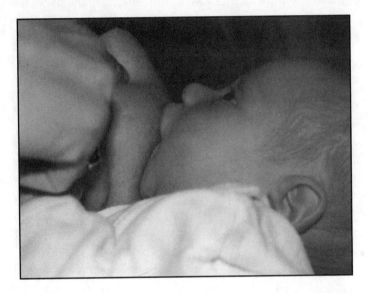

Your nurse or doula should be trained to help with these first feedings for your baby. If not, ask for someone trained in lactation to assist you with some of your feedings. Have your spouse or birth partner help you to check with each feeding, too. It may be difficult for you to see a good latch-on by yourself.

Breast Beware

Avoid watching the clock when you start your breastfeeding. It may help to cover the clock or to turn your back to it. You should not limit your baby's time at your breast. Allow your baby all the time in the world to learn breastfeeding.

With your baby latched on, relax and let your baby suckle as long as it wants. The longer, the better. The first feeding and the ones to follow should last as long as your baby wants to suckle. This won't hurt your nipples as long as your baby is latched on properly to your breast. It is very normal for feedings in these first hours, and in these first few days, to last a long time. This allows baby and you plenty of time to learn. Don't watch the clock: watch your baby. Relax and close your eyes. Take a deep breath in through your nose. Focus only on breastfeeding. Your baby will release your breast or fall asleep when it's satisfied from the feeding.

When baby finishes with the first breast, you want to burp your baby and then offer the other breast. Air can fill the stomach and take the place of milk. Your baby may not have any burps if little or no crying occurs and small amounts of colostrum are suckled.

Place your baby with its tummy against your shoulder. Now gently pat its bottom or back. This helps to release any air pockets. It also stimulates your baby to waken if asleep. You should then offer your other breast to your baby. This enables your baby to get plenty of breast milk and good stimulation from breastfeeding. This first breast-feeding and the ones that follow helps make an imprint. Remember that the frequency of suckling releases hormones, too, that help establish your milk supply.

Your baby might want to suckle from just one breast with each feeding. It's a good idea to offer your other breast. Perhaps your baby will want a little bit more. It's okay, though, for your baby to turn down the offer. Just start with your other breast next feeding.

To offer your baby the other breast, position your baby in your other arm. Bring baby up to your chest level. Baby should face you, and its tummy should touch yours. Hold your breast with your free hand. Touch baby's lower lip with your nipple. When its mouth is wide open, quickly pull baby into your breast again. You want baby to latch on over the milk sinuses. Suckling should begin after baby latches on. Again, let your baby suckle until the breast is released and your baby appears satisfied from feeding.

After your baby suckles from your other breast, try burping again. You can sit your baby in your lap, supporting the chin, and gently rubbing its back. If you have any breast milk on your nipple after feeding, rub it over your nipple and areola. You'll want to air-dry your nipples and areola after each feeding.

LactFact

Research has shown that early and frequent feedings at the breast establish a mother's milk supply within 24 to 48 hours. A breastfed baby typically feeds more frequently, unlike a baby fed formula who is often regulated by the clock. Studies by Goodine and Fried in 1984 and Winikoff, et al. in 1986 showed that mothers who breastfeed early and often, and who don't restrict their baby's feedings, report longer durations of breastfeeding.

Is baby getting anything with these first feedings? If you answered "colostrum," then you've learned something up to this point! The first breast milk, called *colostrum*, measures up to a small amount. Perhaps your baby will suckle only a teaspoonful. This small amount of first milk is part of the plan. Your baby suckles awhile to get this first milk and to stimulate your breast. Stimulation means a release of prolactin and oxytocin. Prolactin and oxytocin cause milk production and milk release. The more, the merrier!

And now, if you've taken your time with baby's first breastfeeding, congratulations! It's time for you and baby to rest, sleep, and get ready for another round. Hold your baby close. These first minutes and hours of motherhood are moments to cherish.

Positions

Proper positioning of your baby at your breast can make a big difference. That's why there are different positions for breastfeeding. I've mentioned the cradle position so far, but there are others to consider.

You'll want to try several of these positions. You may prefer one to another. Your baby may prefer one to another. You will learn which positions are best as you practice more breastfeeding. Think of these positions as different ways that you eat your meal, such as sitting up, lying down, or eating while on your side.

Nursing Mom's Notes

Proper positioning of your baby at the breast and a good latch greatly reduces your chance of nipple soreness.

You may feel quite awkward at first with these positions for breastfeeding. Lots of practice will help remedy this. You may need an extra set of hands to help with your first feedings. Have some throw pillows as well as sleeping pillows handy for comfortable positioning.

Various positions to try when breastfeeding include the following:

➤ Cradle hold

➤ Cross-cradle hold

➤ Clutch or football hold

➤ Side-lying hold

Cradle Hold

The cradle hold is somewhat standard. Perhaps you've seen pictures or images of a mother cradling her baby in her arms. Baby's head is positioned at your elbow with your forearm supporting its back, and your hand holding its buttocks. Your other arm and hand are free to support your breast for feeding. This hold positions your baby's mouth at your breast level. It also helps you position your baby's tummy against your tummy. Some mothers have said this is the only position they use.

Clutch or Football Hold

If you clutch your baby like you're carrying a football, you have the football hold. Your baby's head is positioned in your hand, and its body is along your left or right side. Baby's feet will point toward your back. This position works well for women who are large-breasted. It is also a suggested hold for mothers who've given birth by cesarean, because this keeps baby's knees and feet from poking the incision. Envision your baby sitting up to the breast with this position. Use a pillow or two to prop your baby up at the level of your breast. It's a great hold for breastfeeding when you're sitting in bed.

Cradling your baby for breastfeeding.

(Source: Bravado! Designs, Inc.)

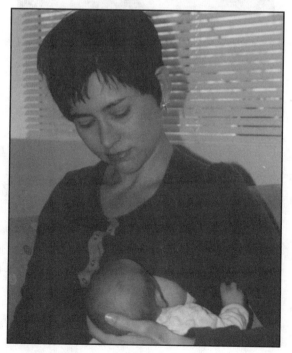

Hold your baby like you're carrying a football.

(Source: Anne P. Mark)

Side-Lying Hold

Lying on your side to breastfeed is the most comfortable position and is very good for your posture! You have your bed or couch to offer support for your back, side, and head. Tuck a pillow under your head, behind your back, and in between your knees, and you're set. Position your baby at your breast and breastfeed away. You may fall asleep, but not to worry. You'll be positioned safely to snooze all you want. If you tuck a rolled receiving blanket behind your baby, baby can safely snooze, too!

The side-lying hold frees up your hands.

(Source: Anne P. Mark)

Cross-Cradle Hold

Last, but not least, is the cross-cradle hold. It's really a cross between the cradle and the football hold. Hold your baby's head in the palm of your hand. Support the baby's back and buttocks with your forearm. Bring your baby across your tummy at breast level to latch on. This hold may help you to position your baby better at the breast.

Try to use various holds with each feeding. It's helpful to rotate your baby's position at the breast. It will help empty different sections of your breast. Different holds rotate the latch-on of your baby. This may also help prevent soreness.

Breast Beware

Don't let your family and friends interrupt your baby's frequent feedings. Explain that breastfeeding every two to three hours is essential as well as typical.

Frequency Factor

You should breastfeed as your baby demands after birth. Every time your baby suckles, it signals release of hormones. These hormones are important for increasing your milk supply and for the release of milk from your breast. These hormones also help control your bleeding after birth. It is typical for your baby to suckle every two to three hours, and sometimes more often than that. No need to question a baby's desire to eat!

Your baby may not demand frequent feedings if it's sleepy. You may have to help a baby who doesn't awaken on its own to breastfeed every two or three hours. A diaper change or undressing a baby can help to stimulate and awaken when it sleeps past three hours.

Because your baby will want to breastfeed so often, it's a great idea to "room in." This means keeping your baby with you as much as possible. It gives you plenty of time to awe and wonder. Your baby loves to be held close. It gives baby a warm, cozy feeling, much like how its pad was on the inside. A baby can smell you, hear you, and see you. The sound of your heartbeat is all too familiar.

Frequency of feeding on this first day is very important. If friends and family come to visit, you'll have to explain that breastfeeding is your baby's number one priority. Mention what it's like to have a full belly. Restrict your visitors, not your baby's feedings. If you feel uncomfortable with an audience, ask them to step out.

The frequency of suckling and swallowing helps with your baby's digestion. This helps the stimulation of the intestines and the passing of a bowel movement. The first bowel movement is a thick greenish-black substance called *meconium*. Colostrum is also a great laxative, which helps with the elimination of this meconium. Your baby needs to pass this to reduce its chance of jaundice. It's hard to believe those small drops of colostrum are packed with nutrition and help with your baby's first poop!

LactFact

It is very typical for a newborn baby to breastfeed eight to twelve times in a day. This means every two to three hours. In some cultures where babies are kept in close contact with their mothers, breastfeeding is done three to four times each hour. That's a lot of breastfeeding in a day's time!

Lactation Lingo

Your baby's first bowel movement is a thick greenish-black substance called **meconium.** Don't be alarmed when you see it—it's normal!

Feeding Cues

There are several ways your baby can say that it needs to eat. Knowing and recognizing these cues are important. A cue is a hint or a sign to grab your attention. A baby's feeding cue can be any of the following:

➤ Rooting

➤ Sucking its fist

➤ Rapid eye movement

➤ Crying

Nursing Mom's Notes

Breastfeed your baby when you recognize feeding cues other than crying. It will make a feeding go more smoothly and reduce the anxiety you may feel when your baby cries.

Breast Beware

Don't offer a pacifier, bottled water, or a breast milk substitute while you're getting breastfeeding established. Water and breast milk substitutes decrease your baby's appetite for breast milk. A pacifier can negatively affect your baby's suckling of your breast. A pacifier cannot offer important nourishment that your breastfeeding does.

Rooting means that your baby will open and close its lips, showing a readiness to latch on. Your baby may nuzzle and nibble at your neck. It may take the edge of the blanket in its mouth, or may try to latch on to dad's nipple! Baby may start to arouse from sleep smacking its lips. Recognizing this cue means you should prepare for a feeding. Baby should latch on easily when you offer your breast.

Babies who suck their fists or fingers are ready to suckle the breast. They may do this while sleeping, and they also can be easily roused. Seeing this cue means to get ready to breastfeed. Breastfeeding before your baby gets fretful and cries reduces any anxiety that you may feel.

A cue that baby shows while sleeping is called "rapid eye movement." Look to see your baby's eyes dancing around under closed eyelids. This is a stage of sleep referred to as rapid eye movement. It means that your baby will rouse from its sleep soon. It also means that you can easily arouse your baby from sleeping by picking up or just changing its diaper!

A baby's cry is the most recognizable cue of hunger. But don't wait until it gets to this point. Look for the other cues to make breastfeeding easy and simple. Sometimes at night you'll have no choice but to wait for the signal of crying. For times when you're not asleep, look for other cues. Be sure your spouse or partner knows to recognize these feeding cues, too.

Help or Hindrance

The success of your first hours and day of breastfeeding is dependent on unrestricted, frequent feedings. If they last a long time, they're supposed to. If you spend most of your time with your baby breastfeeding, this is good. You may be tempted or encouraged to send your baby to the nursery. You'll rest better with your baby at your side, in your room. Your spouse or partner can team up with you to get the job done. Responding quickly to your baby's signals to breastfeed makes a big difference.

There are some other things that may tempt you or be offered to you that aren't helpful toward breastfeeding. If someone suggests a breast milk substitute, a pacifier, or some sterile water, just say no. All of these can interfere with the nature of your baby's breastfeeding. They can decrease or discourage your baby from frequent breastfeeding. A breast milk substitute fills the stomach and decreases your baby's appetite. It may also cause an unnecessary sensitivity or allergy. Water can also delay the good frequent feedings necessary for your milk supply. And pacifiers are often popped in a baby's mouth when it roots or finger-sucks. It's a sign that your baby is ready to breastfeed, not to suck on a pacifier.

Be clear with your health care providers that any baby formula, water, and pacifiers are unwanted. These just don't help get breastfeeding off to the best start. Some parents find that a note card or sticker denoting breastfeeding is helpful. Ask your baby's doctor under what circumstances a breast milk substitute is given when a mother is breastfeeding. Define what 'medical necessity' is, and ask how your breastfeeding will be managed if baby formula becomes medically necessary. Take advantage of rooming in for the best opportunity to breastfeed on demand and best start at breastfeeding.

The Least You Need to Know

➤ Start breastfeeding within the first hour after childbirth.

➤ Breastfeed as your baby demands about every two to three hours.

➤ Learn proper latch-on to help prevent any discomfort.

➤ Remember that frequent suckling is essential.

➤ Try various breastfeeding positions

➤ Don't offer your baby a pacifier, water, or breast milk substitute in place of breastfeeding.

Chapter 11

Your First Week

In This Chapter

➤ Your increase in milk quantity

➤ Signs of reassurance

➤ Caring for yourself

➤ What's in baby's diaper

➤ Baby's weight gain

You've gotten through day one. Now it's on to days two, three, and more. You'll be breastfeeding frequently. It's important that your breasts are stimulated and emptied often. Your baby should show feeding cues and be breastfed at least 8 to 12 times in 24 hours. Remember not to limit your baby's feedings. Breastfeeding should be good and plentiful.

It's especially important to have someone take care of you during these early days of mothering. You'll benefit greatly from one or many who can "mother" you! I've seen so many mothers try to go it alone and become overwhelmed with it all. Whatever you can arrange is essential to help you transition into parenting. Your partner, family, and friends should know that your priorities will be sleeping, eating, and breastfeeding your new baby.

You've Got Breast Milk!

By your second and third day of breastfeeding you'll undoubtedly have questions and concerns. You will probably ask some of these questions:

➤ Is my baby getting anything?

➤ Is my baby getting enough?

➤ Is this breast milk?

➤ How long will my baby breastfeed?

➤ How often will my baby breastfeed?

Remember that your baby is getting colostrum from the start of breastfeeding. Colostrum *is* breast milk. The power of its small quantity cannot be understated. Somewhere between day two and day three, the amount or volume of your breast milk should increase. Breastfeeding every two to three hours around the clock helps this to happen. Moms often say that their *milk's come in* when the quantity of milk increases. Don't be concerned that it wasn't ever there. It's just that you can feel it now. Your breasts become fuller and heavier as breast cells make and secrete more milk.

The color of your breast milk changes from a yellowish colostrum to a white liquid much like condensed milk. You can actually squeeze this milk from your breasts. Water makes up a large part of your breast milk quantity.

Lactation Lingo

Milk's in refers to the feeling that a mother gets when the quantity of her milk has increased. Breast milk quantity usually increases between 24 and 48 hours after birth. Colostrum, or early milk, is viscous and very rich in protein and minerals. It satisfies a baby in the first days as breast milk quantity increases. Colostrum volume averages about 40 milliliters, or 3 tablespoons, in the first 24 hours. Breast milk volume increases to about 500 milliliters by day five when the "milk's in!"

Your milk volume should increase as a result of frequent feedings. These early feedings may take a lot of time. You are learning to breastfeed and so is your baby. Take your time and be patient. Expect your breastfeeding from both breasts to last between

30 and 50 minutes. Your baby will release the breast or fall asleep at the breast when it is satisfied. With your breasts fuller and heavier with milk, allow your baby to feed long enough to empty them. At the end of each feeding your breasts should feel softer than when you began.

LactFact

Eighty-seven percent of breast milk is water. Carbohydrates, namely lactose, make up about 7 percent. Protein content is a little less than 1 percent. About 4 percent makes up the fat content. You'll also find an abundance of immunoglobulins and infection-fighting cells like macrophages and lymphocytes. And don't forget there are plenty of enzymes, growth factors, minerals, and vitamins all packed into breast milk!

As milk volume increases, your baby's feeding pattern will change too. You should hear your baby swallow more. This should reassure you that your baby is getting something. Suckling and letdown, or your release of milk, will cause your baby to "gulp." Hearing these gulps, or swallows, tells you that you've got breast milk!

Your baby will also learn to coordinate feeding and breathing. It may swallow some air. Occasionally your baby will pull off the breast coughing because it was trying to swallow and breathe at the same time. Calm your baby and help your baby latch on to your breast again. It's important to burp your baby after each feeding. Offer both breasts to be certain your baby has filled its tummy. Both of your breasts will benefit from being stimulated and emptied. Sometimes a baby prefers one breast to the other. It's okay for your baby to have a favorite side!

Nursing Mom's Notes

Listen for your baby's swallows. Your baby will swallow when liquid or food is pulled to the back of its mouth. It's breast milk your baby is swallowing!

How Much Milk Is My Baby Getting?

But how much does a baby really eat? You can't see through your breasts to know how much was taken. This is the biggest worry a new parent, and a grandparent, has about breastfeeding. Well, a new baby's stomach is about the size of a ping-pong or golf ball. If we measure that amount, it's somewhere between one and three ounces. A baby will suckle your breast to fill its stomach. So that means one to three ounces.

It's not unusual for a baby to lose weight in the first few days after birth. Expect it. A newborn baby can lose up to 10 percent of its birthweight. It's mostly a fluid loss and the excess is meant to be shed. Water evaporates from its skin. Your baby will urinate and also pass its first stool, called meconium. This loss of fluid means weighing less on the scale. Your baby has two to three weeks to regain its birth weight. Be patient and don't panic. Lots of breastfeeding with adequate breast milk transfer helps a baby to regain its weight.

By your second and third day, in the hospital or birth center, ask for an experienced lactation professional to see you. He or she can watch your baby feeding at the breast, and can offer advice and help assure you of your ability to make breast milk and to breastfeed. If one isn't available, ask your doctor or another experienced health care provider to help. Ask about signs to determine that your milk volume has increased or will increase. Get reassurance and answers to your questions before you head home with your baby. It's typical for a new parent to worry, especially when it comes to feeding your baby. You need to be reassured that you have breast milk and that your baby is feeding. Ask your baby's doctor about a weight check or lactation services available during your first week.

LactFact

A newborn baby's stomach is about the size of a golf ball. It can hold between one and three ounces. As a baby grows and develops, its stomach capacity increases. This allows a baby to consume more breast milk and reduce the number of frequent feedings.

Many babies can be sleepy in the first 24 to 72 hours after their birth. After all, it was quite an ordeal for your baby to experience labor, too. If medication or an anesthetic was used during labor, your baby may snooze even more. It's just like jet lag. It may take a few days to sleep it off. You'll need to help awaken your sleepy baby if it sleeps past four hours. Undress your baby. Change its diaper. Take a wet washcloth and gently wipe your baby's face. You can also gently rub the bottom of baby's feet. If your baby is sleepy and not breastfeeding effectively in the first 24 hours, express your breast milk with a medical grade piston breast pump. You should use it following every breastfeeding attempt. It will stimulate and empty milk from your breasts effectively.

You will be discharged to go home between 48 and 72 hours, depending on your type of delivery. Guess what? Your milk should "come in" about the same time. With an increased amount of milk, you will need for your baby to breastfeed often. Not emptying your breasts of this milk frequently and effectively contributes to engorgement. You should be using the electric piston breast pump if you are not empty after each feeding. You should continue to express your milk with a piston pump following every breastfeeding if you have a sleepy baby. Refer to Chapter 23, "My Breast Are Huge!" about engorgement.

Great Expectations

The reality of being sent home may be met with mixed reservations. No more bedside care morning, noon, and night. Panic may set in. Can I really do this myself? No one around to look over my shoulder and tell me I'm doing it right? For some of you it may be smooth sailing. Others may need a boat, oars, and a life vest to stay afloat. Let's look at what to expect while breastfeeding once you're back home again.

Once you get home you're on your own. No early morning doctor rounds. You can sleep in. You can eat what you want. No call lights or beepers. No one in the other bed talking your arm off. Phew! But being on your own can be scary and downright tough. This is where it really helps to be prepared and have your resources in place.

First of all, expect to be tired. You probably didn't rest or sleep well in the hospital. Your baby has many needs. Breastfeeding is one of them. Being a new parent around the clock is tiring. Minimize your tasks. Dish out as many tasks as you can to helpful family and friends. The priorities for both you and your baby should be eating, sleeping, and diaper changing! You care for your baby and have someone else care for you. Reread the previous sentence. Rest and sleep as much as your body tells you to.

Expect to breastfeed your baby at least every two to three hours. Some babies may cluster, or group, their feedings together. This means several feedings about an hour apart and then perhaps a three-hour pause. Feeding clusters can especially occur at night. Your milk-making hormone, prolactin, can be higher at night. And that means you make more breast milk. If your baby figures this out, expect to keep the night-kitchen open!

Nursing Mom's Notes

Undress your baby down to its diaper before breastfeeding. You usually radiate a lot of heat while you're breastfeeding. Your blood supply and hormones help turn up your thermostat. Heat can make your baby fall asleep and not feed well enough.

Nursing Mom's Notes

Cluster feedings can come at night, especially when your milk-making hormone is plentiful. It's not unusual for these cluster feedings to occur during your first and second week of breast-feeding. These feedings typically "uncluster" after your second or third week.

Expect your baby's breastfeeding sessions to last about 20 to 45 minutes. Some babies may be quick and efficient eaters. Others may "gourmet" at the breast. They take their time to really enjoy their meal. Remember to be patient and to let your baby learn to master breastfeeding.

Lactation Lingo

Engorgement is a swelling of the breasts caused by increased breast milk, blood supply, and lymph in the mammary gland. It can prevent an infant from suckling. It is usually caused by a delay or restriction in duration and frequency of breastfeeding.

Breastfeeding frequently and emptying your breasts will help to ease or prevent any *engorgement* from developing. Breast fullness is normal; engorgement is not and may present a problem for you and your baby. Engorgement is a swelling of the breasts caused by increased fluids in the mammary gland. These fluids include your breast milk, blood supply, and lymph. If you do experience engorgement, expect it about day four or five. Refer to Chapter 23 for more information about managing engorgement.

You should expect to be concerned about your baby getting enough during this first week. Every breastfeeding parent asks this question. Your baby should be hungry at the start of a feeding, and literally pass out when satisfied. A good friend refers to this as a "food coma." They're ravenous, they eat, and then they pass out in a deep sleep. It's a very good sign that your baby has eaten enough.

Measures of Success

As you work your way through this first week of breastfeeding, you are bound to look for feedback. You'll need signs that things are on track. You'll want results for your efforts so far. Your sleep loss, frequent feeding, feeding, feeding, and diaper changes. Has this amounted to anything?

The following are all signs of feedback:

➤ Urine

➤ Bowel movement

➤ Weight gain

I'll bet you never thought you'd become an expert on poop and pee! Well, the truth is, they are all measures of your success. What goes in must come out. It's all in the diaper!

Wee Wee

When it comes to your baby's urine, there is a basic count for wet diapers. Your baby should have one wet diaper for every day of its age. For example, one on day one, two on day two, and so forth. Once your milk supply increases, you should see five to six wet cloth diapers from your baby by the fifth day. Super-absorbent paper diapers usually hold more moisture. This may change your diaper count to three or four wet diapers.

Wet diapers indicate that your baby is eating enough. It also means that you have a good milk supply.

The Poop Scoop

The scoop on poop is number, too! Or is that two? Your baby should pass at least two or more bowel movements in its diaper each day. This should happen after four to five days of age. Fresh, warm breast milk stimulates digestion. It is absorbed quickly and easily from the stomach. Digestion means that it stimulates the bowels to empty. And that means poop as an end result.

Frequent feedings usually result in frequent stools. It's not unusual for your baby to have a bowel movement with each breastfeeding. If you're breastfeeding 8 to 12 times a day, guess how many diapers you'll change? Some babies, though, may only pass one bowel movement every other day. This is not a problem as long as it is a typical bowel movement from breast milk.

I've got to tell you about color and texture. Yes, I'm talking about poop. You need to know so you don't think something's wrong. The first bowel movement your baby passes is meconium. It's the material left over from the making of the intestinal tract. It is a dark, greenish black color and is very sticky, like tar. The good news is that it doesn't stink! Passing these first bowel movements helps reduce your baby's chance of developing *jaundice*. Lots of breastfeeding and breast milk helps this happen.

Meconium continues to pass through the third or fourth day. Once your milk supply increases, the color and texture of the bowel movement changes. The stool becomes runny and a yellowish green color. It may be the consistency of pea soup or have little curd-like lumps. My nephew says it looks like mustard with cottage cheese mixed in! This is a typical breast milk stool. By day seven, it's

Nursing Mom's Notes

It's hard to tell in the first few days with absorbent paper diapers that your baby has urinated. Place a paper nose-tissue inside your baby's diaper. If it's wet when you change it, it's from urine.

Lactation Lingo

Jaundice is a yellowish skin color in newborns caused by the breakdown of excess red blood cells. Red blood cells release bilirubin when they break down. A yellow color appears on the skin because a newborn's liver cannot process the bilirubin very quickly. Jaundice is very common and appears in about 80 percent of term newborn babies.

109

a seedy, runny yellow bowel movement. Don't mistake the runny consistency with diarrhea. Diarrhea is mostly water. A breast milk stool is liquid, but not watery.

Your Baby's Weight Gain

The last measure of your breastfeeding success is weight gain. Remember that it's typical for your baby to have weight loss after birth. Expect it. Once your milk supply increases, the water and fat components help your baby to regain its weight. Fat helps to satisfy your baby's appetite.

Your baby's weight gain is a good measure of your breastfeeding success. Your baby should regain its birth weight by two to three weeks. Some parents can't wait that long. You may be reassured if you have your baby weighed by the third or fourth day.

The Least You Need to Know

➤ Your breast milk volume increases between the second and fifth day of breast-feeding.

➤ Newborn babies typically lose weight after delivery.

➤ Sleepy babies need to be awakened to breastfeed.

➤ A medical grade piston breast pump will stimulate and empty your breasts if your baby doesn't.

➤ You measure breast milk consumption by urine and bowel movement quantities.

➤ Your baby should regain its birth weight by two to three weeks of age.

Chapter 12

The Next Three Weeks

In This Chapter

➤ Twenty-one days of breastfeeding

➤ Coping with frequent feedings

➤ Position and posture while breastfeeding

➤ Signs of adequate breastfeeding

➤ Feeling comfortable and confident with breastfeeding

➤ Your growing baby

Good job! Making it through the first week is worth a celebration. The first week is the biggest challenge for most new parents. Whether you're a first time parent or a return veteran, a new baby brings many changes in your life. Not only are you busy improving your breastfeeding skills but also the skills of being a parent.

You may have had tears and moments of frustration. You'll also have lots of questions and concerns as you experience the next three weeks. This chapter will take a look at the ins and outs of breastfeeding during this time. We'll review feeding positions and patterns, and take a look at changes in your baby's growth and development. We'll also look at getting you out and about with your breastfeeding baby.

How's It Going?

The next 21 days of your breastfeeding experience are very important. It's a time to program your hardware for the quantity and quality of breast milk. It's also a busy time for your baby's growth and development. Frequent feedings and your love and attention all help to meet your baby's needs right now.

You may feel that all you do is eat, feed, sleep, and change diapers at this point. Well, you're right. Remember the basic human needs that I talked about in the beginning of this book? Food, sleep, and shelter are among those basics. Breastfeeding provides your baby with liquid nourishment and a satisfied belly. Providing a warm place to cuddle up to gives baby a chance sleep soundly after a satisfying meal.

Nursing Mom's Notes

If your daily routine becomes monotonous, dress it up. Turn your bed or living room floor into a picnic spot. Throw down a bright floral tablecloth, use paper plates and plastic utensils, eat some picnic foods and enjoy what nature has brought you.

Frequency Factor

I think it's important to repeat that these frequent breastfeedings are very normal. Every time your baby's suckling stimulates your breasts, you release the milk-making and milk-releasing hormones. This signal helps to set your milk supply from here on out. A good milk supply helps with your baby's growth and development. It's very normal for your baby to want to breastfeed at this point, every two to three hours.

This frequency of feedings continues around the clock. Do not expect your baby to sleep through the night. At this point it is not good for your baby to do this. Its demand for food needs to be met morning, noon, and night. Remember that its tummy can only hold so much. Its feedings may be clustered, or grouped, especially during the night.

Probably your biggest question right now is: "When will my baby sleep through the night?" Don't expect this until after the first month. For some babies it may be two or three months before they sleep a good five to six hours at night. Body weight, stomach capacity, and blood sugar levels all play a role in your baby's sleep patterns.

Check Baby's Latch-On

Your baby's latch-on to your breast is important to look at again. Because of the frequent feedings, it's helpful to make sure that latch-on is correct. Improper latch-on can lead to soreness and discomfort. Uncomfortable breastfeeding discourages you from continuing!

At this point, take the time with each feeding to check for the following:

➤ Mouth wide open

➤ Lips flared and sealed around the areola

➤ Nipple and areola centered in mouth

➤ Nose and chin touching breast

➤ Ear, shoulder, and hip aligned

With each feeding, your baby should open its mouth wide and seal its lips around most of your areola. Your nipple should be centered in its mouth. Baby draws your breast deep into its mouth, pulling your nipple to the back of its throat. Its jaws compress and its tongue pulls or "milks" the breast. When breast milk is pulled to the back of its mouth, your baby swallows.

You should feel your baby's gums compress your areola. If you feel that your nipple is being compressed instead, unlatch your baby and position again. Your baby's tongue should draw the nipple back toward the soft part of its mouth. You should also feel your baby's tongue stroking or massaging around your breast. A baby's breastfeeding should create a good "tug" at your breast.

Your baby will unlatch from your breast when it's done with its feeding. Releasing the breast from its mouth or falling sound asleep means "I'm finished." You don't want to watch the clock for each feeding. A feeding from one of your breasts typically lasts from 10 to 20 minutes during this time. Some babies take more time latching on to the breast. Remember to be patient and allow your baby time to improve its breastfeeding skills.

Breast Beware

Improper positioning and latch-on to the breast in the early weeks often leads to soreness and discomfort.

Check Your Position and Posture

It's a good idea to take a look again at the positions for breastfeeding. These holds are as follows:

➤ Cradle hold

➤ Football hold

➤ Cross-cradle hold

➤ Side-lying hold

You'll want to try all of these holds with breastfeeding to vary the way that your baby empties milk from your breast. Imagine if you were to divide your breast into four sections. These holds help to stimulate and empty each breast section, depending on how your baby is held. If you have a particular area of your breast that feels full, use a hold that positions your baby's nose toward that area.

Take a look at your posture. Choose an appropriate place, such as a chair, a couch, or a bed that will give your back and shoulders good support while breastfeeding. Shoulder and upper-back strain are often a result of poor posture. When breastfeeding, your shoulders should be relaxed and held back. Place enough pillows around you to support your arms, back, and shoulder. If you find a pillow designed for breastfeeding helpful, use it. Always bring your baby up to the level of your breasts.

And the Color Is?

I hope I got your attention! At this time, the color of your breast milk transitions to white. It can be distinguished from cow's milk by its hue of blue-gray. If you have expressed any breast milk up until now, you will notice the milk fat will separate and rise to the surface over time. Store-bought cow's milk is homogenized by a dairy and will not separate.

Breast milk can also be divided into two types: foremilk and hind milk. The *foremilk* is readily produced at the beginning of a feeding. It may be thin and watery because it consists mostly of water. This helps to quench your baby's thirst at the beginning of its meal. *Hind milk* is produced later in the feeding. Fat globules take a little more time to prepare. That's why it's important to let your baby suckle as long as it will at your breast. Fat helps satisfy your baby's appetite and keeps baby content between feedings.

How Much Milk Is Your Baby Getting?

How much, how much, how much? Every parent asks this question. We've come to rely on visual amounts so much that we find it hard to rely on our gut feeling or instinct. You just can't see through your breast or your baby's tummy to tell how much breast milk you're producing.

At this point a breastfeeding baby may consume between two and four ounces each feeding. If the number of wet and soiled diapers isn't enough to reassure you, and you are concerned about quantity, then you may consider the following:

➤ Weigh your baby.

➤ Collect your breast milk.

Most breastfed babies are scheduled for a doctor's visit by one week of age. You may be able just to weigh your baby at your doctor's office with each week of breastfeeding. A great measure of quantity is to weigh your baby before and after a feeding. You'll need to use a scale that can measure in incremental ounces. This will tell you and your health care provider about how much was consumed in ounces with a breastfeeding.

Secondly, you may consider using a breast pump to express your breast milk. Be aware that what you pump will not equal what your baby consumes with each feeding. Your baby's appetite determines how much breast milk is consumed with breastfeeding. Pumping your milk at this point following a feeding or in between feedings can offer you reassurance. An electric piston breast pump is your best choice if you choose to pump. It closely resembles your baby's suckling pattern. Refer to Chapters 13, "Express Yourself," and 14, "Collection and Storage," on milk expression and use of a breast pump.

Cruise Control

Breastfeeding should ease into somewhat of a pattern by your second, third, and fourth weeks. You'll be able to make plans and accomplish simple tasks if you identify your baby's feeding pattern. Does your baby like to feed a lot in the morning? Are there long snoozes in the afternoon? It's time to consider cruise control when you can say "yes" to most of the following:

➤ My baby wakes up to feed 8 to 12 times in 24 hours.

➤ My baby latches on properly to my breast.

➤ My baby feeds from one or both breasts.

➤ Breastfeeding is not painful.

➤ My baby is satisfied after breastfeeding.

➤ My baby has four or more bowel movements a day.

➤ My baby has five or more wet diapers a day.

➤ My baby has regained its birth weight by two to three weeks.

If you said "no" to two or more, it may not be time for cruise control. It's not yet time to sit back, relax, and just expect to steer. You should probably choose the "help" button to connect you to one of your professional resources. Your best resource is the lactation professional capable of identifying and helping to resolve your breastfeeding concerns.

Nursing Mom's Notes

If you experience painful breast-feeding or question your milk supply, schedule an evaluation with a lactation professional. Professional evaluation and management can resolve many breastfeeding problems and concerns.

Breast Beware

Do not breastfeed your baby while traveling in a motor vehicle. Do not operate a motor vehicle while breastfeeding your baby. Your baby should always be restrained in the proper infant carrier when traveling in a motor vehicle.

Being comfortable now with breastfeeding means you can add one or two activities to your basic tasks. Maybe you would like to prepare a meal, or perhaps wash a load of laundry. How about a good, long shower? Invite over a friend who will listen to your birth story and the challenges of being a new parent. Ease into your new task or reward, along with breastfeeding.

Out and About

If cruise control is going well, you may consider getting out. Yes, get out for a change of scenery, some fresh air, or a visit with a neighbor. Getting out can make a world of difference in the way you feel about yourself and being a new parent. Breastfeeding can challenge your mental and physical well-being. A break in the routine can make you feel a whole lot better and renew your commitment to breastfeeding.

It's important to keep your first few outings simple. Just getting out can be tiring. Doing too much can exhaust you. Keep in mind that your baby may want to breast-feed when you are out. Unfamiliar sights and sounds to your baby may stimulate its need to breastfeed. At first your baby may sense that something's different and turn to breastfeeding for comfort and security.

If getting out requires transportation, see if someone else can do the driving. That frees you up to tend to your baby. Check with your doctor to see when you are permitted to drive. Make sure that your baby is restrained in the proper car seat. Do not, under any circumstance, breastfeed your baby while your motor vehicle is moving. A baby can be thrown from your arms in seconds. If your baby is hungry or fussy, use your finger to pacify it until the vehicle is completely stopped.

Growth Spurts

It is very normal for your baby to need more feedings than usual. These are called growth spurts. The demand for calories increases because the body is growing. They can occur between two and three weeks of age, and again between four and six weeks. Your baby will show familiar feeding cues, as well as cry from hunger. It's not unusual for baby to take on a "marathon" approach to breastfeeding. This will last one to three days.

Your baby may be especially fussy during these growth spurts. Late afternoon or early evening may be a typical time. Your baby will cry because of hunger, fatigue, loneliness, or boredom. An appetite spurt may increase your baby's crying to alert you to its hunger. Try these things for a fussy baby:

1. Nourish and comfort your baby with breastfeeding.
2. Burp your baby frequently.
3. Wrap it snugly in a light blanket.
4. Carry your baby in a sling.
5. Try walking, rocking, or swinging your baby.
6. Offer some background noise from a radio, a tape recording, or the hum of an appliance.

LactFact

Colic is a term for extreme irritability that continues day after day. Painful crying may last for long periods each day, perhaps at certain times. This crying can occur for any number of reasons. A baby may be hungry, tired, or just need to be held. Other reasons for colic may be intestinal gas, yeast infection, medications, dietary supplements, or a baby's temperament. Babies with colic are best comforted when held in a fetal position with their knees drawn up into their tummy. Carrying a baby in a sling can keep a baby tucked in at mom's or dad's side.

Many mothers interpret crying and fussiness as something gone wrong. Just when you've identified your baby's feeding pattern, they're hungry when you least expect it. Don't worry. More breastfeeding will meet your baby's need. A few days of increased feedings helps to satisfy this increased growth.

The Least You Need to Know

➤ Babies continue to breastfeed every two to three hours during this time.

➤ Proper positioning and good posture is essential when breastfeeding.

➤ Wet diapers, bowel movements, and weight gain indicate adequate breast-feeding. A baby satisfied with each breastfeeding is also a good indicator.

➤ Lactation professionals can evaluate your breastfeeding problems and concerns. They can also reassure you and help boost your confidence about breastfeeding.

➤ Ease into simple tasks and getting out once breastfeeding is going well.

➤ Growth spurts are typical between two and three weeks, and again at six weeks of age.

Part 4
Supply and Demand

Once you've got breast milk, you'll think it's the next best thing since sliced bread. You'll want everyone to ooh and aah over your homemade goodies. You'll definitely be thinking of ways to store and save your tasty supply.

Using the best technique to collect your own creation is important. Timing can also make or break your collection efforts. A little guidance in the milk-expression department will help you find the right tools and techniques for collecting mother's milk.

You'll find out how to handle any low or abundant milk volumes along the way. You'll find out some interesting tips and techniques to use with your breast milk expression. And best of all, you'll find out the storage and shelf life of human breast milk. It will truly amaze you!

Chapter 13

Express Yourself

In This Chapter

➤ Beginning to express breast milk

➤ Methods for milk expression

➤ Choosing a breast pump

➤ Techniques for hand expression

➤ Other means of self-expression

The excitement you'll experience when you see your own breast milk is a momentous event. Words to exclaim your amazement will abound. You'll call out to everyone in your household, maybe to the whole neighborhood. Expressing yourself in more ways than one will certainly boost your milk supply!

Milk Expression

You can begin regular milk expression when a good milk supply is established, usually three to four weeks after you begin breastfeeding. If your breastfeeding is delayed for more than four hours after you deliver your baby, however, it is essential that you begin to express your milk as soon as possible. There are also certain circumstances that require breast milk expression in the first two weeks following delivery. These circumstances include the following:

➤ Breastfeeding problems

➤ Baby unable to breastfeed

➤ A low milk supply

➤ Separation from your baby

I will discuss in later chapters about different breastfeeding problems such as sore nipples, engorgement, and mastitis. These problems can alter or prevent an effective stimulation and emptying of your breast. Altering or preventing good stimulation and emptying will affect your milk supply. Breastfeeding problems are often managed and resolved in combination with expression of your breast milk.

Nursing Mom's Notes

If the start of your breastfeeding is delayed for four or more hours after delivery, begin expression of your breast milk with a hospital-grade electric piston breast pump.

When your baby is unable to actually breastfeed, you will have to express your breast milk to establish a supply. Premature babies and hospitalized infants may not be able to suckle effectively. Expressed breast milk for these babies has proven vital to their health and well-being. Some babies are born with a medical condition that prevents them from suckling, but always benefit from the breast milk you provide them.

A small percentage of women truly experience a low milk supply. It's not unusual, though, to question the amount you do produce. A lactation professional can help you to determine if your milk supply is adequate. If you do have a low milk supply, breast milk expression usually remedies the situation. The basic law of *supply and demand* means that stimulating and emptying your breasts helps increase and maintain your milk supply. It's a simple solution if you're coming up short. Frequent demand and emptying breast milk should increase your supply.

Lactation Lingo

Supply and demand of breast milk production means that the more that milk is emptied from the breast, the more milk the breast supplies.

Separation from your baby, even for one feeding, means that you should plan to express your breast milk. If your baby is less than four months old, you will need to express your milk for at least every three- to four-hour intervals. This is the best way to maintain your milk supply. If you do happen to miss or delay a "session of expression," resume your three- to four-hour intervals as soon as possible.

Mechanical Expression

The word "mechanical" means to produce or operate by machine. Expressing your breast milk mechanically means that you use a breast pump. Breast pumping for milk expression has become increasingly popular over the years with breastfeeding mothers. There are several reasons for this. A breast pump can often simulate the suction and rhythm that your baby uses when suckling the breast. This is essential to create the stimulation for hormone release. A breast pump can provide a mechanical source of vacuum and rhythm for expressing your breast milk. This provides a reliable means of milk expression if you don't want to or can't hand express your milk.

Most moms choose a breast pump for their mechanical milk expression. You can create a vacuum to match your baby's suction at the breast. You can also cycle the vacuum to match the rhythm your baby uses. Combining mechanical vacuum and cycles creates the suckling pattern of your baby. What you're doing is fooling the breast by creating a feeling most like that of your baby.

I have listed the different types of breast pumps in Chapter 7, "Tools of the Trade." However, a brief review is in order. You need to understand the difference between breast pumps to choose which one's right for you. You should match the right breast pump with the right circumstance for successful mechanical expression.

Mechanical expression of breast milk can be done with any of the following breast pumps:

➤ Hospital-grade piston pump

➤ Electric breast pump

➤ Battery breast pump

➤ Manual breast pump

Each of these breast pumps provides the mechanics for milk expression. The vacuum is created mechanically. This vacuum is applied to the breast by placing a shield or flange over your breast. The vacuum control enables you to adjust the amount of suction applied to your breast. The frequency of vacuum application is the key to your success with mechanical expression.

Nursing Mom's Notes

If you want to express more milk in a shorter period of time, choose a breast pump that provides vacuum to both breasts simultaneously.

Choosing a Pump

Your best breast pump is one that enables you to adjust your amount of vacuum and your frequency of vacuum. The vacuum frequency or cycle should be just like the frequency of your baby. At the start of a feeding, a baby suckles between 50 and 90 times a minute. Its rate slows down when milk release occurs. Before you use a breast pump, it's helpful to feel and to watch the pattern of your baby's suckling.

Your hospital-grade piston breast pump will perform most like your baby. It's a breast pump found in most hospitals and follow-up clinics. This type of pump is durable and is designed for multiple users. Each user must have a separate collection kit. This prevents cross-contamination and maintains personal hygiene. This is your breast pump of choice if you experience any of the following:

➤ Encounter a breastfeeding problem during your first month

➤ Need to express breast milk for a preterm or hospitalized baby

➤ Experience a low milk supply anytime while breastfeeding

➤ Will miss two or more feedings for two or more days

➤ Have never used a breast pump

Milk Collection

Electric breast pumps designed for single users usually include your collection kit. This type of breast pump is designed for a mother whose breast milk supply is well established. Choose this breast pump for milk expression if you are breastfeeding comfortably by your third or fourth week. Do not use an electric breast pump that someone else has used. Bacterial or viral contamination can pose a risk to you and your baby.

> **Breast Beware**
>
> Don't take the risk of bacterial or viral contamination from a breast pump that someone else has used. Breast milk or its condensation can contaminate the motor and accessories. Only sterilization with an autoclave can completely eliminate bacteria and viruses. An electric piston breast pump requires a milk collection kit for each user that prevents cross-contamination and maintains hygiene.

> **LactFact**
>
> The major carbohydrate in breast milk is lactose. It is a milk sugar. Other carbohydrates present in breast milk are monosaccharides, oligosaccharides, peptides, and protein-bound carbohydrates. Small amounts of glucose and galactose are present. Lactose regulates the amount of milk produced. By the fifth day of breastfeeding, milk volume is about 500 milliliters per day. That's about 2$\frac{1}{4}$ cups. Full breastfeeding at three to five months yields about 750 milliliters per day. A wet nurse has been documented to produce about 3,500 milliliters of breast milk in a day. Yes, almost a gallon!

Batteries are the power source in a battery breast pump. You can use this pump if you need to express your breast milk once or twice during a week once your milk supply is well established. Most battery breast pumps can only cycle 8 to 10 frequencies per minute. Compare this to the 30- to 60-cycle range of the electric and hospital piston breast pumps. This limits your stimulation and can result in very little milk expression.

A manual breast pump requires that you be the motor source! Your hand operates the handle or plunger to create the vacuum. You can also control your cycles. With practice, you may find that this is a convenient and easy breast pump to use. It is a pump to choose for occasional use. Without need for electricity or batteries, this means it's very portable. You may find, though, that you grow tired of plunging or squeezing and that it takes 20 to 30 minutes to express your milk.

Hand Expression

It is always possible to express breast milk using your hands. This technique is also referred to as manual expression. It is a quick and simple way of expressing milk from your breast. If you don't have a breast pump or can't access a power source, hand expression can come to your rescue. All you need are your hands!

The best way to hand express milk from your breasts is to imitate your baby's suckling pattern. Your baby stimulates the breast with its mouth applying suction and massage. The jaw compresses the milk sinuses. Stimulation of the nipple and areola also causes hormone release. Milk is then made and released with these hormones present.

HAND EXPRESSION OF BREAST MILK

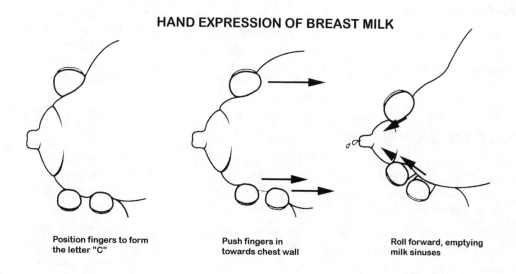

Position fingers to form the letter "C"

Push fingers in towards chest wall

Roll forward, emptying milk sinuses

Milk expression by hand.

To begin hand expression you must first use your hands to gently massage your breast. Gentle breast massage will help your milk to let down. Place both of your hands around one of your breasts. Gently massage with your fingers and thumb. Stroke in the direction of your nipple.

Nursing Mom's Notes

Practice hand expression while you're in the shower, or with your free breast while breast-feeding.

Nursing Mom's Notes

Find a support group or an on-line chat room with mothers who are expressing breast milk.

Then place your thumb on top of the areola, and index and middle fingers underneath, about $1^1/_2$ inches behind your nipple. This is where the milk sinuses are located. Push your thumb and fingers back toward your chest. Then squeeze your fingers together while lifting your nipple outward. Keep your fingers in place over the milk sinuses. Your thumb and fingers should not slide across the nipple.

As with any new skill, several practice sessions will help you improve your technique. You may want to practice hand expression while your baby is suckling. Practice on your free side while your baby stimulates letdown. Place a towel or cloth diaper underneath your breast to catch any milk. You can also practice in the shower while the warm water massages your breasts and helps stimulate letdown.

Once you have the hang of it, rotate the position of your thumb and fingers around the areola to empty other milk sinuses. Hold a clean container such as a bowl or a cup underneath your breast to collect breast milk. Switch back and forth between breasts when the flow of milk slows down. This helps you express greater amounts. You can also save time by hand expressing both breasts at once. Have two containers placed on a table in front of you for milk collection. Hand expression may take between 20 and 30 minutes for breast milk collection.

Creative Expression

There are other ways you can express yourself when it comes to breast milk collection. I'm talking about telling the world about it. Some mothers feel it's helpful to write or verbalize about breast milk expression. After all, it's quite an amazing feat and is something that should be recognized.

You can express yourself in writing through a journal entry, a baby book, or just by keeping a running tally on a sheet of paper. It helps to look over your entries, especially when you have a down day. It's also entertaining to read them after your baby grows up and wants to know what breastfeeding was like. You may also find an online chat room to share with mothers who express breast milk. This may be very helpful, especially if you are expressing for a premature or hospitalized baby.

Verbalize or share with someone about expressing breast milk. It can really boost your self-esteem and provide the support you may need. You'll also benefit from another mother who expresses milk using a method like you do. If you're both using hand expression, you could share tips and discuss any particular concerns you may have. Pumping alongside another mother could also prove helpful. I've learned a lot from my clients by discussing and watching their particular methods of breast milk expression. Just talking about a new skill is bound to improve anyone's technique!

The Least You Need to Know

➤ You should begin milk expression as soon as your first day, if your baby cannot or will not breastfeed. Otherwise, wait until your third or fourth week to start milk expression. Your breastfeeding and milk supply should be well established by this time.

➤ Breastfeeding problems, hospitalized infants, and a low milk supply, all require mechanical expression.

➤ Mechanical as well as hand expression of your breast milk is possible. It's a skill that can be learned.

➤ The right breast pump is essential for successful mechanical expression.

➤ You can benefit from writing or chatting about your breast milk expression.

Chapter 14

Collection and Storage

In This Chapter

➤ Collection basics

➤ Best times for collection

➤ Storage containers and storage locations

➤ Length of storage

Now that you know the different techniques for expressing breast milk, you're ready to start your collection. You'll feel more secure with a backup supply of milk. If you plan to return to work you'll want to tap into your plentiful supply during your early weeks of breastfeeding.

Your backup supply or stockpile will give you an opportunity to get out while someone else watches your baby. Perhaps your spouse or partner wants a turn with your breastfeeding baby. Maybe grandma or grandpa want the honors. Breast milk is your baby's favorite food and a stored supply offers you plenty of security. Stored milk can also be used with solid foods when the time comes.

Basic Collection

One of the first things to do with a product you have purchased is to read the instructions. If you have chosen a mechanical means of expressing your breast milk you will want to make certain that all parts are present and that the product is operational. Place your finger against the port, or hole, of an electric breast pump to check that

Breast Beware

Always wash your hands before breastfeeding and expressing milk. Hand washing is the best way to reduce the spread of germs.

Lactation Lingo

The **flange** of a breast shield should be the proper size for your breast. The flange is the part of the breast shield that's placed over your nipple and areola. It is cone-shaped to create a good seal around the breast. A **breast shield** is the plastic or glass component of a collection assembly. When placed over your breast it allows vacuum to be applied.

vacuum is present. If you have a manual breast pump, place the flange over a soft part of your tummy and operate the handle. You should feel a draw of vacuum.

After assembling any collection equipment that's needed, wash your hands with soap and water. You may want to use a nailbrush to clean under your fingernails. With a new baby in your household you'll want to wash your hands frequently. You do not need to wash your breasts or nipples before you express breast milk. You can cleanse your breasts with soap and water during your daily bath or shower.

When using any breast pump for milk expression, you'll need a container to collect your breast milk. Choose a container that's easy for you to handle. If you will be hand-expressing, a large bowl works well because milk will spray in many directions.

If you have chosen a breast pump that enables you to collect milk from both of your breasts, it may be easier your first few times to collect from just one breast. Remember, it's the collection kit that's considered double or dual, not the breast pump. Using only one of your breasts to learn the skill of breast milk collection makes it easy on you. After you have mastered one breast, add the other collection kit to double up. This enables you to apply the vacuum for collection to both of your breasts.

Make sure the *flange* of the *breast shield* is the right size for your breast. You want it to fit properly. You want to compress your milk sinuses as your baby does. Most flanges of breast shields will fit if you have an average breast size. Remember that breasts come in all shapes and sizes. If you are large-breasted you may need a larger breast shield. If you have smaller breasts, a reducing insert may work well for you. Check with your lactation professional if you have any questions.

When using a breast pump for milk collection, always center the flange of the breast shield over your nipple and areola. Use your hands to hold and support your breast just as if you were breastfeeding your baby. Also remember to support your back and arms like you do while breastfeeding. Massage your breast, take in a deep breath and, most of all, relax! Tension and stress can keep you from releasing your breast milk. Close your eyes and think about the feel of your baby breastfeeding. Other techniques that help with milk release include listening to music, seeing a picture of your baby, or the scent from your baby's clothing.

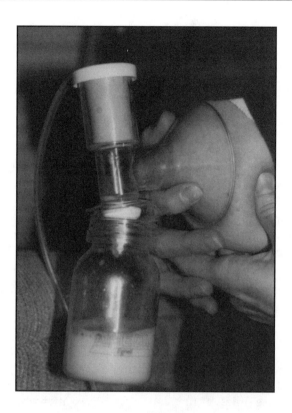

Your breast shield should fit properly over your nipple and areola.

(Source: Anne P. Mark)

After expressing milk or using a breast pump, wash and rinse everything that has touched your breast and breast milk. This includes any parts of your collection kit or the pump itself that collect breast milk or its moisture. It's best to read the manufacturer's instructions about cleaning, for a better understanding. Most parts can be washed using hot water and liquid dishwashing soap. Rinse in clear, hot water and place on a towel to air-dry. You may only need to sterilize the collection kit or breast shield if you or your baby's medical condition warrants. Check your manual to see if it recommends cleaning in a dishwasher. Don't forget to wash your hands after all is said and done.

Breast Beware

Do not submerge an electric breast pump in water when cleaning. Parts and pieces that come in contact with the breast and breast milk need cleaning. These include the breast shield, flange, valve, and collection container.

LactFact

The sterilization of containers and bottles is a procedure adapted from the handling of breast milk substitutes. The increase in formula consumption set the standard for sterilizing bottles, rubber nipples, and other feeding devices to decrease risk of contamination. Sterilization is also referred to as home-sanitization. Components are sanitized in boiling water for 20 minutes and then air-dried. Components used in the health care industry are sterilized with an autoclave. An autoclave uses gas and heat to kill bacteria and viruses. This ensures that any virus or bacteria resistant to boiling is eliminated.

The Breast of Times

Your best time to collect breast milk depends on the pattern of feeding that your baby has developed. You can start by expressing after your baby finishes a feeding. Your results may be only an ounce or less at first, but will increase after you express more often. Allow this milk expression to happen over three to five days. Your milk supply will increase the more you stimulate your breasts through breastfeeding and milk expression. If your baby has a good three- to four-hour nap you can try to express an hour and a half into naptime. Sometimes early in the morning after you have slept is a good time for milk expression.

Nursing Mom's Notes

Express your milk early in the morning after a feeding or while your baby naps. Don't try milk expression when you are tired or at night when you're ready to sleep.

You minimize collection time when you express milk from both breasts simultaneously. If you are using a breast pump and collecting from both breasts, it will take about 15 minutes or less. One breast at a time using a breast pump will take about 15 to 20 minutes. Hand expression will take between 20 and 30 minutes. When you are just getting started, remember to take your time. Feeling pressured or timed against the clock can bring you disappointing results.

Choosing Containers

Your collection of breast milk means that you now have the opportunity to store it. Breast milk should be handled and stored as you would any perishable food item. There are several containers suitable for breast milk storage. Storage containers for breast milk include the following:

- ➤ Plastic bottles
- ➤ Plastic bags
- ➤ Glass containers
- ➤ Food-storage containers

The two types of plastic bottles are polycarbonate and polypropylene. Polycarbonate plastic is clear, hard, and see-through. It's your best choice in bottles if you plan to freeze your breast milk in them. You will probably pay more for them but it's worth it. Polypropylene plastic looks frosted and you can't see through it as well. It's also softer and more pliable. Either type of plastic bottle is suitable for refrigeration or freezing.

Breast Beware

Disposable bottle bags or liners are not intended for freezing. Your breast milk may get freezer burn, or the bag may split or burst when frozen.

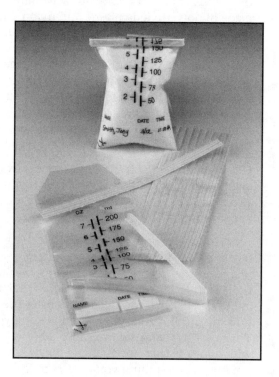

Freezer bags for breast milk storage.

(Source: Hollister, Inc.)

Nursing Mom's Notes

The cream or fat in breast milk will rise to the top over time. This will happen with refrigerated or frozen breast milk, as well as milk left to sit at room temperature. Before feeding your baby expressed breast milk, gently shake the container to mix the cream back into the milk.

Nursing Mom's Notes

Freezer bags filled with breast milk take up less room in your freezer than bottles. Ice cube trays can also be used for breast milk storage. Seal your tray inside a gallon freezer bag.

Breast Beware

Do not thaw or warm breast milk in the microwave. It can change the milk's composition and has the potential to burn your baby.

You can use plastic bags such as freezer bags or disposable bags for breast milk storage. Freezer bags intended for breast milk are ideal, especially if you'll be collecting several containers of breast milk and storing over time. Freezer bags suitable for breast milk storage are made of polyethylene plastic and nylon. This makes them durable, and prevents them from bursting under freezing conditions. They also prevent freezer burn. A freezer bag designed for breast milk storage will cost you more. Don't confuse these with disposable plastic bags or liners. Disposable bags should be used only if you will store your breast milk in the refrigerator. When using a breast pump, you can pump directly into a freezer bag or a disposable plastic bag.

Glass is also a suitable container for breast milk storage. Its drawback is that it can break if you drop it. It's also heavier if you need to carry several of these containers at once.

Food-storage containers also work well for keeping breast milk. These containers can be refrigerated or placed in the freezer. Any food container with a tight-fitting lid will suffice. The drawback to these containers is that you need to transfer the breast milk to another container when feeding your baby. This usually means pouring into a bottle or cup, which means that you increase your chance of contaminating or spilling your breast milk.

Location and Expiration

You have several possibilities for storing your breast milk. Where you should store your milk depends on how long you plan to store it. There are several possible locations for breast milk storage. You should consider the quantities you're storing as well as how you're preparing to store it.

Refrigerator Storage

You can store human breast milk in your refrigerator, in any of the containers already discussed. It will keep between five and seven days at 39°F. After this time period you should freeze or discard your milk. This storage location works well if you plan to use your expressed breast milk within a few days.

You want to store your breast milk in amounts your baby takes at a feeding. Store in two-ounce quantities if your baby is less than one month old. You can take breast milk out of the refrigerator just before you plan to use it. Gradually, over a period of 5 to 10 minutes, warm your breast milk in a container of warm water. Gently shake the breast milk to mix the fat that has risen to the top. Do not warm your breast milk in a microwave or on the stove.

Freezer Storage

Human breast milk can be stored in a freezer in any of the containers already discussed, except for disposable bottle liners. If possible, use a freezer with a separate door from your refrigerator. You can store breast milk between three and four months. A deep freeze of –20°C or less can store breast milk between 6 and 12 months.

You should store in the amounts your baby takes at a feeding. Babies between two and four months consume between two and five ounces each feeding. You can layer frozen milk. Chill the milk first in the refrigerator, and then you can add it to your frozen milk. Do not put warm milk on frozen milk, so that you don't thaw the frozen milk.

Nursing Mom's Notes

Label any collected breast milk with your baby's name and the date of collection. When using from your breast milk storage, you'll want to select the oldest milk first.

Breast Beware

Do not refreeze breast milk once it's been thawed. Like other perishable food items, thawed breast milk should be consumed within 24 hours. You risk contamination if it's refrozen.

Lactation Lingo

Lipase is an enzyme in breast milk that breaks down fat. This enzyme will break down fat to make it more digestible.

Use the milk with the oldest date first. Thaw one container of milk at a time. If you need more, another container will thaw quickly. You can thaw frozen milk overnight in your refrigerator. You can also thaw frozen milk under warm tap water or by placing it in a bowl of warm water. Do not warm your breast milk in a microwave or on the stove. Once you warm your milk, discard whatever amounts your baby doesn't consume in an hour.

Cooler Storage

You can store breast milk in a cooler with ice for up to 24 hours. This is an alternative if a refrigerator is not available. You can also transport your breast milk from one location to another in a cooler.

If you will use your breast milk within four to six hours, it can remain at a room temperature of 66° to 72°F. Human breast milk is very stable when compared to baby formula. However, it is still recommended that you refrigerate it as soon as possible. Fresh, refrigerated breast milk is best for your baby since it retains more antibodies than frozen milk. Older, frozen breast milk should always be used, though, over a breast milk substitute.

Sometimes you'll find that your expressed milk may have an unpleasant smell or taste. Certain vitamin and mineral supplements may cause this. If the fat has broken down, it can take on a soapy smell. The enzyme *lipase* breaks down the fat in milk. An excess of this enzyme will break down the fat and cause it to take on a soapy smell. If you find that this happens you can chill your milk before you place it in the freezer, or just place it directly in the freezer.

LactFact

Fresh, refrigerated breast milk is best for your baby since it retains more antibodies than frozen breast milk. Freezing can destroy a small percentage of immunity factor and antibodies present in breast milk.

The Least You Need to Know

➤ Start collecting breast milk when you have a good milk supply. Your third, fourth, or fifth week of breastfeeding is ideal.

➤ Collecting milk from both breasts simultaneously is fast and efficient.

➤ You can use bottles, bags, and food containers for breast milk storage.

➤ You can store breast milk in a refrigerator, a freezer, a cooler, and at room temperature. Breast milk keeps in a refrigerator up to seven days, three to four months in a freezer, and six months or longer in a deep freezer.

➤ Store breast milk in quantities that your baby takes at a feeding. Three to four ounce quantities are appropriate for babies older than one month.

Chapter 15

Your Milk Supply

In This Chapter

➤ Not producing enough milk?

➤ Using herbal remedies

➤ Producing too much milk?

➤ Human milk donations

If you're like most mothers, when it comes to milk production you'll wonder if there's enough or too much. You'll ask what to do if there's not enough. You'll ask what to do when your cups runneth over. Let's take a look at producing too little and too much breast milk.

You may also like to know about possible remedies to improve any low or abundant milk supply. You'll learn more about herbs and their uses for breastfeeding. Find out about human milk banks as well as how and why to be a donor. Read on for more information to use for yourself or to share with others.

Too Little

First off, let's consider a low milk supply. There may be several reasons and situations that could contribute to your low milk supply. Remember that an adequate milk supply results from how effectively you stimulate and how efficiently you remove milk. The key words are effective and efficient. If you or your baby don't stimulate your breasts well enough or frequently enough, the signal necessary for hormone release is minimized, and this will ultimately affect your supply. To increase a low supply, you must first identify the reason for decreased stimulation. You need to improve stimulation, and you can complement it with one or several remedies. You might consider an evaluation from a lactation professional. This could help determine the reason for your low milk supply.

If your milk supply is low in the first few days or first week of breastfeeding, there could be a couple of reasons why. It could be that your baby isn't stimulating your breast effectively. Sleepy babies, preemies, and babies with jaundice just don't eat well. It's also possible that something is blocking the release of your milk-making hormone. Remember that pain can interfere with the release of prolactin. And stress, too, can affect your milk supply.

Nursing Mom's Notes

During the first two weeks, you should breastfeed and empty your breasts at least 8 to 12 times in 24 hours. After this time, make sure that you are breastfeeding and emptying your breasts at least 7 or 8 times within 24 hours for an adequate milk supply.

Home Remedies

You can sometimes boost a low milk supply with a change in your breastfeeding technique. When your baby's swallowing slows down during breastfeeding, switch and offer your other breast. If your baby is sleepy, try to awaken with a burp before offering your other breast. Try to hand massage your breasts while breastfeeding. Use some deep breathing and relaxation exercises. A good shoulder massage while breastfeeding could melt away your tension.

Another remedy is using a breast pump to increase the stimulation and the emptying of your breasts. If you experience a low supply during your first week of breastfeeding be sure to select a hospital-grade piston breast pump for use. This type of pump enables you to make adjustments to provide a comfortable and stimulating vacuum. It's designed for frequent use, ideally for every time you breastfeed. Using a single collection kit, you can pump and breastfeed your baby at the same time. This helps remedy a low milk supply if you follow it for three to five days.

Nursing Mom's Notes

Use a single collection kit to express your milk after breastfeeding. Switch the collection kit to your other breast when your milk flow slows down. Try breastfeeding and emptying your other breast at the same time. This can really help boost a low supply.

If you experience a low milk supply any time after your breast milk has been well established, you've probably had some infrequent feedings or emptying of your breast milk. You can remedy this with more frequent pumping or by just allowing your baby to breastfeed more frequently. Again, this remedy works best if you pump following every feeding over three to five days. Consider an additional breastfeeding to your daily routine. Allow three to five days before you expect to see an increase in your milk supply.

Herbal Remedies

Most herbs have uses as medicinal plants. Medicinal plants are used to treat and heal medical conditions. Pharmaceutical companies have often developed drugs based on the medicinal actions of herbs. Medicinal herbs have often been recommended to mothers experiencing a low milk supply.

Herbs can be used and consumed in several ways. You can prepare and use them in any of the following forms:

➤ An herbal tea

➤ A tincture

➤ Vinegar preserves

➤ A poultice

➤ A compress

➤ A salve

➤ Aromatherapy

It is best that you consult an experienced and knowledgeable expert for help to select the right herb for the right result. Herb sources and active ingredients can vary. It is also important to consult your physician before using any herbal remedy, especially if you take prescribed medications and supplements.

The two types of herbal teas are *infusions* and *decoctions*. Infusions work best for leaf and flower material because these yield higher plant or *phytochemicals*. A decoction is typically used for root and twig material because they can be harder to extract the medicinal phytochemicals from. When preparing an infusion, start with fresh water, bring it to a boil, and steep your medicinal herb(s) until the water is cool. If you like it hot, then gently reheat your tea. If you prefer, add some lemon and honey to sweeten your tea. For a decoction, use fresh water and boil or simmer your herbal material for 10 to 20 minutes.

Lactation Lingo

A **phytochemical** is a chemical derived from a plant source. It can be good for us when it offers our body protection and helps to heal any ailments. A phytochemical is bad for us when used in excess or when it interacts with any prescribed medications. **Galactagogue** is a material or action that stimulates the production of milk. Several herbs can act as galactogogues.

Here's a Tongue Twister—Galactagogues

Galactagogue is a material or action that stimulates the production of milk. There are several medicinal herbs that are used as a galactogogue. Herbs that help to increase milk production usually contain *phytoestrogens*. These are plant chemicals that are similar to the female hormone estrogen. Estrogen works in the human body to stimulate the production of human breast cells. Breast cells are the source of milk production. When stimulated, breast cells will produce milk. The following are reported plant sources that might help to increase your milk supply:

➤ Fenugreek

➤ Fennel

➤ Anise

➤ Caraway

➤ Chasteberry

➤ Lemongrass

Fenugreek (*Trigonella foenum-graecum*), also known as Greek hay, has been used since biblical times to increase a mother's milk production. It contains diosgenin, an estrogen-like compound, which helps to increase milk flow. Fenugreek is commonly used in Middle Eastern cooking. It adds flavor and enhances the aroma of food. Fenugreek also contains mucilage. It soothes the stomach and adds fiber to help with digestion. Fenugreek has been known to ease colic, the painful stomach spasms that infants experience.

LactFact

Fenugreek contains phytoestrogens that can stimulate the production of human breast cells. Fenugreek is less effective if the breast is not completely emptied of breast milk. Take two to three fenugreek capsules by mouth three times each day. Look for an increase in your milk supply over one to three days. Fenugreek produces a maple-like scent in your sweat and urine.

The seed of fenugreek contains the active ingredient, but you can also consume the leaves and flower of the plant. You can take the fenugreek seed as a tea infusion, in capsule form, or added liberally to the foods you are cooking. Fenugreek is also available as a tincture. Many women report that it can be quite effective!

Fennel (*Foeniculum vulgare*) contains compounds that are also similar to estrogen. It has also been used for centuries to stimulate milk production. Do not confuse fennel with fennel oil. The oil has been known to cause miscarriage, and consuming quantities greater than a teaspoon can be toxic.

Anise, caraway, chasteberry, and lemongrass are also known to enhance milk production. Chinese herbalists recommend the consumption of peanuts (*Arachis hypogaea*) and roasted sesame seeds (*Sesamum indicum*) to women who produce little milk. Since legumes contain several estrogenic compounds, the seed from the pod is given to help with milk production.

Breast Beware

Do not confuse fennel with fennel oil. The oil has been known to cause miscarriage, and consuming quantities greater than a teaspoon can be toxic.

Got Milk?

There is always a possibility that you can produce too much milk. This can only be seen as a bad thing if recurring mastitis or plugged ducts plague you. Mastitis is an infection of the breast that occurs when your breast is not emptied thoroughly of its produced milk. Milk ducts can become full and swollen from retained breast milk. An overabundance of milk can contribute to milk stasis, in which residual milk is left in the milk ducts and the alveoli. Milk stasis can lead to infection. Bacteria that thrive on the milk sugars can often cause an infection.

A good milk supply can be misinterpreted as an overabundance of breast milk. I've had mothers comment that they don't want to create too much milk. Consult a lactation professional to help identify whether you have an overabundance of milk. Your body takes the opportunity, especially at the start of breastfeeding, to make plenty of milk for your baby. Your breasts will supply in response to stimulation. If your baby consumes everything on the plate, then great. If only three-quarters are eaten, then anything left over should be emptied from your breast and stored. It usually takes a good three to six weeks from the start of breastfeeding for your supply to even out.

An overabundance can be caused by a pituitary disorder that usually requires medical attention. Prolactinomas are pituitary tumors that cause an excess of hormone release. This results in increased milk production, which sometimes can be excessive. Emotional and stressful events can also cause an overproduction of breast milk.

Milk Inhibitors

It's best to use a hospital-quality electric piston breast pump to help reduce an overabundant milk supply. Again, you can adjust the vacuum for effective stimulation and efficient emptying of your breast. When using a piston breast pump, you remove just enough milk from your breast to feel comfortable. This helps to prevent milk stasis from any residual milk and reduces your chance of mastitis or plugged milk ducts. In the case of weaning, emptying just enough milk to feel comfortable helps with the slow and gradual reduction of your milk supply. I'll refer to measures for weaning in Chapter 30, "Weaning Your Baby."

To suppress your milk flow, either for weaning or to reduce an overabundance, try the following herbal remedies:

➤ Parsley

➤ Sage

➤ Jasmine

Nursing Mom's Notes

Before you take measures to inhibit an overabundant milk supply, consider donating to a milk bank.

You can take parsley and sage as tea infusions. You might also try a tabouli salad. Its main ingredient is parsley! You can actually crush the jasmine flower and rub it around the breast for absorption into the skin. I should also add that cabbage leaves, even though not an herb, are commonly used to inhibit milk production and relieve engorgement. You chill the leaves from green cabbage in the refrigerator and then place them on the breast for 10 to 15 minutes.

You must take caution with any plant source not to obtain results that you don't want. In other words, too much of these herbs can cause a drastic reduction or cessation of your milk production. Be sure that you consult a lactation professional or your physician before using any remedy to reduce your milk supply.

Become a Milk Donor

By now, you are well aware that a mother's milk is the best food for any infant, if not every infant. The nutrition from human milk cannot be replicated. Antibodies and white cells fight infection and boost the immune system. Your baby benefits from good growth and development, minimal allergies, and enhanced brain function.

The opportunity for and availability of donated breast milk has been used for centuries. Donor milk is breast milk that's been given or provided to someone in need. Human breast milk can provide nourishment for infants as well as older children and adults. There have been many recipients of donated milk and no documented cases of milk-related illness. Now that's a proven track record.

Donor milk recipients include infants, children, and adults with the following conditions:

➤ Prematurity

➤ Kidney failure

➤ Cardiac problems

➤ Burn victims

➤ Organ-transplant recipients

➤ Intestinal diseases

Human Milk Bank

We've got banks for money, blood, sperm, and, yes, human milk. In years past, people thought nothing about offering breast milk directly from a lactating woman. No one batted an eyelash. In several countries around the world it happens every day. Wet nursing or cross nursing are the methods of providing breast milk directly to a baby. Cross nursing is the breastfeeding by a lactating woman to a baby who is not her own. Human milk donation today is handled through a milk bank, which operates much like a blood bank. A milk bank can provide a supply of human milk to recipients with medical need.

A human milk bank adheres to the following guidelines for donated human milk:

➤ *Pasteurize* and freeze human breast milk for storage.

➤ Require a prescription showing medical need from a physician or health care provider.

➤ Request documentation from baby's health care provider that growth and development is appropriate.

➤ Screen donors about their health and lifestyle.

➤ Follow operational guidelines and recommendations established by the Human Milk Banking Association.

Donors are the backbone, or should I say the breastbone, of a human milk bank. Donors provide a continuous supply of valuable milk for recipients. A typical donor is in good health, motivated, and has excess milk. Donors may express several ounces of milk for days and weeks while they breastfeed. They may make a one-time donation or supply milk in batches. Donors pump their breast milk and deliver it frozen to the milk bank. The milk is then thawed, cultured, and pasteurized.

Donors are screened by the following means:

➤ Initial telephone query

➤ Written questionnaire about their general health and lifestyle

Lactation Lingo

Pasteurization is the sterilization of milk by heating it to 140°F or above and then cooling. French chemist and biologist, Louis Pasteur, developed this process.

➤ Verification by health care provider of mother's and baby's health

➤ Blood tested for infections

The donation of breast milk is entirely voluntary. Donors believe that human milk is vital, and they motivate others to do the same. Some may have benefited from donor milk and want to give back any way they can. Mothers whose infants have died find that donating milk helps them heal from the loss they have experienced.

The Human Milk Banking Association of North America, Incorporated (HMBANA) is a nonprofit organization established in 1985. Its purpose is to provide operational guidelines for milk banks as well as to advocate, educate, and coordinate the distribution of donor milk. The following human milk banks are operational and members of the HMBANA:

Mother's Milk Bank
Valley Medical Center
P.O. Box 5730
San Jose, CA 85150
408-998-4550

Mother's Milk Bank
HealthOne
1719 East 19th Avenue
Denver, CO 80218
303-869-1888

Mother's Milk Bank
Christiana Hospital
4755 Ogleton-Stanton Road
Newark, DE 19718
1-800-NICU-101

Umass/Memorial Medical Center
119 Belmont Street
Worcester, MA 01605
508-793-6005

Mother's Milk Bank at WakeMed
3000 New Burn Avenue
Raleigh, NC 27610
919-350-8599

Mother's Milk Bank of Austin
900 East 30th Street, Suite 101
Austin, TX 78705
512-494-0800

Lactation Support Service
British Columbia Children's Hospital
4480 Oak Street
Vancouver, BC V6H 3V4 Canada
604-875-2345

Cost and Reimbursement

There are costs associated with the operation of a milk bank. Fees are charged to help cover processing and shipping. They may help fund research and cover any clinician fees. Presently, the processing fees for human donor milk in the United States range from $2.00 to $2.75 per ounce. Many human milk banks operate within a university or hospital department. Donors aren't paid because the fees charged often only cover operational and handling expenses. Some donors receive perks or services in kind, such as use of breastfeeding equipment and supplies.

Insurance reimbursement and coverage for donor milk may vary. Recipients must have a medical need for breast milk. Third-party payers or Medicaid may cover the fees associated with donor milk. If your baby requires human milk, then it's definitely worth filing a claim with your insurance company for your expenses. Like human blood, human milk can save lives.

The Least You Need to Know

➤ Remedies for a low milk supply include increased breastfeeding, herbs, and the use of a breast pump.

➤ Remedies for a low milk supply should be used for at least three to five days before you see some results.

➤ An overabundant milk supply should be expressed and stored. Caution should be used when using remedies to decrease an abundant milk supply.

➤ Donated human milk is available for anyone with a medical need.

Part 5

It's Back to Work

There are some things for you to consider if you are a working mother. You can choose to continue breastfeeding along with your return to work. If you are going to work full time and breastfeed, you'll need some guidance to help you with the collection and storage of your breast milk.

Some co-workers or even your boss may greet your breastfeeding with mixed reactions. You'll need to know how to handle these situations and what your best line of defense will be. There's a chapter to help ease you back in the workplace with tips and solutions for many circumstances.

It's every mother's right to breastfeed. And it's also a baby's right to eat. But what are the legal implications surrounding breastfeeding for a mother and her baby? In this part, you'll gain some insight about legal circumstances and learn which laws protect you as a breastfeeding mother.

Chapter 16

Working Mother

In This Chapter

➤ Choosing to work and breastfeed

➤ Employment options that work

➤ Breastfeeding awareness in the workplace

➤ Preparations for breastfeeding and working

➤ Feeding alternatives

You'll have many decisions to make for your baby before as well as after birth. Returning to work after your baby is born is a big decision for any new mom. How can anyone replace the love and care that you provide for your very own baby? You may wonder if you can combine your breastfeeding with your work schedule. Well, you certainly can. All it takes is some creative planning and your commitment to continue breastfeeding.

Remember that breastfeeding provides you many advantages as a working mother. The continued health benefits and the immunity your breast milk provides your baby are the best bargains around. You can "grow" your own breast milk and not have to buy baby formula in a can. Your breast milk prevents the allergic responses in your baby that a cow's milk formula can cause. Your commitment to continued breastfeeding could help you overcome any anxiety about returning to work or having another person care for your baby. You can stay connected. Only you can provide this valuable resource for your baby. Let's consider what it takes to be a working, breastfeeding mother.

Decisions, Decisions

There are many special advantages that breastfeeding offers any working mother. Others can help to care for your baby, but only you and you alone can provide nature's best resource for your baby. You may enjoy the private time that breastfeeding provides. It helps you take time out for some peace and quiet with your baby. You may like the feeling of closeness with your baby that breastfeeding offers. There's nothing better than looking into your baby's eyes and seeing the "thank you" beam from within. That's all the reason to want to keep on breastfeeding and coordinating it with your work schedule.

The first thing to consider is whether you want and need to return to work. The questions to ask yourself are "Do I want to work?" and "Do I need to return to work?"

Nursing Mom's Notes

You need a desire and a commitment toward breastfeeding to combine it successfully with working.

You have to answer these questions before you can proceed. Oftentimes the "need to work" answer is yes and the "want to work" answer is no. If I had it to do all over again, I would have carefully considered and answered these two questions myself.

You see, if you want to return to work and you can honestly answer "yes," then there's an important element of desire within you. Desire is very important when it comes to combining your breastfeeding with your work performance. Your success with continuing to breastfeed is determined by wanting to make it happen. If you don't really want to return to work you won't be motivated to do what it takes to keep breastfeeding.

LactFact

Signed into law in 1993, the federal Family and Medical Leave Act (FMLA) guarantees employees 12 weeks of unpaid time off to care for a newborn or adopted child. Companies with 50 or more employees have this. An employee must have been on the job for at least one year to qualify. Also, the employee must have worked 1,250 hours throughout the year. During the employee's leave the employer must continue medical benefits. Some employers require that an employee use paid vacation, or any other accrued leave, during their 12-week period.

Your other consideration is whether you need to work. Many households today depend on dual incomes to maintain a desired lifestyle. If you like certain services and conveniences that modern life has to offer, then you need the money to pay for them. If you are the primary source of income for your household, then you may have to return to work. Health insurance may be something to consider, especially if you are the sole carrier. Draft a family budget and compare it to life without your income contribution. Visualizing the reality of your finances may help with your decision.

Creative Scheduling

Once you've made the decision to return to work, you'll need to consider how much work you want to do. There are several possible work schedules from which to choose. You can combine breastfeeding with any of them. A number of jobs today lend themselves to creative and flexible opportunities for working, breastfeeding mothers.

Full Time

To be employed on a full-time basis usually entails a 40-hour workweek. When and how those 40 hours are accomplished is dependent on your employer and the work task at hand. Some full-time jobs are Monday through Friday from eight or nine in the morning to four or five in the afternoon. Another week's work may be four 10-hour days. Then there are schedules with afternoon or night shifts of work. Some employers offer 12 hours of shift work over three days' time, and compensate for a 40-hour workweek. Full-time work can come in several package options.

A full week's work may be necessary to be eligible for benefits. If your employer requires that eligibility for benefits include 40 hours of work, you'll have to comply if you need the benefits. If benefits aren't an issue, then perhaps your job description requires 40 hours each week. If you don't know, you'll need to find out. Full-time work will be the most challenging schedule to combine with breastfeeding.

Full-time work can sometimes be more than 40 hours each week. Your employer may require mandatory attendance for meetings, presentations, additional training, and overtime. So, 40 hours can become 50 before long. Seasonal work can also bring concentrated work hours into your week, too, so keep that in mind. Be well aware of what your full-time commitment is before you choose to return.

Breast Beware

Combining breastfeeding with full-time work will be a challenging accomplishment for any new mother.

If you are a working professional, you may need to continue working on a full-time basis. You can't help it if you're in demand! You may feel it's necessary to keep up with your professional skills and that only full-time work can satisfy this. You may find that your client base requires that you provide full-time hours. If so, you may not have a choice about your work schedule.

Part Time

The beauty of this type of work is the flexibility that part-time hours have to offer. This really could be a working mom's dream. Flexibility means that work time can bend around the schedule you choose. It may offer you just the right amount of work time and mom time to keep you happy. If you are a mother who wants to return to work, but you don't like the commitment of full-time hours, you should strongly consider part-time hours.

Find out or ask your employer if any work is available with *part-time* hours. If benefits are offered to part-time employees, find out how many work hours are necessary to be eligible. You might as well cover all your bases and collect as much information as you can to help make your choice. Ask if there are any new mothers who have returned to work part time at your place of business. Better yet, ask if there are mothers who have returned to work and are breast-feeding. That's what you'd like to do. Talk to these mothers and get some feedback, if possible. It really helps to hear from someone who's making it happen.

Part time may range from one to four days, evenings, or nights. It could be five or six days for four or five hours. Any number of combinations might be available. In some cases, you might be the one to make an offer. Think about what kind of work schedule would really make you want to return to work. Jot it down on paper. Talk it over with your spouse or partner. Get some input, especially if he or she will provide the care for your baby. Approach your boss with a proposal for viable part-time work. There's nothing better than for you to present a working plan to upper management. It shows your commitment, desire, and creativity to return to work.

If part-time work is not available with your present employer, you may consider the following sources for part-time employment:

Nursing Mom's Notes

The best type of work for a breastfeeding mother is a job or position where you can create your schedule of work hours. That means you are accountable and you report to yourself. When it's time to breastfeed or express your milk, you can do it.

Lactation Lingo

Full-time employment is often a 40-hour workweek. **Part-time employment** is less than 30 hours worked each week. **Job-share** is a job or position shared between at least two people.

➤ Nonprofit corporations

➤ Small businesses

➤ Employment agency

Nonprofit corporations may pay you less but may be very receptive to your need for flexible hours. They usually want to attract and retain employees. You may be in the best position to bargain for the work hours and position you want. Small businesses with fewer than 100 employees are also great to target because you can be a great asset to them. If you present them with an offer for what you can do for them, in the hours that you are available, it could be a present for an employer with a bow on top. Keep in mind that women-owned businesses might have been started because they wanted the flexibility and part-time hours just like you do. Offer up that you are looking to balance your breastfeeding and work hours, and see if that doesn't strike up their interest in you. An employment agency that specializes in placing part-time positions may be worth investigating. This type of agency works in your best interests. They will place you in a position that you want and ensure that your work hours satisfy what you requested.

Another type of part-time work is *job sharing*. You split the position with another employee and function as one unit. Some split the work as one week on, and one week off. Some work three days one week, and two days the next week. If holidays need to be worked, you choose who works what, in a calm, grown-up manner! Find out if benefits are available with job sharing. If not, and you need them, you'll have to nix this work possibility.

Part-time work has some drawbacks that you may want to consider. Time with your baby and family may be satisfied, but your opportunity to move up may be diminished. Promotions and advancements may not be available to you when you work an abbreviated workweek. Identify your work goals. Think long and hard about the pros and cons before you pursue a part-time work schedule.

Breast Beware

If you choose to job share, find out if any benefits are available for you and the other employee. Some employers do not offer paid benefits when a position is shared.

Home Work

If you are an enthusiastic, flexible, and disciplined worker, then this job's for you. Working from home or your home base can offer the best of family and work life. Making it happen and planning your work strategies can prove this work choice a winner.

Several job opportunities lend themselves to working from home. If you are presently employed, see if your position can be operated from a home base. Your employer may jump at the chance to save on the costs for office space, insurance, and other benefits.

Telecommuting is becoming very popular with today's workforce. It can keep you on the home front, eliminate the time taken to travel to your place of business, and allow you to be more productive. Being at home enables you to continue with your baby's breastfeeding pattern without interruption. You can breastfeed while punching away on the keyboard or while talking "hands-free" on a speakerphone. Many employers want to retain employees whom they have taken the time to train and groom, and who are assets to the company. Give it a go. It never hurts to ask.

You might consider turning some of your unique skills into an independent contractor position. That means offering your specialized skills with products or services that you can capitalize on. Ask yourself what service or product that you can provide from a home base. Many popular freelance positions are in demand within the market today. Many companies rely on outside sources to provide services that aren't performed by their staff. The following positions may lend well to your possibility of working from home:

➤ Designers

➤ Accountants

➤ Writers

➤ Editors

➤ Computer experts

Keep in mind that, as an independent contractor, you provide the location, equipment, and insurance necessary to complete the job at hand. You become self-employed. You are your own boss. It does take the discipline and time management to complete what you need to. Being your own boss, though, gives you the freedom to continue with breastfeeding your baby, and to provide the love and care that's most important.

Hey Boss, I'm Breastfeeding

Once you've considered your working choices, it's time to approach your boss with a proposal and negotiations. This may very well be the hardest part for you. You know what you want. You've looked at it from every possible angle. You've weighed the pros against the cons. You want to be well received and to walk away with what you want. But it may not go as you envision.

You will need to tell your boss that you've made the tough decision to return to work and to continue breastfeeding your baby. "Is she crazy?" I hear you ask. She doesn't know my boss! I'm telling you this because that's where I went wrong when I returned to work. I didn't breathe a word. I kept it a secret. Looking back, I had no support and no one to listen when the going got tough. Every breastfeeding, working mother deserves the respect and recognition for taking on her commitment. You not only raise awareness about breastfeeding, but also empower yourself for the choice you have made.

"My boss is a man! There's no way I can speak a word about such a personal thing like breastfeeding." Okay, okay. We're walking on thin ice. I don't want for you to be embarrassed. The opportunity for a male boss to take this "breast" thing and run with it can be tempting. Consider the approach of explaining that breastfeeding offers so many health advantages. You can say that you will be spending your breaks and lunch hours doing something healthy for you and your baby. You might consider taking your spouse or partner along for support and to help by talking man-to-man. It may be that your male boss is most uncomfortable with the discussion of breastfeeding. He may not want to know any details; he just wants to know if you'll get the job done.

On the flip side of the coin you tell me that your boss is a woman. She thinks that breastfeeding is gross and a waste of time. You'll definitely be faced with a challenge here. Try using the "healthy mom, healthy baby" approach and emphasize what breastfeeding means to you. Again, it really helps to raise awareness of breastfeeding and its advantages, regardless of someone's opinion.

Nursing Mom's Notes

Prepare a list of things you want to talk about with your boss. Include breastfeeding in the number two or three slot. Be ready with an alternative on your wish list if something is declined.

Be sure to point out to your employer the advantages that breastfeeding offers. Continued breastfeeding helps protect you against breast and gynecological cancers. For your employer this means a healthy employee. The unique factors in breast milk provide your baby with immunity and protect against infection. A healthy baby means you'll take fewer sick days to care for your baby's illness. Healthy employees, and their healthy babies, keep an employer's cost of health care insurance at a minimum. Satisfying your desire to keep on breastfeeding will also motivate you. In return, you'll offer your best work performance.

In addition to your boss, it's a great idea to share with one or two of your co-workers that you'll be breastfeeding. You might find someone who's recently had a baby and who has continued breastfeeding. Perhaps a male co-worker will respect what you're trying to do. Be open about the health advantages, reduced costs, and the happy mother-baby duo. Just by chatting about breastfeeding, you'll help to educate and to advocate the "breast" thing since sliced bread!

Your Breast Scenario

Okay, you've made your decision, you have a work plan in place, and the boss encounter is behind you. Now you need to know what to do to make breastfeeding and working happen. Your early weeks of breastfeeding with your baby help you to get off to a good start. You'll need to spend as much time breastfeeding your baby as you can to set up a good milk supply. Make sure that you rest and sleep as your body tells you to. You should eat foods that offer a good balance of nutrition and energy. Take a look at Chapter 29, "Stepping Out," on what to eat while breastfeeding. Satisfy your thirst, and remember that water is essential for your body. Drink up!

It's important to start early to prepare for your return to work. Your third, fourth, or fifth week after delivery is the ideal time to express your breast milk to stash and store. You'll not only need a starter supply but your breasts will respond to making more milk at this time. Any breast milk that you express you can store long term in the freezer.

Breast Beware

Don't purchase a breast pump off the shelf just because it says it's electric. Find out the type of pump, the vacuum mechanics, and the number of cycles available per minute. Be an educated consumer.

If you choose not to hand express your breast milk, then now is the time to rent or purchase a breast pump. A breast pump enables you to mechanically express your breast milk. You will need a durable and dependable breast pump. I strongly recommend a medical-grade electric piston breast pump; it's your best choice for breast milk expression. It is durable, dependable, and offers you the best stimulation for expression and collection. It's well worth the rental fee if you use it often. If you will be using a breast pump for the first time, this is also your best bet. You could rent and then purchase your breast pump of choice. See if your retailer or supplier offers a discount toward a purchase if you choose to buy later on. It's important to use the best equipment to help make your milk collection successful. I've listed for you the following quality electric piston breast pumps to consider for rent.

Electric Piston Breast Pumps for Rent

Manufacturer	Brand	Accessory Kit
Ameda®	SMB	HygieniKit Dual or Single
	Lact-e	HygieniKit Dual or Single
	Elite	HygieniKit Dual or Single
Medela®	Classic	Universal Pumping System
		Manualectric® Breastpump System
	Lactina Plus	Universal or Double Pumping System
		Manualectric Breastpump System
	Lactina Select	Universal or Double Pumping System
		Manualectric Breastpump System

You may consider the purchase of a breast pump at this time, but you'll need to make sure it's a pump designed for use two or three times each day. By three or four weeks postpartum you can start pumping after your first and second morning feeding. With this frequency of milk expression be sure that you purchase a breast pump intended for this frequency of use. Even if you intend to return to work part time, you will need to purchase a breast pump that withstands your daily use. I've listed for you the following quality breast pumps to consider for purchase:

Personal Breast Pumps for Affordable Purchase

Manufacturer	Brand
Ameda®	Purely Yours
	One Hand Breast Pump
Avent®	Isis Breast Pump
Medela®	SpringExpress
	ManualEase
	Pump In Style®
	DoubleEase
	MiniElectric

Use It or Lose It

The time to start your daily milk expression is during your third, fourth, or fifth week after your start of breastfeeding. It may be helpful to review the chapter on breast milk expression. Expressing your breast milk at this time will program your breasts to make enough milk for your baby and for your return to work. Don't worry about making too much milk. It will be just the right amount. This is milk that you should save and store, regardless of when you plan to return to work. You need to tap into what you're capable of making right now.

About an hour after your first morning breastfeeding you should try to express your breast milk. You may not collect a great amount of milk when you first start, so don't worry. Be patient and remember that expressing your breast milk is learned, just like breastfeeding is. The quantity will add up with your continued collection times. Try to pump

Nursing Mom's Notes

Your third, fourth, or fifth week of breastfeeding is the best time to start expressing milk for your return to work. Even if you won't return until your 14th week, the best time to tap into your supply is between weeks three, four, and five. You have to trust me on this one!

Lactation Lingo

Prolactin is your hormone that stimulates milk production. Its peak release from your pituitary gland can be between 2 and 5 A.M.

Breast Beware

You should be consistent with the times that you express your breast milk. Skipped or missed pumping will result in less milk.

again an hour after the third time you breastfeed in the morning or in the early afternoon. You may find that you express more milk early in the day and less milk toward the end of the day. Your milk-making hormone, *prolactin,* can be highest at night between 2 and 5 A.M. and this may account for more milk in the morning.

Store your breast milk in two to four-ounce quantities, especially if your baby will consume it at two or three months of age. Any milk that you collect can be stored in the refrigerator for five to seven days. You can combine amounts to make two to four ounces. Just remember to add chilled milk to chilled milk, not freshly expressed warm milk to chilled milk.

You need to be consistent with the times that you express your breast milk. Each time you stimulate your breasts to produce breast milk it is interpreted as a feeding. It's important not to miss these times. Your breasts will begin to make less milk if you miss or skip a breastfeeding. The same will happen if you miss or skip your times to express your breast milk.

Remember to take it one day at a time. If your baby seems to want to breastfeed more often, and experiences a growth spurt, then focus on just breastfeeding your baby. That's the best thing about starting so early. You can allow a few days for just breastfeeding and then return to your breast milk collection routine.

Feeding Baby Sans Breast

Your biggest question now is how to give your baby breast milk without offering it from your breast. You don't want to confuse your baby after you've worked so hard to master the skill of breastfeeding. The following are alternatives for offering your breast milk to your baby:

➤ Bottle-feeding

➤ Eyedropper feeding

➤ Cup feeding

➤ Finger feeding

➤ Spoon feeding

160

Bottle-feeding is perhaps the most preferred means of giving any milk to a baby. After all, baby formula helped to introduce bottles to the market. You can choose between different types of bottles as well as an endless number of artificial nipples or teats. Try a silicone nipple over latex; it smells and tastes better. Also, look for a nipple that stretches like your nipple during a breastfeeding. Consider an orthodontic nipple as well as a nipple with a slow liquid flow.

If your breastfeeding is well established and baby is breastfeeding well from your breasts, a bottle can be introduced by about four weeks of age. Let someone else introduce your baby to bottle-feeding. Your spouse, partner, or a grandparent will probably jump at the chance. You want your baby to connect the love and warmth of breastfeeding with you.

Nursing Mom's Notes

Try a silicone nipple over latex; it smells and tastes better to your baby.

Breastfeeding babies will often gulp down the breast milk when they are offered it from a bottle. Remember that they have perfected the skill of stimulating, compressing, and drawing milk from the breast with suction. Breast milk in a bottle can come quickly and easily with the slightest of vacuum and a bit of gravity to boot. If your baby drinks from its bottle too quickly and still seems hungry, your baby will need to take several rest periods during its feeding. You may also try an artificial nipple with a smaller hole. One that's got a slow, slow flow!

Feeding with an eyedropper can be easy for the person feeding. It's a great alternative for the baby who refuses a bottle. Breast milk is drawn up through the tube with a bulb syringe and then inserted along the side of baby's mouth. With a gentle squeeze and some suction from the baby, breast milk can be drawn out and swallowed. If necessary, you can also easily measure the amount that baby takes since most eyedroppers or medicine droppers have graduated volume markings.

Cup feeding and finger feeding require more patience and persistence from the person feeding the baby. Cup feedings work well for the four to six-month-old baby, although cup or bowl feedings to premature babies have been documented. Smaller cups designed for breast milk feedings are on the market as well as videotapes showing you the technique. Finger feeding uses a small, flexible silastic feeding tube attached to a syringe or bottle containing breast milk. The tubing can be wrapped around your finger and inserted into baby's mouth. The bottle is held at chest level, and the syringe is slowly advanced as baby suckles your finger like the breast. Spoon feeding is a simple alternative to try but its success, too, depends on the age of your baby. It lends itself well to the older baby.

The Least You Need to Know

➤ You can successfully combine breastfeeding and working.

➤ Several work combinations are available to the breastfeeding mother.

➤ Supervisor and co-worker support is very helpful.

➤ Start your breast milk collection during your third, fourth, or fifth week after delivery.

➤ Select and use a quality breast pump for your milk expression. Choose the right breast pump for the right circumstance.

➤ Methods for offering expressed breast milk include bottle, cup, dropper, and finger feeding.

Chapter 17

On the Job

In This Chapter

➤ Childcare options for breastfeeding mothers

➤ Types of childcare providers

➤ Preparations for breastfeeding and working

➤ Breast milk expression for working mothers

➤ Locations for expressing breast milk

Before your actual return to the workplace, you'll have to do some footwork and phone work to make sure everything is in place. You'll need to consider who will care for your baby, the time line of your workday, your work environment, and any supplies needed for you and your baby. You're a busy mom, and managing your time wisely is essential. I'm going to point out the important logistics for you to accomplish before you head back to work.

Preparing to go back to work is like getting ready for a trip. You have more than just yourself to get ready. There will be a checklist of things you need, things that baby needs, things to do, and things to get in order. It's very important to start your preparations as soon as you have committed to your return. Let's look at the important concerns on your "to do" list.

B.Y.O.B.

Is it possible for you to bring your own baby to work with you? More and more businesses are becoming family-friendly and may agree to allow you and your baby at work together. This is an ideal circumstance for any breastfeeding mother. It provides you the opportunity to breastfeed at almost any time while you work. Your baby's feeding routine has no interruption. No need to express your milk, to store, and to worry about your baby's refusal to breastfeed. This alone can make you more than a happy camper! It's a great opportunity if you'll be working three to five hours. Eight hours of work with your breastfeeding baby may be too much for you. Of course, the kind of work you do and the environment that you work in may determine if this is possible. If there are environmental circumstances or you need to dash off at a moment's notice, this can't be an option. The important question for you to answer is whether you can take care of your baby and can get your work done. Your employer won't be happy if you can't cut the mustard. Know what I mean? If your work requires your undivided attention and you can't work efficiently with your baby at your side, then don't consider this as an option.

There are a few things you'll need to consider to care for your breastfeeding baby at your work place. Your baby will need a car seat or portable crib to catch some z's. Let's face it, you will get tired of holding your baby all the time. And you shouldn't rely on your co-workers to help hold your baby. Many moms find that a baby sling is an excellent way to "wear" your baby while working. A baby sling works just like a hammock. You wear a wide fabric sash designed for carrying a baby. Your baby can sleep, breastfeed, and stay attached to you while hanging out in your sling. And the bonus is that your hands are free! You can answer the phone, use a computer keyboard, and complete tasks that require the use of your hands.

Nursing Mom's Notes

Use a baby sling to hold, carry, and breastfeed your baby while you're on the job. It's also great to use around the house and for running errands with your baby.

You'll need access to a bathroom for diaper changes and for washing your hands. The availability of a baby-changing station is great. If not, you'll need a changing mat and a place to lay your baby down for a change. You may have to dispose of soiled diapers somewhere other than the bathroom, especially if there isn't an appropriate container. Don't forget an ample supply of diapers and wipes. You don't want to get caught short on the job.

An extra change of clothes for you and your baby is a good idea to have on hand. Accidents do happen. You'll need to be prepared with something clean and dry to change into if necessary. Try to bring yourself snacks or a meal. You may find that you want to eat at your desk or in a break room instead of going out for food. And don't forget plenty to drink. You'll get thirsty during your time at work and with breastfeeding.

Sling Ezee™ baby sling for wearing your baby.

(Source: Parenting Concepts)

There's one drawback to having your baby with you while on the job. It works great for a baby up to about six months of age. When they start to get mobile, though, it becomes a whole new ballgame. They don't want to be contained and are ready to explore. Crawling turns into walking. Then your baby will want to get into everything. So keep this in mind for long-term planning. Bringing your own baby to work can be great in the first months of infancy, but you may need to go back to the drawing board before the end of baby's first year.

Nursing Mom's Notes

An employee came to work for me with one special request: She wanted to bring her then five-month-old son to work with her. She knew that expressing her milk was an option but didn't want to be separated from her baby. She wanted to actually maintain her breastfeeding relationship. Sounded like a workable plan to me. I agreed to her request. And Jack came to work with his mom. He peered out of his sling and observed business activity. She took breaks for breastfeeding as often as she needed. Several customers were encouraged, surprised, and perhaps a bit jealous that a working mom had her baby right at her side.

Home Sweet Home

The opportunity to keep your breastfeeding baby at home with a caregiver while you work cannot be understated. Even if it's your neighbor's home or even Grandma's place, home offers the safety and comfort for any new baby. It gives you the peace of mind to focus on your work, knowing that your baby is safe and sound.

You can manage your breast milk inventory in your own home quite easily. There's no room for error when giving your baby your breast milk. No chance of mistakes, no one to discard your precious supply except you. You get to be boss when it comes to policies and procedures for the care of your breastfeeding baby.

Is it possible that your spouse or partner has the time and wants to be the care provider? There's nothing better than knowing and trusting someone close to you. Like most new mothers, you'll be most comfortable with a spouse, family member, or close friend taking care of your baby. Look into all of your options for care in your own home or at the home of a close relative or neighbor. Someone you know and trust. Maybe you'll get lucky and someone will volunteer to fill the position!

Another consideration is to hire someone to care for your baby in your home. This will involve searching, seeking, and some paperwork, but the time spent is worth the reward. You can employ someone in your own home whom you feel will provide the next best thing to your care. Be sure to offer that you are breastfeeding and will be providing expressed breast milk for your baby. Pay attention to his or her reaction; it may help you decide whom to hire. There's nothing worse than someone sending you a message of disapproval. You don't need his or her opinion or dissertation about breastfeeding. That decision has already been made. You want someone who will follow your instructions and fulfill the requirements of the job.

Breast Beware

Consider any local laws and ordinances regarding an employee in your own home. Inquire about liability insurance and any other safeguards to protect yourself in the event that unforeseen circumstances should arise.

I can offer to you, from personal experience, to proceed carefully when contracting someone for care in your own home. Call and check his or her references. Enlist the services of a legal professional to draft a work agreement. The lawyer can also help defend you if a deal goes sour. The last thing you need is a battle in court in addition to breastfeeding, parenting, and working. As the saying goes, better safe than sorry.

Childcare Providers

Businesses that provide childcare are also an option for the care of your baby. Some offer part-time enrollment while others require a full week's care. Whether it's a home day care or a full-service facility, a business that specializes in childcare is usually licensed and insured. Hours of operation are usually set and you don't have to worry about someone canceling on you. If someone must care for your baby, a childcare business may be your only solution.

Ideally you should find a childcare provider who is supportive of breastfeeding. Your success with working and breastfeeding may be strongly influenced by your baby's caregiver. The following are questions to ask of a childcare provider to help with your choice:

➤ Do you care for babies whose mothers are breastfeeding?

➤ Are you comfortable with handling breast milk?

➤ Will you give my breast milk to my baby in a bottle, a cup, a syringe, a spoon, or an eyedropper that I supply?

➤ Where will you store and offer the breast milk that I provide?

➤ Do you have a place where I can breastfeed before or after work?

Nursing Mom's Notes

Find out if your employer or company offers an on-site childcare facility. Many working mothers find that they can continue breastfeeding with their baby in close proximity to their workplace.

Getting answers to these questions will probably help you narrow down the possibilities right away. Listen to your heart and go with your instinct. If you don't get a good feeling then move forward and look for another. Ask around for recommendations from other breastfeeding mothers. Don't overlook any contacts or networks you have established.

Home Business

There are definitely some things to consider in a childcare business that's operated in someone's home. The price may be right but not necessarily the circumstances. First and foremost is to check on a valid license. If he or she comes highly recommended and he or she isn't licensed, find out why. Schedule a visit on sight to get a feel for the location and its operation. Make sure that you take your spouse or partner. His input and impression is extremely valuable. You may want for this to work for you because you really want to return to work. In reality you may overlook some important details.

Be sure to ask about any pets on the premises and their access to the babies and children. Determine what the ratio is for provider to babies and children. Ask how many babies are enrolled and their approximate ages. Find out if anyone smokes and whether smoking is inside or outside. Look for any safety measures like fire alarms

167

and fire extinguishers. Inspect any cribs, highchairs, and strollers that might be used for your baby. Are they safe and do they pass your inspection?

When it comes to breastfeeding, the advantages of a home-childcare business are the homey atmosphere and relaxed setting that it provides. You may want this for your baby. The provider may be very familiar with the care of a breastfeeding baby. This is a definite bonus. If you need only a few hours of care, you may be able to get a customized schedule. Be honest and open about your needs from the start, to avoid any disappointments later on.

Breast Beware

Pets and smoking can be health hazards in a home-childcare facility. Be sure to ask if anyone smokes inside the house or around the premises. Ask about any pets and where they are kept during childcare hours.

Lactation Lingo

Fringe benefits are payments, allowances, or perks given in addition to an employee's regular salary.

Business Facility

You may find that the most reliable and convenient solution is a business facility that specializes in childcare. One may be close to or on your way to work. If it's within five minutes of your workplace or you have a flexible schedule, you may be able to breastfeed your baby during a break or at lunch. Your company may also provide a childcare facility for its employees. Several large companies have built a childcare facility on their premises to attract and retain valuable employees. It may be one of the *fringe benefits* that your employer offers you. Your company may also subsidize your childcare fees when you choose a facility they are partnered with. It's important to ask about any childcare benefits for which you are eligible.

The consequences of choosing such a facility may be the "institutional" and impersonal feeling you get when you walk through the door. The baby-to-provider ratio may be more than you desire. The employee turnover rate at some facilities can be extremely high. Illnesses and infections can run rampant in these childcare centers. Fortunately, your breastfeeding will provide immunity and help to protect your baby. The policies and procedures for dispensing breast milk may be too strict or outdated. I was called in to consult with our state health department when several city daycare centers were found discarding mothers' breast milk after 24 hours. Talk about an uproar.

Again, it's extremely helpful to visit a facility and talk to the employees. Be sure to offer that you will provide expressed breast milk for your baby and pay attention to their response. Your spouse or partner should definitely take a look because any additional input is valuable. It's important to feel comfortable with your decision. If you don't think you've made the right choice, it's okay to try something else and move on.

While I'm Away

The decisions have been made and you'll be busy preparing for your return to work. It's a great idea to schedule some practice runs before you're really back on the job. See if some half days are possible with your childcare provider before your first time back at work. You can practice gathering the things you'll need and walk through your planned routine. If your spouse or partner is part of the childcare plan he'll have the opportunity to experience bringing or picking your baby up from the provider. If your childcare provider will come to your home, you can show him or her around and resolve any questions or concerns he or she may have. A trial run helps put everyone at ease.

Several practice sessions will help with the tears and guilt that you'll experience when putting your work plan into action. The hormones of breastfeeding and motherhood could put you on an emotional roller coaster. It's the truth. You realize that someone else is taking your place while you are away from your baby. You'll ask yourself if you've made the right decision. Will this person do as good a job? Will my baby still love me when I come back? The lump in your throat and the pang in your heart may be hard to handle but that's why you're making a practice run. You have to believe in yourself and your decision.

It's best to give your childcare provider an idea of your baby's feeding pattern. Better yet, give him or her a written record of your baby's typical pattern or schedule. Feeding frequency and quantities are the important points to cover. Many childcare providers are not familiar with the dining preferences of breastfeeding babies. Breast milk digests in about an hour and a half, so your breastfeeding baby will want more frequent feedings than a formula-fed baby will. The quantity of breast milk your baby consumes may range from two to five ounces with each feeding. This amount will depend on the age of your baby when you return to work. The following table may be helpful for you to determine these amounts.

Nursing Mom's Notes

Draw up a business card for your childcare provider, listing all of your contact information. List the telephone numbers where you can be reached and indicate which one you answer readily. Consider listing your spouse or partner's information if he can be contacted with questions or concerns about your baby.

Baby's Breast Milk Consumption

Age	Each Feeding	Daily Average
0–2 mos	2–5 oz	26 oz
2–4 mos	4–6 oz	30 oz
4–6 mos	5–7 oz	31 oz

Weight	Daily Average	
8 lb/3600 gm	21.3 oz/639 ml	
9 lb/4000 gm	24.0 oz/720 ml	
10 lb/4500 gm	26.7 oz/801 ml	
11 lb/4900 gm	29.3 oz/879 ml	
12 lb/5400 gm	32.0 oz/960 ml	
14 lb/6400 gm	37.3 oz/1019 ml	
16 lb/7300 gm	42.7 oz/1280 ml	

It's also important to inform your childcare provider that your breastfeeding baby breastfeeds for reasons other than just food. Your baby may not need to eat but just wants to be held. Remember that breastfeeding comforts and soothes and that holding can help meet that need. Your provider may find that a baby sling is helpful for carrying your baby. Your baby may sense your absence and will feel more secure being held. Your breastfeeding baby may want to suck and not necessarily eat. Your provider could offer a pacifier to help with this need.

Offer up any pointers about your breastfeeding baby that you feel are important. Do you sit in a rocker and breastfeed or find that you burp your baby a certain way? You might want to provide your childcare provider with a cloth diaper or receiving blanket that smells of you, for use while feeding your baby. Include a favorite toy or some music, to simulate what it's like when you are there.

Communication will be the key while you are away from your baby. Childcare facilities often record the number of feedings, the amount, and the times of day they were taken. If you have someone in your home or are using a home-childcare facility, you might provide a daily plan or notebook to fill in with your

Breast Beware

If you need to use baby formula to supplement your breast milk supply, your childcare provider should give it early in the day. It takes twice as long for a baby to digest baby formula as it does with human milk. If a formula feeding is given just before you return from work, your baby may not want to breastfeed.

baby's routine. Make sure your provider can speak to you personally while on the job if immediate feedback is necessary. The best you can do is to take a deep breath, relax, and not worry!

I'm Off to Work

It's best to try to develop a breastfeeding routine for your return to work. You should continue to express a couple of times each day and store that milk. While you're not at work, you'll want to breastfeed as much as possible whenever you and your baby are together. This helps you to maintain an adequate supply of breast milk. Once you're back to work you might try the following routine to help with breastfeeding and working:

➤ Allow your baby to breastfeed leisurely at the start of your day.

➤ Breastfeed again before leaving home or leaving your childcare location.

➤ Breastfeed after work at childcare, or once you're back home from work.

➤ Transition to home after work by holding and cuddling your baby.

➤ Breastfeed on demand during weekends and any days off.

Be prepared and ready for the work that you've committed to. Make a list of any personal items that you will need while at work. It won't look good if you forget necessary items for expressing breast milk, especially if extra time is taken from your work in order to get them. If you'll express your breast milk at work, write down all the supplies or equipment that you'll need. Have your checklist handy for your first few weeks of work. It will help keep you organized and minimize forgotten items. You'll have it memorized before too long.

Nursing Mom's Notes

If you'll be working full time, try to start back to work in the middle of the week, like a Wednesday. Your first week back will be stressful. You'll benefit from a shortened workweek.

If you will express your breast milk while at work, consider bringing these items:

➤ Breast pump

➤ Pump-accessory kit, if needed

➤ Storage containers

➤ Your baby's picture

➤ A meal

➤ Snacks

➤ Liquid nourishment

➤ Extra blouse or shirt

➤ Breast pads

➤ Extra bra

➤ Sweater

If a refrigerator is not available for storing your breast milk, you may need a cooler or an insulated tote with ice. Remember that breast milk can stand at room temperature for four to six hours, but you'll probably feel at ease if you can keep it cool. It makes it easier to transport for return to your childcare location or to home.

Nursing Mom's Notes

You can store freshly pumped breast milk in a small cooler with freezer packs for about 24 hours.

To be a working and breastfeeding mother you must have support. It's quite a load and a commitment to handle. Your work will be a job and your breastfeeding will be a job. You will need support and help with the responsibilities of your household and your baby. Ask your spouse or partner to share the tasks of meal preparation, laundry, shopping, cleaning, and any other chores around your house. The demands of a new baby, working, and breastfeeding will be hectic but worth it in the long run. You'll sit back one day and look back on your accomplishments. I do all the time!

Give Me a Break

To keep breastfeeding while you're on the job means that you need to express your breast milk when your baby would be breastfeeding. You'll need to take the time and to find a place to do this. Depending on your baby's age and feeding pattern, your break may be as often as every three to four hours.

How frequently you should express your breast milk will depends on the number of hours you are away from your baby. Plan to express at least twice during an eight-hour work shift.

You will need to take a break in order to express your breast milk. Realistically you should plan on about 20 minutes. Consider the time involved to walk somewhere or to set up in your office. It takes time to wash your hands, relax and express, store your milk, wash your supplies, and use the bathroom.

The best break times to use may be your coffee break and lunch hour. If you only get a lunch hour during your shift, see if you can split it up during the hours you work. Twenty minutes in the morning and 40 minutes in the afternoon are realistic break times. If your co-workers take breaks to smoke, then you deserve a break to do something healthy for you and your baby! Remember this if anyone harasses you about what you do on your break time.

Lactation Room

Your type of work may make expressing difficult, but look for any possible places and times to express. Scout any quiet, private places at work. You might have to be creative. See if an executive bathroom, a lounge, or an unoccupied office is available. Ideally, a room with a place to wash your hands is great, but you can always stop in the bathroom somewhere to wash up. If you look hard and ask about an available location, something's bound to surface.

Many companies are becoming mother-friendly and have created a specific place for lactation. Sometimes called a new mother's lounge, it's a room designed for working women who are breastfeeding to stop, drop, and pump. They are private, secure, and usually have the electrical outlet you've been hunting for.

LactFact

Some companies have a room or lounge designated for a working mother's use to express or pump her breast milk. If your workplace does not provide such accommodations, consider a proposal to your human resources or personnel department requesting one. Include the number of staff members currently breastfeeding and any future employees who will use the facility. A lactation room should provide the following items:

➤ A small room with an inside door lock

➤ A comfortable chair

➤ A small table

➤ An electrical outlet

A sink, a small refrigerator, and a telephone can enhance the room but are not necessary items. Include any location or room that could be considered appropriate for use.

There is a possibility that your company may be really progressive and have medical-grade piston breast pumps available for your use. With more businesses looking to offer perks for employee retention, several businesses will invest in such a breast pump and deduct it as a business expense. All you need is the accessory kit to connect to the breast pump and any additional supplies for collection and storage. Ask your contact in human resources or your boss about availability. Better yet, propose the idea, and you may get what you wish for without having to click your red heels three times!

The Least You Need to Know

➤ Consider all childcare options before you return to work.

➤ Find a childcare provider who's supportive of breastfeeding.

➤ Rehearse your routine before you return to work.

➤ Use any breaks during work to express milk or breastfeed your baby.

➤ Inquire about a lactation room at your place of employment.

Legislation Today

When I returned to work after my first baby, I had a charge nurse who made it very clear to me that I should not expect any break during the workday to express milk for my baby. Since the unit was busy around-the-clock, breaks were usually not allowed. I had taken three months of disability during my pregnancy and she implied that it was time for me to carry my load. She also despised breastfeeding. To her it was a lewd, crude act that she saw as "not normal."

My first week back she followed through with her intent. A break for lunch sometimes came around two o'clock and she instructed me to "eat quickly" and get back as soon as possible. After the weeks that followed, I couldn't take much more. I spoke with my unit manager. Unfortunately this, too, was a dead end.

"What were my rights?" I asked. What sort of legal recourse could I take? All I wanted to do was to continue to provide breast milk for the health and well-being of my baby. I couldn't believe this was really happening, particularly at a large metropolitan hospital.

What Is the Law?

The legislation we have today has been enacted because the rights of a breastfeeding mother were in question. Over one third of the states in the United States have legislation in place that specifically addresses the question of breastfeeding in public.

LactFact

The purpose of any legislation is to spell out what is legal. Legislation often results from an incident or incidences where an act's permissibility is questioned. The natural act of breastfeeding has consistently been challenged and questioned in the public, the private, and the employment setting.

The choice to breastfeed is a basic human right. You may choose to breastfeed because of your lifestyle. You may also choose to breastfeed because of the health and medicinal effects that it provides to you and your baby. You may choose to breastfeed for other reasons, too. Predominant evidence and research are available that support any parent's choice of breast-feeding:

➤ The American Academy of Pediatrics states that human milk feeding protects against several diseases, some of them life threatening. Your baby's growth and development are greatly enhanced by the benefits that human milk provides.

➤ The World Health Organization and UNICEF also recommend that globally all infants should be fed breast milk exclusively, from their birth to at least six months of age. They also recommend that breastfeeding continue with complementary foods up to two years of age or longer.

With the AAP, WHO, and UNICEF all endorsing breastfeeding, who's saying that women can't and shouldn't breastfeed? Who says that this basic human act is questionable and that laws must be made to permit breastfeeding? The answer, my friends, is the people around us who don't believe, don't know, or refuse to accept the facts about breastfeeding. It's the collective group of people who don't or won't breastfeed who want to make up rules and regulations about breastfeeding. It's ignorance, it's lack of education, and it is prejudice that all contribute the idea that breastfeeding can't and shouldn't take place. Our society pressures new parents to accept the use of bottle-feeding and baby formula as normal. The public at large has planted the idea that the act of breastfeeding is indecent and lewd. And parents who want easy living choose to feed their new baby canned food.

Parents who make the choice to breastfeed must turn to the law to protect and defend their freedom of choice. Several states have enacted legislation to protect and defend parents who breastfeed. Presently 27 states in the Unites States have laws that specifically address breastfeeding rights. You don't have to breastfeed behind closed doors just because someone doesn't want to see you. These laws help endorse as well as educate everyone by clearly defining and addressing the what, where, and when about breastfeeding. It should be comforting to know that whether a law is in place or not, you have every right to breastfeed. The purpose of breastfeeding legislation is not to legalize it but to state that you do have the right to breastfeed. Law or no law, you can do it wherever and whenever you want.

Public Performance

Rest assured that you can breastfeed your baby anywhere that you can be with your baby. That's right. The grocery store, a movie theater, the city park, or your local swimming pool are perfect examples of places where you can breastfeed. When you breastfeed in a public place, you are not committing an offensive act. Where the thought or idea came from—that a mother exposes herself indecently by breastfeeding—is beyond me. The message that legislation sends to our society is that breastfeeding anywhere is not a lewd or indecent act.

LactFact

A client was distraught over an incident that occurred while breastfeeding in public. She ventured out to an exhibit at our metropolitan art museum and sat down on a gallery bench for her son's breastfeeding. A male security guard approached and reminded her that "no food or drink" was permitted in the gallery and asked that she leave. She moved to another gallery. Seated on a bench in the middle of this gallery, a female security guard approached her. Again the circumstance of "no food or drink" was cited and she was asked to leave. My client asked what food or drink she was referring to. "Well, you know—your breastfeeding," the guard replied. "You might squirt milk on a painting."

Twenty-seven states specifically address the question of whether the United States permits public breastfeeding. The following are states that have enacted breastfeeding legislation. Can you find yours?

- ➤ Alaska
- ➤ California
- ➤ Connecticut
- ➤ Delaware

- ➤ Florida
- ➤ Georgia
- ➤ Hawaii
- ➤ Idaho

- ➤ Illinois
- ➤ Iowa
- ➤ Michigan
- ➤ Minnesota
- ➤ Montana
- ➤ Nevada
- ➤ New Hampshire
- ➤ New Jersey
- ➤ New Mexico
- ➤ New York

- ➤ North Carolina
- ➤ Oregon
- ➤ Pennsylvania
- ➤ Rhode Island
- ➤ Tennessee
- ➤ Texas
- ➤ Utah
- ➤ Virginia
- ➤ Wisconsin

Many of these states specifically outline that a mother breastfeeding in public does not commit a *lewd, lascivious,* or indecent act. Many also address that if the mother is permitted on the premises or location with her child that she has the right to breastfeed there. Some of these laws state that the exposure of the mother's nipple and areola while breastfeeding is not considered an exposure of *sexual organs*. The restriction or limitation of a mother to breastfeed is considered an act of discrimination in some of these states. A fine may be levied if an owner or manager of a public resort, amusement center, or other accommodation does not allow a mother to breastfeed in his or her public location.

The circumstance of reporting and serving as a juror is also outlined in several states' laws. Dismissal from jury duty usually requires a written request. Even if your state doesn't address jury duty, or just plain doesn't have a law, you should consider other exemptions that your state laws may have. Look for laws that speak about parents as sole caregivers or parents responsible for the direct care of young children at home.

Lactation Lingo

Lewd refers to being obscene or indecent. The meaning of **lascivious** is being loose or lustful. **Sexual organs** are also known as the genitals.

Congresswoman Carolyn B. Maloney of New York introduced a federal bill ensuring a woman's right to breastfeed her child anywhere on federal property that she and her child are entitled to be. It was enacted into law in September of 1999. You will find it as part of the Treasury-Postal Appropriations House bill number 2490. Legislation is a small but powerful tool to use in raising public awareness about the rights of breastfeeding mothers. Even though laws are in place, taking legal recourse if necessary is very time consuming. One has to weigh the importance of protecting her breastfeeding rights versus allowing the same occurrence to continue.

LactFact

Carolyn B. Maloney has also introduced in the House of Representatives an amendment to the Pregnancy Discrimination Act. House bill number 3861 proposes that breastfeeding be protected under civil rights law. It requires that a woman cannot be fired or discriminated against for expressing her breast milk in the workplace. She cannot be fired for breastfeeding or pumping during her own lunch time or break time. This bill proposal has presently been referred to the Education and Workforce Committee. You can contact Carolyn B. Maloney (D–NY) electronically at www.house.gov/maloney/issues/breastfeeding.htm.

If you are like me and your state doesn't have laws specific to breastfeeding rights, look for any city or county ordinances that may have been amended that could apply to breastfeeding. You may find that any discrimination or segregation because of breastfeeding can be used in your favor. Overall, breastfeeding in public should be accepted if your child is allowed with you on the premise or location and if the bottle-feeding of a child is also permitted in that location. You can use the legislation enacted in another state to support your claim for breastfeeding rights if you are ever challenged. It's a great opportunity to educate and a small step to take toward overall change.

Nursing Mom's Notes

If the bottle-feeding of a child is permitted in a public or private place, then breastfeeding is permitted, too.

Performance at Work

The fact of the matter about continuing your breastfeeding when you return to work is the difficulty that you may encounter with your employer or your place of employment. Co-workers can make your life pretty difficult, too, especially if they believe that breastfeeding or pumping is unacceptable in the work place. Things can get downright ugly. Your employer may try to prevent you from expressing your milk. I found that out all too quickly when I returned to work. Neither my charge nurse nor my manager supported my choice to express breast milk for my baby. There just wasn't a thing they could do to help me. They told me that things just couldn't be changed. No effort was made to help me make a change. Supervisors and managers can frustrate your efforts by making your situation very difficult.

So, what's a working breastfeeding mother to do? It's a real challenge to express your breast milk if there isn't a quiet, convenient place to do it. Hey, we don't eat our meals in a toilet stall, so why should you settle for a toilet stall to prepare a meal for your baby? Fortunately, many states are encouraging or mandating that employers accommodate breastfeeding mothers upon their return to work. By simply providing a clean, private room or lounge for new mothers, an employer is making an effort to support employees who return to work and maintain breastfeeding. Many employers who have taken these measures have found that their retention of employees is relatively high. Just for taking the initiative, it acknowledges that this is the most important benefit they can offer to a new mother returning to work.

Fewer than 10 states are required to accommodate any mother who returns to work and who continues to breastfeed. Six states have legislation that addresses the employed breastfeeding mother and what employers are required to provide to them. It's a fact that the fastest growing segments of today's work force are women with infants and toddlers. Over half of these women return to the work force by the time their babies are three months old. So it's definitely in the employers' best interest to create a "mother-friendly" workplace to attract and retain this segment of the work force.

The state law in Texas says that a business can designate itself as "mother-friendly" if its workplace includes all of the following:

➤ Flexible work schedules

➤ Access to private room or lounge

➤ Access to a clean, safe water supply

➤ Hygienic storage location for mother's breast milk

Breaks and work patterns can be scheduled to provide a mother with time to express her breast milk. Any breastfeeding mother can tell you that successful milk expression comes from using a quiet, private location. Having access to a sink to wash your hands and your pump accessories is a nominal reward. Working, breastfeeding mothers aren't asking for anything too outrageous that an employer can't provide them.

The advantages of returning to work and continuing to breastfeed are many. Your choice to breastfeed helps your family, your employer, and the public at large. Employers can miss out on an important benefit for women if they don't offer any lactation programs or support. Studies show that women who do maintain their breastfeeding with breast milk expression miss less time from work. The babies are happy and healthy from the breast milk's benefits and their mother's efforts. If an employer offers a worksite lactation program and other perks for breastfeeding, he or she will have mothers beating the doors down to work there. Who wouldn't want to work where the location, the equipment, the health care professional, and the environment were all lactation-friendly?

Congresswoman Carolyn B. Maloney of New York introduced an important federal bill for breast-feeding during the 106th Congress. It is the Breast-feeding Promotion and Employers' Tax Incentive Act. It encourages employers to set up a safe, private, and sanitary environment for women to express their breast milk. Tax credits are awarded to employers who set up a specific area for lactation. If they purchase or rent lactation-related equipment, hire a lactation consultant, or promote a lactation-friendly workplace, additional tax credits are awarded.

It involves a lot if you decide to take legal action for discrimination against you for breastfeeding in the workplace. The best advice I can offer you is to consult with an attorney before you take action. There can be time limits for filing a lawsuit against any employer in question. You collect most of your evidence and information necessary for a case while on the job. If the possibility of getting fired looms over you, then consider if this is the best decision for you and your family. If you have the time to record, document, and pursue legal recourse, then more power to you. On the other hand, if all you have time to do is work, and you are finding the time and place to express breast milk, then just focus on that and keep things quiet. Your first priority should be your baby and yourself. Maybe next time around you can find an employer who doesn't discriminate or harass over lactation issues. Maybe new laws will protect and provide the ideal working, breastfeeding circumstance.

Nursing Mom's Notes

Talk tax credits to your company's accountant or business manager for a workplace lactation program. Equipment rental or purchase, a lactation room, and hired lactation specialists can all qualify under the Employer's Tax Incentive Act.

Breast Beware

If you choose to take legal action for discrimination or harassment regarding breastfeeding, consult an attorney. An attorney can represent you and help determine your legal rights.

A Parent's Right

Each and every parent has the right to choose breastfeeding for his or her baby. It is a basic human right. If the father wants the infant breastfed, but the mother refuses, this becomes a very complex circumstance. The best course of action is to educate and counsel the mother about the health, growth, and development factors that breastfeeding provides to an infant. A father could try to supply expressed breast milk from a milk bank or other source, but this invariably becomes a cumbersome if not costly ordeal.

At this time, there isn't any legislation regarding breastfeeding and divorce or paternity cases. I have personally been called as a lactation consultant on cases of baby/toddler visitation where the question of breastfeeding continuation was involved. Depending on the age of the infant or child, if breast milk is the primary source of nourishment, a decision is usually made in favor of the breastfeeding mother. If the question becomes that of breastfeeding versus a father's bond with his child, decisions are usually made in favor of a father's direct contact with the infant or child. If the breastfeeding is not vital for the child's growth and development, dad usually wins out. Breastfeeding is encouraged to continue as long as the father can maintain a significant relationship with his infant or child.

There may be circumstances where a mother tries to use breastfeeding in her favor and refuses to allow any contact between a father and his baby. If legal circumstances aren't involved, it's important that others be able to hold and interact with your baby. It's important to point out here that your spouse or partner can care for your baby when you are not feeding directly at the breast. Although it's your right to breastfeed, you don't need to hog your baby all of the time. Don't use breastfeeding to prevent others from cuddling and loving your baby, too. Time out from holding and handling is therapeutic for your mind and soul. They may not do it just like you, but handling by others helps improve the socialization of your baby. It also helps your baby to learn more about him or herself.

Nursing Mom's Notes

You may be exempt from jury duty while you are breastfeeding. Ask to be excused if you are breastfeeding and are responsible for the direct care of your infant or child. Jury service may prevent you from breastfeeding or expressing your milk and could contribute to a breast infection.

The Least You Need to Know

➤ Breastfeeding is a human right.

➤ Several states have enacted laws that protect breastfeeding.

➤ Congressional bill proposals address breastfeeding discrimination and company tax credits.

➤ Breastfeeding rights arise with separation and divorce cases.

➤ Fines and lawsuits have occurred in breastfeeding discrimination cases.

Part 6

The Unexpected

As a new parent, you'll have hopes, dreams, and ideas about yourself and the birth of your baby. Many mothers can get breastfeeding off to a great start. Being prepared for what to expect and having support lined up helps tremendously.

Sometimes, despite your very best efforts, a problem related to your breasts or feeding can arise. Some can be simple and easily resolved. Some can be more complex, requiring the combined help of a lactation professional and your health care provider.

This section offers you guidance and information about breastfeeding problems. If your breastfeeding is progressing smoothly, there's no need to sneak a peak in this part. Sometimes a mother can create a problem for herself just by reading. Look for information and some plans for action in this part.

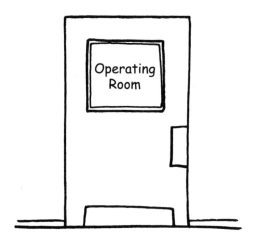
Operating Room

Chapter 19

Surgical Delivery

> ## In This Chapter
>
> ➤ Breastfeeding after cesarean section
>
> ➤ What to expect after surgery
>
> ➤ Enlisting help from family and friends
>
> ➤ Using an electric piston breast pump
>
> ➤ Tips for recovery at home

Over the years that I've worked as an obstetrics nurse, I've heard many words and phrases that refer to a cesarean section delivery. During moments of labor transition or pushing, a woman would plead with those of us attending her birth to, "Take the baby!" I always thought to myself, "Where would we take it?" Obviously it means to remove it or take it out of the uterus via surgical incision.

As an obstetrics nurse, the question of breastfeeding after a cesarean would always come up, too. Moms would say, "I planned to breastfeed. Can I still do that?" Basically, cesarean delivery and breastfeeding are very compatible. But there's some important information that will help you with your breastfeeding after experiencing this type of major surgery. That's what I'm going to share with you throughout this chapter.

What's Happened Here?

The birth of your baby by cesarean delivery can happen for any number of reasons. A cesarean or C-section is the delivery of a baby through a surgical incision made in the mother's abdomen and uterus. It is major surgery and can have potential complications that arise from this type of delivery. It is the safest form of delivery for any baby who cannot deliver through the woman's vagina.

Your physician may decide that a cesarean delivery is necessary for some of the following reasons:

➤ A large baby

➤ Signs of distress to the baby during labor

➤ Inability to deliver by forceps or vacuum

➤ Baby's position is not head first

➤ Repeat cesarean

➤ Premature baby

The hardest thing to contend with about a cesarean may be that it's not what you wanted. And it can be downright scary. In anticipation of your baby's birth, you may have spent a lot of time preparing for a vaginal delivery. Some women block it out or put it on the back shelf of their mind. It's very easy to ignore the possibility. Aren't all babies supposed to come out from down below?

LactFact

According to Greek mythology, Apollo mastered the first cesarean by removing Asclepius from his mother's abdomen. It is possible that the term "cesarean" derived from the surgical birth of Julius Caesar. It was under Roman law that Caesar required a child be cut from its dead or dying mother. Religious practice also required that an infant be buried separately from its mother. The Latin verb *caedare* means to cut. The term "section" came from a 1500s midwifery book and replaced the word "operation."

I would reassure parents in childbirth class that a cesarean delivery is a safe way out. I've seen the lives of many babies saved because of this delivery. Remember, the most important point is a healthy outcome for mother and baby. Your physician's role is to protect the health and well-being of you and your baby. Let your doctor help you decide to C or not to C!

The whole procedure may only take about 45 minutes. You'll probably have an *epidural* or spinal anesthesia to block your pain during surgery. Very rarely, general anesthesia is used, meaning that you are put to sleep for the delivery. Your epidural anesthesia may be used if it's already in place from your labor. If time permits and they're given the choice, most women opt to use an epidural anesthesia. It allows you to stay awake during delivery. Oftentimes a general anesthetic is used for emergency C-sections or in cases where an epidural anesthetic isn't possible.

When your baby is delivered, your doctor may suction amniotic fluid from its nose and mouth with a small tube. Some hospitals use additional health care professionals to then care for your baby at delivery. A team from the Newborn Intensive Care Unit (NICU) may then examine your baby. It's possible that they'll admit your baby to the NICU. Admission to the NICU is possible if your baby shows any of these symptoms:

Lactation Lingo

Medications that produce a loss of sensation are anesthetics. General anesthesia puts someone to sleep to block the pain. A spinal or **epidural** anesthesia blocks the pain below the waist.

➤ A fast or slow heart rate

➤ Fast or slow breathing

➤ Fever

➤ Low blood sugar

➤ Physical abnormalities

➤ Possible infection

If your baby is admitted to the Newborn Intensive Care Unit (NICU) after the delivery, more than likely you will not be able to breastfeed right away. They may perform tests. They may apply monitors for your baby's heart rate and breathing rate. There is also a possibility that they may also place a tube for breathing assistance. This will probably delay your opportunity to initiate breastfeeding within your first hour after birth.

It's very important to emphasize to the NICU team that you are breastfeeding. Ask when the first opportunity to breastfeed will be. Ask to be informed if baby formula will be given. Remind the team that your first breastfeeding and subsequent feedings are very important.

They may start an intravenous fluid in the NICU if your baby needs nutrients or fluids. There is a possibility that they'll give glucose water or baby formula. Be sure to ask if your baby's doctor has ordered the glucose water or baby formula. Unfortunately, glucose water or baby formula is often given through a bottle with an artificial nipple. If your baby needs these fluids, you might ask or suggest that they use a syringe, finger feeding, or eyedropper. And never, never stop asking when you can start to breastfeed.

Breast Beware

Remind the Newborn Intensive Care Unit (NICU) team that you will breastfeed. Ask to be informed if the need to give baby formula to your baby arises. Also inform your maternity nurse and ask for help expressing your breast milk using the electric piston breast pump. Your baby needs you and your milk to get better. A result of using an artificial teat or nipple may cause nipple confusion for your baby. Your lactation consultant or NICU nurse should offer you help to restore effective suckling for breastfeeding.

Can I Still Breastfeed?

Congratulations! The attending doctor gives your baby a clean bill of health following your surgery. Now you can breastfeed. If you are still in the surgery room and your condition warrants it, someone might help you position your new baby for breastfeeding. It's possible, though, that nausea and vomiting may flare up when the surgeon stitches up your abdomen. This definitely isn't the best time to start breastfeeding.

Once your surgery is finished and the final stitch or staple has been placed, you'll be wheeled off to the recovery room. See if you can hold your new baby. If you have some uncontrollable shaking after your C-section, this won't be possible. Shivering and shaking may happen from blood loss, fluid loss, or temperature change, but it's short-lived. I can tell you that a nice warm blanket helps to settle the symptoms. Have your spouse or partner hold your baby until it subsides.

If you've had a general anesthetic, you may not be awake enough to hold your baby. A general anesthetic puts you to sleep and it may take some time for you to rouse. As soon as you are awake and alert, try to offer your baby your breast for its first feeding.

There are quite a few things to keep an eye on in the recovery room. As a postoperative patient, your blood pressure, heart rate, and breathing rate all need to be monitored. Your surgical incision as well as your uterus need to be checked frequently for bleeding. Once these have been checked and recorded you can start your first breastfeeding. The nurse or surgery tech will be busy recording your vital signs, but emphasize how important it is for you to start breastfeeding. Demonstrating that you can breastfeed helps to minimize the disappointment you may feel about a cesarean delivery.

You'll have to work around the tubes and wires with your first breastfeeding. Your intravenous line will be with you for at least a few days. It's your liquid nourishment. Postoperative patients may only have ice chips or clear liquids by mouth as ordered by your doctor. You have to pass gas before they feed you anything. Your appetite probably won't be ravenous after all that you've been through. You may also have a blood pressure cuff around your arm and an oxygen monitor around your finger. You might ask if the cuff could be relocated to your leg and the oxygen sensor to your toe because you'll want your arms free for breastfeeding. You'll need to deal with the intravenous line in your arm.

Nursing Mom's Notes

Begin to breastfeed in the recovery room after your cesarean. It will cause your uterus to contract and help control any bleeding. Both you and your baby will be satisfied with your ability to breastfeed. If you are unable to breastfeed your baby right away because of NICU admission, you should begin to stimulate and express your breast milk. Use a medical-grade electric piston breast pump and start using the pump at least six hours after delivery.

For your first breastfeeding, you have the option of a side-lying or a football-hold position. If you can't tolerate the head of your bed being raised, then I suggest the lying-down position. Ask the nurse or surgery assistant for help getting positioned. If you've had an epidural anesthetic, you'll be numb from your waist to your toes. You won't be able to move without help. Remember to use several pillows to position your baby at your breast level. This will help with back and shoulder strain.

A quick review for latching your baby to the breast goes like this:

1. Using the football hold, position your baby at your side with its head in your hand and its feet pointed behind you.

2. Bring your baby close to your breast with its nose pointed upward.

3. Holding your breast with your free hand, touch your nipple to your baby's lower lip.

4. When your baby opens its mouth like a yawn, quickly pull your baby on to your breast.

5. Your baby's lips should seal over most of your areola. You'll feel the tongue stroking and a good tug at your breast.

Once your baby has latched on, let this first breastfeeding last until baby releases your breast or falls asleep. Let your spouse or partner burp your baby. This enables your nurse or surgery tech to check your uterus and incision. Then you'll want to reposition and offer your other breast to your baby. If your baby declines your offer to suckle your other breast, it's okay. Offer it for the next feeding. Allow for plenty of time and really enjoy your first time with your new baby.

Breastfeeding after a C-section helps to contract your uterus. The intravenous fluid that you've been given will probably have a synthetic hormone called Pitocin. It acts just like oxytocin to help keep your uterus firm and your bleeding minimal. More than likely you will need pain medication for at least 72 hours after your C-section. If you've had an epidural anesthetic, morphine may have been added to give you prolonged pain relief following your surgery. There are other drugs that may be ordered for your pain. These are fast-acting and are eliminated from your system quickly. It is best to take them immediately after breastfeeding to allow the level to peak before another feeding. Medications in this category include …

➤ Ibuprofen

➤ Acetaminophen

➤ Codeine

Don't be afraid to take your pain medication.

It's important that your pain be controlled to enable you to let down during breastfeeding. Pain can work against you and not permit relaxation, including your release of *colostrum* and milk from the alveoli.

Expect This

Plan to camp out in the hospital for at least three days. If you are recovering well following your surgery your doctor may release you before three days. Your

Breast Beware

The composition of your colostrum will not be affected by any medications taken. Don't withhold your early feedings because of this concern. Some medications can pass into your breast milk if taken just prior to breastfeeding or pumping your milk. Taking a medication after breastfeeding or pumping is completed gives you time to excrete it from your system.

Lactation Lingo

Colostrum is the thick, yellowish fluid in the breast that's the first milk. It has highly concentrated proteins, immunoglobulins, vitamins, and minerals.

diet should progress from ice chips to liquids to solid foods. You may remain on bed rest for a while or be able to sit in a chair within six hours following surgery. It's very important to try to ambulate or walk as soon as your doctor orders. Walking will help you to recover faster and get your internal system moving again.

You will want to breastfeed often after your cesarean, just as with a vaginal delivery. Your baby may or may not show a readiness to breastfeed often. You should strive for at least eight times in 24 hours. That should be about every two to three hours. If your baby does not want to breastfeed every two to three hours, you will need to awaken your baby.

To help you breastfeed often you should practice *rooming in* with your baby. Keep your baby in your room. Better yet, put up the side rails on your bed and keep your baby in bed with you. Ask your spouse or partner to help you with side-lying and football-hold positions. Use plenty of pillows to prop and position your baby properly at your breast. Try the cradle hold, too, if it's comfortable for you.

Your baby may be very sleepy, especially if you had a prolonged labor and a lot of pushing prior to your C-section. It's not unusual for babies to be sleepy anyway in the first 24 hours, regardless of their mode of delivery. Your baby may have some major jet lag if it was exposed to several drugs and medications throughout your labor and cesarean delivery. Your baby may not breastfeed well right now. Your milk should still "come in," though, by your third or fourth day.

Expect to be very tired in the days following your C-section. You'll also feel like something major has happened. Some of your feedings will be satisfying while others will not be. The ups and downs in your baby's feeding pattern are typical whether you've had a vaginal or cesarean birth. Ask for a lactation consultant or a nurse to help evaluate your baby during a breastfeeding. You will benefit from your longer stay in the hospital recovering from a C-section. Ask as many questions as needed to feel comfortable with your breastfeeding.

Of utmost importance during your recovery is to rest, rest, and rest. Recovery from a major surgery like a cesarean takes lots of rest and sleep. Keep

Lactation Lingo

Rooming in means keeping your baby in your room with you while in a hospital or birth center. This enables you and your partner to observe for your baby's feeding cues. Your baby's feeding cues will help ensure frequent feedings. You might also rest and sleep more easily with your baby close by.

Breast Beware

If your baby is still sleepy and won't breastfeed by your second day, you'll need to take action. Wake your baby more often and start to express your colostrum with the electric piston breast pump. Baby needs to awaken and breastfeed before your milk comes in.

your visitors to a minimum, as well as any celebrating. There will be a time and a place for these later on. For now you need to practice plenty of breastfeeding and to sleep as much as possible.

If your baby has been admitted to the NICU you will need to begin stimulation of your breasts with an electric piston breast pump. This should be a medical or hospital-grade type that offers adjustable and intermittent suction. You will need your own accessory or milk collection kit. This maintains hygiene and prevents cross contamination. You should first use the breast pump with a single kit; you can add another kit for dual pumping once you've mastered single pumping.

If your baby is not able to breastfeed directly you should try to use the electric piston breast pump, preferably within six hours after your delivery. If you are too sick or physically unable to pump, a nurse, lactation consultant, or your partner could help you to use the pump and collect your colostrum. It is important that you start expressing your milk when you are physically and emotionally ready.

Nursing Mom's Notes

Start to pump your breasts soon after your surgery if your baby cannot breastfeed. You should also use the electric piston breast pump if your baby is not breastfeeding effectively by your second day. Any colostrum that you collect can be saved and stored. This early breast milk can also be fed to your baby if necessary.

A sufficient pumping session should last about 10 to 15 minutes. Be sure to read the manual or directions included with your accessory or collection kit. If your nurse or lactation consultant doesn't show you how to pump, read the instructions. In your first few days after delivery you will get drops of colostrum in the collection container. This is what to expect. More will come with more pumping. Don't be discouraged. Don't feel that the whole bottle needs filling. Be patient. Your milk supply will increase. You should pump every three hours while awake and at least once during the night. This will simulate the frequency that your baby would be breastfeeding.

It may be extremely helpful to use an electric piston breast pump if your baby seems very sleepy and breastfeeding is ineffective. You want to try to get as much breastfeeding accomplished as you can, but some of these babies fall back to sleep quickly. It will take a few days for them to shake the jet lag. You should use the electric piston breast pump following any short or ineffective feedings by your second or third day.

If you can only get about 5-minutes' worth of breastfeeding from your baby after lots of effort, you should plan to pump about another 10 to 15 minutes.

Your Game Plan

Going home can be a very anxious event for a new mother, let alone a postoperative breastfeeding mother! You will need to plan for a few basic things before you get home. Being able to organize and manage once you're home will make your life easier. Having the following in place can make for a smooth transition:

➤ Relative or friend to help

➤ Quiet, comfortable room

➤ Bed or couch on ground level

➤ Hospital-grade electric breast pump, if needed

➤ Groceries and food supplies

The key to recovering quickly after a C-section is getting sufficient rest. It is imperative that your spouse or partner and relatives understand this. You will be breastfeeding every two to three hours to nourish your baby and to bring in a good milk supply. Don't be afraid to say no to visitors. The fun and games can come later. Your partner, a relative, or a friend can do some light housekeeping, cooking, and laundry. Don't feel obligated to cook and clean. For now you have a very basic but simple agenda. Breastfeeding around the clock will keep you busy. Remember that you take care of your baby and someone else will need to take care of you.

Once at home you should set up a breastfeeding base camp. Your bed, couch, or a comfortable chair is a great location. Try to keep these items at your campsite:

➤ Food and snacks

➤ Water and liquids

➤ Telephone

➤ TV remote control

➤ Radio

➤ Diapers and wipes

➤ Burp cloth

➤ Baby clothes

Nursing Mom's Notes

Back at home, set up a base camp around your bed, couch, or chair with items you need for breastfeeding and baby care.

Keeping up with your fluids is important for your recovery from major surgery. Your body has an incision and a uterus that need to heal. Water is your best choice. Milk and juice will do, too. Strive for six to eight glassfuls of fluid each day. Limit any caffeine consumption to 200 mg or less each day. Your appetite may be minimal but do your best to eat a variety of protein, carbohydrates, fruits, and vegetables.

Take some short walks to get yourself moving around. Build up gradually to cover more ground. Get outside for a few minutes of fresh air each day regardless of the weather. It will benefit your psyche. Try some stretching exercises indoors on days that you just can't get it all together. Yoga is a great way to relax both mentally and physically.

Plan to rent an electric piston breast pump if your baby cannot or will not latch on and breastfeed. If you had a delay in your start to breastfeeding, your milk may be delayed coming in. I highly recommend that you use your rental breast pump to pump colostrum and stimulate your breasts. Should you still have a sleepy baby on your hands you will find the breast pump very useful when your milk comes in.

The Least You Need to Know

➤ You can breastfeed after a cesarean section delivery. Just like with a vaginal delivery, expect to breastfeed your baby every two to three hours.

➤ After your cesarean delivery you will be tired, uncomfortable, and maybe a little disappointed. Start moving as soon as your doctor allows. Begin to walk for small doses of exercise.

➤ Begin to express and save your colostrum soon after delivery if your baby cannot breastfeed.

➤ If your baby is still sleepy by your second day and not breastfeeding well, you may need to use a piston breast pump.

➤ Plan for help with chores and meal preparation once you are home.

➤ Medication that your doctor has ordered is generally safe for breastfeeding.

Early, yes... but I still need breast milk!

Chapter 20

Early Delivery

In This Chapter

➤ Breastfeeding benefits for premature babies

➤ Breast milk expression, collection, and storage for your premature baby

➤ Techniques for maintaining your milk supply

➤ Insurance coverage for durable medical equipment

➤ Breastfeeding your premature baby

➤ What to expect from your premature baby after hospital discharge

It's not what you had expected and certainly wasn't what you had dreamed about. But the fact may be that you have or will deliver a premature baby. Your role as a parent will be different now. You'll want to provide your breast milk for your premature baby because it's extremely beneficial. It gives you an active role and helps fulfill something that you may have planned for your baby.

What's Happened Here?

You are faced with so much when your baby or babies deliver prematurely. It's disappointing, it's scary, and can be downright overwhelming. It's the last thing on your wish list for parenthood. The first person you want to blame is yourself. Getting breastfeeding started will help you to overcome the fear and disappointment you may feel resulting from a premature delivery.

You're Early, Baby!

A *premature* baby is one born before 37 weeks of gestation. It may be tiny and fragile or appear hearty and healthy to you from the outside. But on the inside, health problems in a premature baby often arise because the baby's system is too immature to function properly. Modern technology can often help a premature baby to overcome these problems. It will take time for a premature baby to grow and mature.

Lactation Lingo

A **premature** infant is a baby born before 37 weeks gestational age, regardless of its birth weight.

Some of the common problems seen in premature babies are

➤ Difficulty with temperature regulation

➤ Irregular breathing rate

➤ Infection

➤ Feeding difficulty

The birth of a premature baby can result from preterm labor. In some cases the physician makes a decision to deliver early. A mother or baby's health may be at risk and warrant an early delivery. You may know in advance that an early delivery is possible. It may also come when you least expect it.

LactFact

The trend in twin and triplet births has produced some remarkable statistics since 1980. According to the National Center for Health Statistics, the number of twin births in the United States rose 52 percent, from 68,339 in 1980 to 104,137 in 1997. Nearly half of these twin pregnancies delivered prematurely. Triplet and higher-order births rose 404 percent, from 1,377 in 1997 to 6,737 in 1997. Women ages 45 to 49 birthed more twins in 1997 than during the entire decade of the 1980s! Connecticut and Massachusetts showed twin birth rates 25 percent higher than the U.S. rate. The triplet and higher birth rates for Nebraska and New Jersey topped out at twice the national level.

Two, Three, and More

It is not uncommon for mothers with multiple babies to deliver early. About half of all twin pregnancies are born prematurely. Triplet and quadruplet pregnancies are usually challenged with preterm labor; your doctor and staff at the hospital usually prepare you well in advance about a premature delivery.

The degree of prematurity depends on the gestational age of your baby or babies at birth. The closer a baby is to term, the better its chance of survival. If there's time before delivery, try to visit the Newborn Intensive Care Unit (NICU). You'll get a feel for the surroundings and see the staff at work. It can make you slightly more at ease knowing where your preemie baby's new digs will be.

Can I Still Breastfeed?

Delivering a premature baby can bring on feelings of fear and guilt under such stressful circumstances. It is very natural for you to feel a loss of control. You may also feel quite helpless.

Fortunately, breastfeeding can offer you a take-charge approach to help overcome your guilt and helplessness. It gives you the opportunity to control the circumstances now. Your breast milk is a gift that only you can provide your premature baby.

Your breast milk benefits a premature baby immensely. It's much easier to digest than baby formula. Your breast milk will protect your premature baby from viral and bacterial infections. It can also help to protect against intestinal diseases that premature babies can get, like diarrhea and necrotizing enterocolitis (NEC). Your own milk contains enzymes, hormones, and growth factors that help your premature baby's digestive and nervous systems to mature.

Your colostrum will help greatly with the excretion of *bilirubin*. Bilirubin is a by-product resulting from the breakdown of excess red blood cells. The excess bilirubin in the blood supply causes jaundice. Premature babies may develop jaundice in the days following their birth.

The contents of your breast milk are specific to your premature baby's gestational age. These components are much higher than what's found in

Breast Beware

Premature infants who don't receive human milk are markedly at risk for developing necrotizing enterocolitis (NEC). This serious complication of premature birth is an inflammation of the intestinal tract, which usually causes the tissue to die.

Lactation Lingo

Bilirubin is a by-product resulting from the breakdown of excess red blood cells. The excess bilirubin in the blood supply causes jaundice.

breast milk for a baby born at term. You'll find these components much higher in a mother's breast milk for her premature baby:

➤ Protein

➤ Sodium

➤ Chloride

➤ Calcium

➤ Iron

➤ Nitrogen

Babies born three to five weeks early can often start breastfeeding right away. Sick or very small babies will usually not be able to breastfeed. Under these circumstances you need to begin to express your breast milk to establish your milk supply. That way you'll have a milk supply ready when your baby is able to breastfeed or be fed your breast milk.

If you deliver more than one baby, you can still breastfeed! Some mother's think the more, the merrier! Your body will produce the milk supply for multiples as long as you stimulate and remove milk from your breasts. I've had many clients who have successfully breastfed twins, triplets, and quadruplets!

Expect This

The age of your premature baby determines when it can begin suckling from the breast. A baby can start to coordinate its suck, swallow, and breathing around 33 weeks of age. This ability needs to be present before you can begin breastfeeding any baby.

Premature babies unable to breastfeed are nourished through an intravenous line as well as given feedings through a tube. If your baby has a breathing or feeding tube in place, your baby will not be able to breastfeed. Expressed breast milk can be given through your baby's feeding tube. This feeding tube may stay in place for days or weeks until your baby learns to take all its feedings by mouth.

To establish and maintain a supply of breast milk you will have to express or pump your milk. You should try to begin within six hours of delivering your premature baby. Complications from your delivery may not enable you to start right away. If this happens, you should begin to pump as soon as you are physically able. Any colostrum that you begin to express is very beneficial for your baby.

Nursing Mom's Notes

It's best if you begin using a medical-grade electric piston breast pump within six hours after you deliver. You should continue to use an electric piston breast pump at least eight times in 24 hours. Pumping will stimulate your milk production and help you to maintain a milk supply for your premature baby.

You will need some time to learn to express your breast milk with a breast pump. With a little practice and some persistence, you will learn it. Go slowly at first and be patient. You will start to get drops in your first days of pumping and then work your way up to a larger volume. A very small baby will need only a small amount of milk at first. Remember that the milk you make is specific to your baby's gestational age. This means that the balances of nutrients are exactly what are needed for each stage of your baby's growth and development.

Plan to pump as often as your baby would be breastfeeding. That's about eight times in 24 hours. This is what it takes to provide the amount of milk your baby will need. Design a plan to ensure that you can pump eight times in 24 hours. If you prefer to sleep through the night, you will have to pump eight times while you are awake. If you set the alarm and awaken through the night to pump, then you can schedule yourself every three hours around the clock. It's helpful to make a plan and commit to it. Otherwise, your milk supply will dwindle with time. Providing breast milk for a premature baby or for multiple babies will involve some effort on your part. It takes a commitment and some dedication to provide your premature baby with a premium source of nutrition.

It is imperative that you use an electric piston breast pump. This type of breast pump is a medical or hospital grade. Don't settle for anything less. This type of breast pump closely mimics the rhythm and suckling action of your baby. You will be able to adjust the suction strength on a medical-grade breast pump. This is the best possible pump to sustain your milk supply while your baby is unable to suckle your breasts. Your maternity floor or NICU should have this type of electric piston breast pump available to you while in the hospital. If one is not available, ask for help in locating this type of pump. Also refer to Appendix C, "Resources," and call one of the breast pump manufacturers. They will be able to refer you to a supplier in your area.

It's best that you pump both of your breasts at the same time. In other words, simultaneous pumping. It saves you time and has been shown to cause higher prolactin levels for a greater amount of milk. You will need a dual-pumping accessory kit to accomplish this. Start out pumping each of your breasts for about five minutes until your milk comes in. When your milk volume starts to increase you will want to pump each breast until the flow of your milk subsides. It's very helpful to massage each breast before you express. Also massage while you pump to help stimulate milk flow, letdown, and a good emptying of your breast. Once your milk volume has increased, expect dual pumping to take about 10 to 15 minutes.

Breast Beware

Don't use anything less than a medical-grade electric piston breast pump. Pumping for a premature baby is serious business. This pump can best match the rhythm and suction of a breast-feeding baby.

The hospital or NICU will have specific guidelines for the collection and storage of your breast milk for a premature baby. Ask for a copy of these guidelines. Here are some basic steps, though, to follow when expressing your breast milk for a premature baby:

Nursing Mom's Notes

Ask the NICU staff or your lactation consultant for the hospital's guidelines on breast milk expression. The collection and storage protocol for premature and hospitalized infants should be included in these guidelines.

LactFact

The Health Care Financing Administration (HCFA) established the first reimbursement code for breastfeeding equipment in January 2000. This code designates the Egnell Elite electric piston breast pump as durable medical equipment. Health care providers are able to bill third-party payers for an electric piston breast pump DME when medically necessary.

1. Wash your hands.
2. Use clean accessories and collection containers.
3. Massage each breast to prepare for pumping.
4. Start with a low vacuum and increase to a comfortable amount of suction.
5. Pump until the flow of milk slows to a drip.
6. Wash all pump accessory parts that touched your breasts or breast milk. Use hot soapy water and rinse well with clean, hot water.
7. Sterilize the pump accessory parts and containers in boiling water or a dishwasher at least once each day.

Once your milk supply is established, try to collect between 15 to 20 ounces of breast milk each day. This may seem like a lot to you but it's best to have an ample reserve. Your collected amounts may vary. Save whatever you can express. You may experience some stress along the way that will decrease your milk supply. With extra milk on hand you won't panic should your milk supply temporarily decrease.

Containers of your breast milk should be labeled with your name, the name of your baby, and the date and time that you collected the milk. If your milk is to be used or given within 24 or 48 hours you can refrigerate it. Otherwise, make sure that you or the hospital staff transfers the milk directly to the freezer. Remember to keep cold any refrigerated milk. Frozen milk should be kept frozen when you transport it to the hospital. Carry your milk in an insulated cooler packed in ice or with ice packs.

Your insurance company should cover your rental expenses for a medical-grade electric piston breast pump and any supplies. Because your premature baby is hospitalized, there is medical need for you to use durable medical equipment (DME) while away from the hospital. Call to inquire of your insurance company if you need prior authorization. They may already have a contracted provider for this type of durable medical equipment. A prescription is usually required from your physician written as "Electric Piston Breast Pump DME."

Your Feeding Plan

It's possible that your premature baby can breastfeed right away. The health care team will probably determine your baby's readiness to suckle at the breast. It certainly doesn't hurt, though, for you to ask when breastfeeding will be possible.

Ready, Set, Breastfeed

Breastfeeding your premature baby for the first time will exhilarate and overwhelm you at the same time. Try using the football or cross-cradle hold for your first feedings. These positions enable you to support your baby's head with your hand. These positions also help to pull your baby onto your breast for a proper latch-on.

It's also very important that you are in a chair or couch that offers good back support. Your posture and position are essential to these first attachments. Use a stool and plenty of pillows to support your baby and to help position your baby at your breast.

At first your baby may just nuzzle and lick your nipple. That's okay. Breastfeeding will be a new skill for your baby to learn. You will need to be patient and understanding. Go ahead and express some milk from your milk sinuses with your fingers. This may rouse some interest and get your baby to smell the breast milk you have to offer. It's not unusual for premature babies to latch on and off the breast with these first breastfeeding sessions. If your baby doesn't breastfeed with these first few attempts, just know that the loving and holding is extremely beneficial. Being able to hold your baby may be a milestone in itself. Patience and time will enable your baby to adjust to breastfeeding.

Once your premature baby is feeding at your breast you'll look for some sign that all's well. Look for these signs with breastfeeding to assure you that things are going well:

➤ You can hear your baby swallowing milk.

➤ Your baby becomes satisfied when finished with breastfeeding.

➤ Your baby gains weight. Expect just about an ounce each day.

Nursing Mom's Notes

Your premature baby may just nuzzle and lick your nipple when offered its first time to breastfeed. Latching on and off your breast during these first breastfeedings can be expected. Express some milk from your nipple to stimulate an aroma of great food!

Once your baby begins to suckle at your breast and take breast milk, you will probably begin to decrease your pumping frequency. It will also depend on the strength of your baby's suckling. A good rule of thumb is to expect to use the pump off and on for about a month after your baby is discharged from the hospital.

Just a Little, Please

When you are able to breastfeed, you can expect your premature baby to be sleepy. This is typical behavior. As a result, your baby may not breastfeed as vigorously as a baby born closer to its due date. Your premature baby will probably fall asleep while breastfeeding before a sufficient meal has been eaten. If this happens, remember to pump afterward to empty your breast and maintain your milk supply.

Breast Beware

A premature baby will typically fall asleep just minutes into a breastfeeding. It's important to continue using your breast pump following a feeding to ensure that your breasts are emptied and to help assure a good milk supply.

Your baby may breastfeed very well with each feeding and throughout the day. Your baby may stay awake throughout its feeding and be alert for awhile following. If not, you will need to continue using an electric piston breast pump after each feeding. Pump for about five minutes after your baby has finished its breastfeeding. This will effectively stimulate and remove any milk that your sleepy baby has not. Store and freeze this milk for later use if necessary.

Some babies need additional nutrients, called fortifiers, because of their small size and immaturity. Additional calcium and phosphorus can be mixed with your breast milk, if necessary, to provide these additional nutrients. Your physician will indicate if your baby's breast milk needs a fortifier. Fortified breast milk can be given in an eyedropper, a bottle, or a supplementation device.

To add some weight to a premature baby, you should also consider expressing just *hind milk*. This offers concentrated calories from the cream for weight gain. To do this, you need to express your breast milk with a breast pump for about two minutes and then switch your containers. You then collect the hind milk that you express, and that's what you feed to your baby. Feeding mostly hind milk to your baby can usually increase its weight in a week or two.

Lactation Lingo

Hind milk is the milk released from the breast near the end of a breastfeeding. The fat content may be two to three times the concentration found in foremilk.

More Than One Mouth to Feed

Breastfeeding more than one baby at the same time is entirely possible. If you get to start breastfeeding in the hospital, be sure you get all hands on deck to help. Ask for the lactation consultant as well as any experienced nurses from the NICU. They can offer suggestions, help you attempt simultaneous breastfeeding, and discuss any supplementary feedings.

Remember that after many days and weeks of pumping it will take a while to be able to breastfeed your multiples exclusively from your breasts. This means that you may have to continue with any alternative feeding until your babies are able to fully breastfeed. Start out breastfeeding one of your babies who's eager to go to the breast. With time, you may find that it's easier to breastfeed two babies at the same time. Not to worry; each baby can get the nourishment needed from just one of your breasts. Use the method that feels most comfortable to you. Don't be afraid to put your maternal instinct to good use.

Being a mother and breastfeeding two or more babies takes a lot of organization. You'll find that it's helpful keeping a daily record of breastfeeding activities. Recording the number of feedings, which breast each baby fed from, and length of feedings, helps to keep you sane with two or more mouths to feed. Keeping track of wet and soiled diapers gives you a way of charting their progress.

Nursing Mom's Notes

As a mother of multiple babies, you will need on-going help completing household chores and daily activities.

LactFact

When one client delivered quadruplets prematurely, she was determined to express her breast milk for her babies. Years earlier, she had breastfed her sons, now teenagers. She pumped her breast milk and carried it daily to the intensive care unit. Once all four babies were home, they breastfed, usually in pairs. Breast milk was offered by bottle to those who couldn't wait their turn! She continued to pump and breastfeed for about seven months. At that time she had to return to work part-time, but continued to breastfeed her four babies in the morning and at night.

An example of a breastfeeding record looks like this:

Breastfeeding Record

Date: _____

Day #: _____

Feeding #	Feeding Length	Which Breast(s) (R = Right; L = Left; B = Both)	Wet Diaper	BM Diaper
❏ 1	_____	R/L/B	❏	❏
❏ 2	_____	R/L/B	❏	❏
❏ 3	_____	R/L/B	❏	❏
❏ 4	_____	R/L/B	❏	❏
❏ 5	_____	R/L/B	❏	❏
❏ 6	_____	R/L/B	❏	❏
❏ 7	_____	R/L/B	❏	❏
❏ 8	_____	R/L/B	❏	❏
❏ 9	_____	R/L/B	❏	❏
❏ 10	_____	R/L/B	❏	❏
❏ 11	_____	R/L/B	❏	❏
❏ 12	_____	R/L/B	❏	❏
_____	Total		_____	_____

You'll need more than just your pair of hands to get started breastfeeding your babies. You'll need someone else to help and to hold babies while you learn your new skills.

Home Sweet Home

The news that your baby is coming home will certainly bring tears to your eyes. You will finally be in charge. You may be overwhelmed and fearful about being on your own, though. After all, you've had constant help and support from the hospital staff. Now it's time to put your parenting and breastfeeding skills to good use.

A premature baby will be released from the hospital when certain criteria are met. This will vary from doctor to doctor and from hospital to hospital. A certain weight may be necessary. The physical condition of a small baby must be satisfactory. Doctors will consider these factors before they discharge a premature baby:

➤ Suck and swallow ability

➤ No illness

➤ No complications

➤ No respiratory problems

Spend an entire day or two with your baby before discharge. Feed on demand to help build your confidence with breastfeeding. Ask for the lactation consultant to watch your baby breastfeed. Get as much advice, and ask as many questions as you need to, before you go home. Inquire about your baby's weight gain. Ask your baby's doctor when you should visit for a weight check. You may want a scale to check and record weight gain if this is of concern.

If you've done your homework, you have already located your electric breast pump supplier. If not, you should ask your hospital staff or pediatrician to recommend a breast pump DME supplier. They should be able to confirm the type of breast pump you need. You'll probably need to continue using your breast pump to help express breast milk after feedings until your baby is breastfeeding and gaining weight well. Be sure to ask your insurance company about follow-up visits for your baby after discharge.

The Least You Need to Know

➤ Your breast milk is nutritionally balanced and age-specific for your premature baby. It protects against bacteria and viruses that cause serious illnesses in premature babies.

➤ Breastfeeding and expressing your milk for multiple infants is possible.

➤ Expressing breast milk for your premature baby or babies should begin within six hours after delivery or when you are physically able. Pump from both breasts eight times every 24 hours. Simultaneous pumping saves time and stimulates greater milk production.

➤ You can establish and maintain your breast milk supply best by using a medical-grade piston breast pump. A dual collection kit enables you to express from both breasts at the same time.

➤ Your insurance company should cover any expenses for electric piston breast pump DME and supplies. Inquire about coverage for medically necessary lactation consultation.

➤ Breastfeeding multiples requires help and more than one pair of hands. Try to breastfeed one at a time or as a pair, whichever feels more comfortable.

➤ It's typical for a premature baby to be sleepy or fall asleep while breastfeeding.

Chapter 21

Hospital Admission

In This Chapter

➤ Reasons for hospitalization

➤ What to expect with admission

➤ Maintaining your milk supply

➤ Circumstances that interrupt breastfeeding

➤ Getting help during your admission

Some of us learn the hard way. We don't think about or consider the possibility that something out of the ordinary can happen to our bodies. We don't keep space open in our planners for getting sick, having an accident, or needing an operation. Some of us may have an inkling that we're not feeling quite right but we choose to ignore it. Then we have to take the time to heal.

Situations can always arise where you or your baby are in need of medical attention. And that attention may have to take place in a medical facility. Your health care provider may be focused solely on your illness or disease. You may be focused solely on your breastfeeding. Let's take a look in this chapter about breastfeeding if an illness or emergency arises that lands you or your baby in the hospital.

What's Happened Here?

If an illness, disease, or emergency occurs, chances are that you and your baby will require a trip to the hospital. With health care costs at an all-time high, cost containment is certainly an issue with many physicians and health care providers. That's why preventative medicine is practiced. It helps to keep you healthy and wise, but I'm not sure about the wealth! An admission to the hospital requires a medical necessity. So if your doc says so, you'll have to go.

In or Out?

Nobody wants to go to the hospital, let alone stay in the hospital for an extended period of time. Depending on your situation, the hospital will provide your medical services in one of two types of patient categories. These types are *outpatient* and *inpatient*.

Outpatient means that you may be cared for in a clinic, in a room, or in an area of the hospital where your stay is quite brief. You become a transient person. If the illness or disease you have can get treated in a relatively short amount of time, you are listed as an outpatient. Your baby could also be admitted as an outpatient if the care provided is brief and relatively simple. Some facilities have a 23-hour observation period where you are released before the clock strikes midnight. This means that you won't be admitted and classified as an "inpatient."

Lactation Lingo

Outpatient is a term that means you may be cared for in a clinic, in a room, or in an area of the hospital where your stay is quite brief. **Inpatient** is a term that means you are assigned a hospital bed and are counted in the number of persons getting bed and room service.

Inpatient means that you are assigned a hospital bed and are counted in the number of persons getting bed and room service. The care that you receive in a hospital is that which usually cannot be provided in your home. You may need constant and intense bedside care from any number of health care professionals. Procedures and equipment may be readily available to help in your treatment and care. If your baby is admitted to the hospital, there's a good chance that care will need to be provided as an inpatient.

Mommy's Not Well

There's always a possibility that the mommy can get sick or develop a condition where hospitalization is necessary. This can happen during pregnancy, with childbirth, or well into the post-delivery time frame. Your family may realize what an incredibly empty household they have without a mommy around.

Some conditions can crop up during pregnancy and childbirth that require a hospital admission. Some of these include the following:

➤ *Preterm labor*

➤ High blood pressure

➤ *Diabetes*

➤ *Anemia*

➤ Delivery complications

Your care with these conditions may only be available as an inpatient. Your length of stay will be as long as your physician deems necessary. Again, it may be that the equipment and medications as well as the trained staff are all on hand in the hospital to care for you. Like or not, you'll have to deal with it.

Lactation Lingo

Preterm labor means labor before the time that actual labor should begin. It's premature or early. **Diabetes** is a disease marked by excess sugar in the bloodstream because the pancreas fails to produce insulin. **Anemia** is the deficiency of blood or hemoglobin.

Something Surgical

Some situations may require surgical intervention. It may be that these arise quite suddenly. The news may drop like a bombshell that you're gonna need an operation. If there's horrendous pain involved, you may welcome the news of surgery. Anything to make you feel better.

Unplanned surgeries for breastfeeding mothers may include any of these:

➤ Appendectomy

➤ Hysterectomy

➤ Cholecystectomy

➤ Cyst removal

You may also plan surgery for after you deliver, so that it won't come as such a surprise. I've seen mothers schedule oral surgery, orthopedic procedures, and hernia repairs that couldn't be done while they were pregnant. Many times you can have these scheduled surgeries performed as an outpatient status. That means you're in and you're out, all in a day's time.

Breast Beware

If your gut feeling tells you that something's not right, call your health care provider. A mother's instinct is usually the best indicator that a problem has arisen. This is especially true about knowing your own baby. Don't be worried if everything ends up okay. It's better to be safe than sorry.

209

Special Care for Baby

When it comes to a baby needing medical intervention, the thought or mention of hospitalization can be devastating to a new parent. Many times a parent will ask over and over, "What could have been done to prevent this from happening?" The truth is that no matter how prepared or how careful you are, things just happen.

Any number of circumstances may require a hospital admission for your baby. In the first few weeks after delivery, any of the following may necessitate a hospital admission:

➤ *Dehydration*

➤ *Jaundice*

➤ Prematurity

➤ Respiratory infection

➤ *Diarrhea*

➤ Surgery

➤ Diagnostic studies

Lactation Lingo

Dehydration means the loss or removal of water. **Jaundice** is a yellowish skin color in newborns caused by the breakdown of excess red blood cells. **Diarrhea** is an excessive and frequent looseness of the bowel.

It will be quite heartbreaking for you, not to mention downright scary, to experience an admission to the hospital with your baby. You will feel so helpless as the health care providers assume the care for your precious gift of life. You'll ask yourself over and over what you could have done to prevent this. Make sure that you have your network of support in place. And most of all, don't blame yourself one bit for what has happened.

Can I Still Breastfeed?

I'll cut to the chase. Breastfeeding can be maintained with most of these hospital admissions provided that your breasts are stimulated and emptied on a regular basis. Remember that it is essential that all of your milk be emptied to prevent any breast infection. It is also important in the regulation of your supply. Regular and frequent emptying prevents your milk from causing irritation of the milk ducts and backup into your milk glands. If milk stasis occurs, then the milk production will wane.

You have two options to stimulate and empty your breasts on a regular basis. Here they are:

➤ Your first option is to continue with your baby suckling your breasts frequently to feed and empty your breast milk. It is helpful for both you and your baby to continue with the breastfeeding you have already established. If you or your baby are unable under the circumstances to do this, you'll have to look at the next option.

➤ Your second option is to empty milk from your breasts with a—you guessed it—medical-grade piston breast pump! If your baby cannot or will not suckle, an electric piston breast pump helps to simulate the suckling action of your baby through its vacuum and cycling action. Plain and simple, it's effective, efficient, and can be used as often as necessary for emptying your breasts.

Be aware that some diagnostic studies or procedures can interfere with or compromise your milk collection. When and if any dye or radioactive material is used, you'll want to check with your physician about its longevity in your body's system. If active feeding from your breast is discouraged or denied, you'll need to maintain your milk supply with mechanical expression.

Surgery will definitely put your breastfeeding on hold temporarily but only for a short while. If you receive a general anesthetic, you'll be able to breastfeed after the gases have been metabolized from your system. That means you'll have to be, in hospital terms, awake, alert, and oriented. You'll have to be able to handle your baby and be alert for breastfeeding to occur. Most anesthesiologists allow breastfeeding within 24 hours of administering an anesthetic. Some allow it within four to six hours of its circulation within your bloodstream. Your best bet is to ask. Call a lactation professional for suggested anesthetics that allow for breastfeeding to resume quickly. Your anesthesiologist may not know. If you can call ahead, that is if your surgery is planned, ask about the time frame for breastfeeding after surgery.

If your baby is the patient, whether inpatient or outpatient status, ask the staff taking care of your baby about breastfeeding. Hopefully, if it's the Newborn Intensive Care Unit, they will be very supportive of your feeding choice. You're what they call the easy customer. If your milk supply is already established, try to continue with breastfeeding your baby if at all possible.

Breast Beware

Some medications and pharmaceuticals used for diagnostic procedures are not compatible with breastfeeding. They can cross over into your breast milk and be harmful to your baby. You may have to "pump and dump" or discard your expressed breast milk. This may last for 48 to 72 hours or until the substance has been excreted from your system.

Nursing Mom's Notes

Look for or ask about a room on the pediatric floor, in the NICU, or on the maternity ward where you can use a medical-grade piston breast pump. You will need your own collection kit for breast milk expression. If you are a patient on a medical or surgical floor, have your nurse call the maternity floor. Depending on your condition, you may need the piston pump at your bedside.

You'll be able to breastfeed if your baby doesn't have difficulty with the combination of breastfeeding and breathing. Your baby will also need to be awake and alert. A sleepy baby, such as one with jaundice, may not be able to latch on and maintain a good and effective stimulation of your breast. Remember that it is essential to have effective and efficient stimulation of your breast to maintain a good milk supply.

LactFact

Jaundice is a condition where bilirubin levels in the blood are high and give the skin a yellow tinge. The breakdown of red blood cells produces iron and bilirubin as byproducts. Many babies have this normal or physiologic jaundice when they are first born. Most of the bilirubin is excreted in the baby's first bowel movements. Colostrum helps with bowel movements by causing a laxative effect. Infrequent and ineffective breastfeeding will cause bilirubin to be absorbed back into the blood. Babies with jaundice are typically very sleepy and must be awakened frequently to breastfeed.

When your circumstances are an emergency, the situation changes ever so much. You'll probably read this after-the-fact. Hopefully not. Alert your spouse or partner that they should reference this book in the event of an emergency. Whether it's you or your baby who has an emergency, someone besides you needs to know about handling breastfeeding under these circumstances.

You, the mother, need to be able to maintain your milk supply when you are physically able to do so. In other words, if you are too sick to hold and suckle your baby at your breast, then actual breastfeeding will not be possible. You must remember that infant safety is a priority. If you cannot handle your baby while breastfeeding, then a mechanical pump will more than likely be necessary.

Here's What Will Happen

I'll start with an explanation of the easiest circumstances to expect and will progress to the harder ones.

Pediatric Unit

If your baby gets readmitted to the hospital following birth, it can be to the pediatric floor or Pediatric Intensive Care Unit or PICU. Admission to the pediatric unit for your baby may be your easiest situation where breastfeeding is concerned. Breast-feeding is not a foreign concept to the staff, nor laughed at, in this department. This means that the pediatric staff will support many of your breastfeeding wants and needs.

If milk expression becomes necessary, most pediatric units in a hospital have a medical-grade piston breast pump. As a matter of fact, they usually have more than one depending on the usual census of babies in their unit. Ask about its location or the room that's designated for pumping. Ask for its guidelines for breast milk storage. Also inquire about any contain-ers or freezer bags available to store your milk. The staff is often glad to talk to you about procedures, to give you milk storage guidelines, and to point out the breast pump on the floor or the designated new mother's room. If you are too overwhelmed, then have your spouse or partner get the scoop.

Nursing Mom's Notes

The best health care professional to contact during your hospital admission is the lactation con-sultant. Ask any of the staff as-signed to your care to telephone or page the "LC." No matter where you are in the hospital, you should be able to talk about your breastfeeding circumstances with a lactation consultant. If an LC is not on staff, ask for an ex-perienced nurse from the mater-nity floor.

Admission to the Medical Surgical Floor

Okay, I said it would get a little more difficult. Suppose you are admitted to a medical surgical floor. And you ask the nurse assigned to your care about a medical-grade breast pump. She looks at you with a blank stare. She doesn't have a clue. Your best bet is to ask for an old one—nurse, that is. She'll probably walk to a closet or make a phone call to round up "Old Silver," the antique breast pump. Don't get too scared. A little polish, and the stainless steel will be shiny in no time.

It's important to know that this type of pump is a real workhorse. Don't let its ap-pearance scare you. All you need is the collection kit, and to assemble and connect, and you're off and pumping. The challenge comes in getting someone to locate this pump. If possible, have the staff contact a lactation consultant within the hospital. He or she can usually seek out or locate what you need. It also won't hurt to have a little review or instruction. There's nothing worse than having all the parts and pieces, and not knowing what to do with them.

Emergency!

The next scenario is your emergency room or surgery suite. If you are a patient in the ER or find yourself admitted and travelling through the halls of surgery, you'll need to find someone who comprehends the words "breast pump." It may not be too often that patients with a need to express breast milk frequent these departments. Ask for someone who may have knowledge about the piston breast pump. Better yet, ask about the possibility of contacting the lactation consultant. You'll need to have a medical-grade piston breast pump and the collection kit to express and collect your breast milk when necessary.

Outpatient Procedures

Last, but certainly not least, is a situation where you are admitted for a test or procedure as an outpatient. Try to keep your baby nearby, with Dad or a caregiver, and continue with breastfeeding as desired. If your baby cannot be with you to breast-feed, you will need to express your breast milk. Again, this means a good old piston pump. The challenge begins in trying to locate one or having someone in the department locate one for you. If possible, you should ask for a lactation consultant, or better yet, call one yourself and ask about pump availability if needed. Don't forget that you'll need a collection kit. These are usually stocked on the maternity or postpartum floor.

Nursing Mom's Notes

If a medical-grade breast pump cannot be located or made available at your facility, you should contact a supplier and bring it into the hospital your-self. Better yet, your spouse or partner could do this for you. Medical-grade breast pumps are usually UL-approved and should be okay for your personal use in the hospital.

Feeding Your Baby from the Hospital

If the opportunity to actually breastfeed your baby under any of these circumstances cannot be accomplished, you'll have to resort to mechanical expression. That means emptying breast milk from your breasts at a frequency that your baby would usually breastfeed. If that frequency is about every two to three hours, then you will have to maintain this during your hospital stay. If your baby's feeding frequency is every three to four hours, you'll have to express your milk this often.

It's essential that you maintain this frequency. If not, you may develop a breast infection. Given what you are being admitted for in the first place, an infection would not be welcome. You may have to explain this to the staff caring for you. Remember that few health care professionals receive formal or adequate training about breastfeeding management. More than likely, you will know more than the staff who are caring for you do.

When surgery is required, it is best to talk to the anesthesiologist prior to your procedure. You'll want to know what anesthetics will be used and about their transfer into your breast milk. I've personally consulted for women whose anesthesiologist had them breastfeeding within two to four hours post-surgery. It does make a difference how often you are emptying your breasts. If you only breastfeed your three-month-old every four hours, it is certainly different from a mother feeding every two hours.

It is best to call ahead, if possible, if you know that a hospital admission is necessary. You can supply them with the date and time of your intended admission. Try to call and talk to the lactation consultant on staff. You may want to share the following information:

➤ The date and time of your procedure or surgery

➤ Any anesthetics, medications, dyes, or radioactive materials that will be used during your care

➤ If you are familiar with the use of a breast pump

➤ The age of your baby

➤ Any pertinent information about your breastfeeding experience

➤ If you have seen or worked with a lactation consultant

A bed is often available in your baby's room so that breastfeeding can continue. If your baby is admitted to the pediatric unit and cannot breastfeed, you will need to express your breast milk for the staff to feed to your baby. This will need to be as often as your baby breastfeeds. Remember that your breast milk has valuable infection-fighting properties. And most sick babies fed breast milk get better faster. The antibodies and immunoglobulins create an incredible line of defense against bacteria and viruses.

An alternative option to offering your baby breast milk, if hospitalized, is donor milk. Your physician can order pasteurized donor milk to the hospital and have it readily available for your baby. Just like blood transfusions, timing is essential for these circumstances. Keep in mind the transport time, availability, and the education of staff about the benefits of breastfeeding and donor milk.

Breast Beware

Many health care professionals do not receive formal training in lactation. You will probably have more knowledge and expertise about breastfeeding than they do. Don't hesitate to get a second opinion from a lactation professional if you are offered conflicting advice about breastfeeding.

Nursing Mom's Notes

Donor milk can be obtained from a milk bank with a physician's prescription. Look in Appendix C, "Resources," for contact information in locating a milk bank.

Actually, every hospital should have a supply of donor milk in its freezer for breast-feeding babies in need of supplementation. This enables a baby to receive only human milk and it eliminates the exposure to a breast milk substitute. This could eliminate a lot of headaches and heartache for parents who choose only the best milk feeding. Unfortunately, most hospitals in the United States do not stock donor breast milk. You might ask your physician, though, about ordering donor milk for your hospital or your baby if it becomes necessary.

The Least You Need to Know

➤ A hospital admission might be scheduled or it might be an emergency circumstance for you or your baby.

➤ You or your baby may be admitted to a hospital as an outpatient or an inpatient, dependent on the type and length of your necessary care.

➤ Try to maintain or continue breastfeeding as desired with a hospital admission. Stay with your baby or keep your baby close by you while in the hospital.

➤ Anytime your breastfeeding frequency becomes interrupted or altered, it may become necessary to stimulate and empty your breasts with a medical-grade piston breast pump.

➤ Any delay or infrequent emptying of your breast milk may result in a breast infection.

➤ Ask the hospital staff to contact a lactation consultant or a maternity nurse with any hospital admission.

➤ Your physician can order donor breast milk for your baby from a milk bank.

Chapter 22

It Hurts

> ## In This Chapter
>
> ➤ Nipple tenderness versus nipple soreness
>
> ➤ The common causes of nipple soreness
>
> ➤ Basic comfort measures
>
> ➤ Remedies for sore nipples

Your breastfeeding is supposed to be an experience that's comfortable and satisfying. After all, why do it if it's uncomfortable and dissatisfying? Breastfeeding mothers seem to have a common complaint, though, that you may have heard about already. And that is nipple soreness.

It's important that you know how it happens, what can be done about it, and how to prevent it from happening to begin with. I've had a mother or two tell me that they gave up breastfeeding because it hurt. Knowing the cause of nipple soreness can help you try to prevent the number one complaint that mothers have about breastfeeding.

What's Happened Here?

You may experience a slight degree of nipple tenderness during your first few days of breastfeeding. After all, the nipple and areolar tissue have never experienced the amount of suction your baby can apply to it. It's like breaking in a new pair of leather shoes. There's a slight amount of discomfort involved. This nipple tenderness is seen in a majority of breastfeeding mothers between day three and day six. It is temporary, or transient, and should get to feeling better. The tenderness should always resolve and not be bothersome. Rest assured that this discomfort is temporary and your condition will improve.

When someone complains beyond the first week that "it hurts," chances are that nipple tenderness has turned into nipple soreness. Nipple soreness that lasts beyond your first week and becomes painful is a warning that something is wrong. Breastfeeding is an activity that occurs between you and your baby. Both you and your baby need to be looked at in order to find the cause and try to correct it.

Basically, there are two different kinds of soreness seen with breastfeeding. In one case, the nipple becomes *irritated*. The other and more severe case is when the nipple becomes *traumatized*. Irritated and traumatized-nipple soreness can happen for a number of reasons. These reasons can be any of the following:

➤ Improper positioning at the breast

➤ Baby has sucked from a rubber teat or pacifier

➤ Vigorous breastfeeding because of infrequent feedings

➤ Baby is taken off the breast without breaking suction

➤ Baby has a tight frenulum

When your baby is not positioned properly at the breast, nipple soreness can definitely result. A blister or crack can result from the abrasion that improper positioning brings on. It may be the baby's tongue, the gums, or the lips that create a stressful contact with your nipple tissue. We usually see stressful contact occur with these circumstances:

➤ Baby's latched on to just the nipple, not the areola.

➤ Baby's mouth not opened wide enough with attachment.

➤ Baby's lip tucked in, not flared out.

➤ Baby's positioned too low on the breast causing stretch and stress to the upper-areolar tissue.

Breast Beware

Nipple tenderness is often noticed between your third and sixth day of breastfeeding. If tenderness becomes soreness, a lactation professional or health care professional should evaluate any nipple soreness you experience beyond your first week.

Lactation Lingo

Irritation is heat and redness in the skin caused by friction. **Trauma** is a wound or bodily injury with a lasting effect caused by a violent force or severe pressure.

If your baby has started to suck from an artificial nipple or teat, the suckling during breastfeeding can sometimes become confused. During a feeding from a bottle, an artificial nipple is held stationary by the baby's gums. The tongue only controls the flow of liquid from the bottle when suction is applied. When this is learned, a baby won't compress the milk sinuses with its gums and won't stroke or pull milk from the breast with its tongue during a breastfeeding. The result with breastfeeding is trauma to the nipple from this learned sucking pattern.

Vigorous breastfeeding results when your baby is very, very hungry. This ravenous hunger will occur if the frequency of feedings is delayed. Your skin tissue may not withstand the vigor of a very hungry baby's suction. Breastfeeding frequently on cue or as desired will keep your baby's hunger satisfied.

If your baby is taken off the breast without first breaking the suction from suckling, this can be traumatic to your nipple. Don't cut feedings short hoping to prevent sore nipples. Sore nipples will not result from long, lengthy feedings. Nor do they come from frequent feedings either. If you hear this from any health care provider, you can take the opportunity to correct them or totally ignore what they tell you.

A condition known as "tongue-tie" can sometimes be the cause of nipple soreness. With this condition, the tip of baby's tongue is held tightly to the floor of the mouth from a thick band of tissue known as the *frenulum*. With the frenulum attached too near the tip of the tongue, it can abrade the nipple and contribute to soreness. The tongue becomes heart shaped when the baby tries to lift and thrust it. The baby can only bite the nipple as a result, and this leads to nipple soreness. Don't overlook this condition as a cause of nipple soreness. It is not a concern with bottle-feeding as a baby typically gums the artificial nipple.

Lactation Lingo

A **frenulum** is a thick band of tissue that attaches the tongue to the floor of the mouth. Tongue-tie refers to a short or very tight frenulum that restricts the thrust of the tongue beyond the gum.

Nursing Mom's Notes

Seek the help of a lactation professional when your nipple soreness lasts beyond one week. A lactation professional can observe your breastfeeding technique and help you determine your options for relief.

Can I Still Breastfeed?

Most of the time with nipple soreness it's not a question of: "Can I still breastfeed?" Depending on the severity of the soreness, the question is: "Can I stop breastfeeding?" The nipple tissue is very sensitive and therefore can be quite uncomfortable when it's rubbed raw or becomes cracked.

Yes, you can still breastfeed, but you'll need to take some action to correct the source of your problem. Your soreness won't improve until the reason for your soreness is found. You can do some troubleshooting on your own to find the source of your soreness. If you take some relief measures it can provide comfort to weary, sore nipples while breastfeeding.

Basic Relief

Good positioning of your baby at your breast while breastfeeding is the most basic remedy to start with. An awkward angle, holding your baby out from your breast, and letting your shoulders slump over your baby, are all positions that you can improve. I haven't had a mother comment yet that a change in position didn't improve the feel of breastfeeding.

Lactation Lingo

An **emollient** is a soothing agent or medicine. Breast milk contains milk fats and proteins that act as emollients when applied to your breast.

LactFact

Apparently sore and traumatized nipples have plagued breastfeeding women throughout the years. A Dutch monk used the following remedies for "injured nipples" in the early 1900s. Women were instructed to apply the following herbs and concoctions to their nipples:

➤ Lily oil

➤ Fresh butter mixed with white wine

➤ Gum arabic dissolved in rosewater

➤ Common houseleek

➤ Rosewater mixed with an equal quantity of French brandy

➤ Lip pomade

➤ Quince seeds dissolved in rosewater

I can't help but wonder if the French brandy and the white wine were used externally or consumed!

220

The basic healing power of breast milk needs to be repeated again. The immunoglobulins, milk fats, and proteins in breast milk all contribute to the healing of your skin cells. Rubbing breast milk into your nipple and areolar skin offers some quick relief and helps to heal your skin.

Keeping dry breast pads against your nipple and areola is essential. Ask anyone who has left a wet diaper on a baby too long what the results are. The skin starts to macerate or break down when exposed to wetness for prolonged periods of time. You should change your pads when they become wet and after every breastfeeding.

And it's extremely helpful to expose your nipple and areola to air with each breastfeeding. This shouldn't take but a few minutes of "air time" after each breastfeeding. Don't be so quick to pull up the flap from your nursing bra. Allow some fresh air to circulate and to dry your skin thoroughly.

Product Relief

Lanolin is an ointment that has been used for hundreds of years to heal skin. Lanolin is derived from sheepskin and offers properties of an *emollient* when applied to your skin. There are many mothers who will offer personal testimonials about the healing power of lanolin.

A breast shell can offer relief to any mother experiencing nipple soreness. You wear a shell over the nipple and hold it in place with a bra. It keeps any clothing from brushing against or sticking to a sore nipple. A shell also has small holes that enable air to circulate. Breast shells should be removed at night and not worn while sleeping.

You may consider taking a mild analgesic to relieve any discomfort or pain. An analgesic is a drug that helps to relieve or alleviate pain. Your physician often prescribes an analgesic for pain relief following childbirth. If you choose an analgesic, it should be taken about 30 minutes before you anticipate breastfeeding.

Breast Beware

Prolonged use of a nipple shield may lead to an inadequate milk supply. A nipple shield should be used under the direct care of a lactation professional or a health care provider.

It is also possible to use a nipple shield to protect your sore nipples during breastfeeding. A nipple shield is a thin, elastic silicone shaped like the human nipple. It is placed over the breast as a cover and allows for breastfeeding. A nipple shield should be used with extreme caution. I highly recommend that you use it under the care of your lactation professional. Use of a shield may not allow for good stimulation and compression of your milk sinuses. This can lead to inadequate emptying of your breast and thus an inadequate milk supply.

The Ameda® nipple shield for relief of nipple soreness.

(Source: Hollister, Inc.)

Expect This

The skin of a sore, irritated nipple will appear pink and irritated. It may also appear slightly reddened and chapped. The tip of your nipple may also look blanched or whitened after your baby unlatches from your breast. Your soreness may start just when your baby latches on to your breast. It should subside after your baby latches to your breast correctly and with the flow of milk.

Nipple soreness may result with your use of an electric breast pump. If you experience nipple soreness at the start of milk expression with a breast pump, the vacuum may be too high. You should adjust the vacuum control to a minimumal amount that's necessary for your milk to let down from your breast. A vacuum that is too high is often the culprit of nipple soreness when mechanical breast pumps are used. It's also extremely important that you use the correct breast shield size for your nipple. The flange and nipple tunnel of your breast shield should fit correctly to avoid nipple abrasion when suction is applied.

The skin of a nipple that's been traumatized will appear cracked or blistered. Sometimes crescent-shaped abrasions or bruising may be present above or below your nipple. Your nipples may be swollen, and often times will burn, especially of they are reddened. This means that breastfeeding will oftentimes hurt. If a crack or a blister opens, you may see a straw-colored fluid ooze from the opening. This will begin a scab formation, so leave it alone. Don't add insult to injury. You can take a cotton ball soaked in warm water to gently dab it clean.

Your soreness should start to improve three or four days after healing measures are taken. You should also

Nursing Mom's Notes

The breast shield for any breast pump should be the correct size for your nipple and areola. The flange and nipple tunnel should fit properly to avoid nipple abrasion.

have identified the cause of your nipple soreness. Continue to work on proper positioning of your baby with every breastfeeding. You may choose to breastfeed from your breast that hurts the least. Milk expression from your other breast can offer some needed relief for a day or two.

Your Feeding Plan

If at any time you cannot tolerate breastfeeding because of the pain, you should seek help from an experienced health care professional or lactation professional. They will watch you breastfeed and try to help solve any problems you have experienced. Don't wait until it's too late to get professional help. When you identify problems with positioning or attachment early in breastfeeding, you can often resume breastfeeding while reducing any discomfort or pain.

Try some of the following techniques to make your breastfeeding more comfortable and to help eliminate any cause for nipple soreness:

➤ Massage your breasts before breastfeeding. This encourages the letdown or release of your milk and helps to satisfy your baby's hunger quickly.

➤ Ensure that your baby is positioned toward you at the level of your breast. Your baby should open its mouth widely and latch on to your areola. Most of your areola should be drawn into its mouth with suckling.

➤ Discontinue the use of any soap or antiseptics when you clean your breasts. With your daily bath or shower cleanse your breasts with only warm tap water.

➤ Rub any residual breast milk on your nipple and areola. Breast milk has some wonderful emollients and immunological factors to help heal your breast tissue.

➤ Keep your nipples exposed to air after each breastfeeding. This enables them to dry thoroughly and helps prevent soreness from wet, moist skin.

➤ Wear a bra that's entirely cotton. Cotton will absorb your body moisture and any dripped milk from your breasts.

➤ Change your breast pads frequently. You must keep dry fabric or paper against your nipple.

➤ Wear a breast shell. It will keep clothing off your nipple in between and after feeding.

➤ Use a purified grade of lanolin. This can be left on your nipple while breastfeeding and works great to heal chapped nipples.

➤ Ask your lactation professional about any product for moist wound healing.

Nursing Mom's Notes

Try the football hold or lying-down position for breastfeeding with sore nipples. Both holds are great positions for keeping your baby positioned at the level of your breast during a breastfeeding.

You or your partner must take a look at your position during breastfeeding. Correct posture and positioning make a world of difference. If you were using the cradle or cross-cradle hold for breastfeeding and got sore nipples, you should probably try the football or lying-down hold for a change. Your baby will attach to your breast with a different position. This should help relieve the contact with some very sore areas.

You should try to follow these simple steps when using the football or clutch hold while breastfeeding:

1. Place one or two pillows along your side to support your arm. It also brings your baby up to breast level.

2. Your baby's head and neck should be held in the palm of your hand. Your forearm should support your baby's upper body.

3. Cup your hand under your breast and touch your nipple to your baby's lower lip.

4. When the mouth is open like a yawn, pull your baby onto your breast.

5. Your baby's lips should encircle most of your areola.

When lying down to breastfeed, try to follow these simple steps:

1. Place several pillows behind your back for support when you lie on your side.

2. Your baby should be placed on its side.

3. Place a rolled blanket behind your baby's back for support.

4. You should be face-to-face and tummy-to-tummy with both you and your baby on your sides.

5. Follow the attachment technique from the football hold.

You should consider the use of an electric piston breast pump if you experience very painful soreness and want to stop breastfeeding. Many women do not want to continue to breastfeed when pain is experienced. A piston breast pump will be effective at maintaining your milk supply while you take a break. It will rest your breast enough to allow your nipples to heal. Use an eyedropper, cup, or finger feed any expressed breast milk to your baby during this time. Resume breastfeeding as soon as you feel your soreness has improved.

You might also try breastfeeding from your breast with the least-sore nipple. Yes, you are supposed to alternate your starting-breast with each feeding. But with sore nipples, I want you to try something different.

Another technique is to try to unlatch your baby from your breast after *nutritive suckling* has stopped.

Lactation Lingo

Nutritive suckling is a breastfeeding that is nourishing or promotes growth.

Remember that nutritive suckling happens with your milk-ejection reflex, and swallows are heard every one to two seconds. With nonnutritive suckling, your baby doesn't use its tongue and jaw to stimulate and remove milk. You usually see or feel a slight quiver of the jaw and you won't feel a good tug. Slip your finger in alongside the corner of the mouth and break any suction. You can let your baby just suck on your finger if necessary.

You might also try to add shorter, more frequent feedings. Instead of eight, try to make it 10 feedings in 24 hours. Make sure you let your baby feed long enough to get satisfied. Don't cut feedings short to guard for soreness. By adding more feedings, you offer your baby a plentiful buffet of food. And a buffet can keep anyone plenty full!

The Least You Need to Know

➤ Nipple tenderness is typical in the first few days of breastfeeding.

➤ Your health care provider or lactation professional should evaluate any nipple soreness that lasts beyond your first week.

➤ Improper positioning can often cause nipple soreness, as can a baby who sucks an artificial teat or is breastfed infrequently.

➤ You should express breast milk with a medical-grade piston breast pump if you experience painfully sore nipples and want to quit breastfeeding.

➤ Relief measures for sore nipples include applying breast milk, air-drying, and changing wet breast pads frequently. Lanolin, breast shells, mild analgesics, and a nipple shield may also provide some relief and help to heal your nipples.

➤ The football hold and lying-down hold may be the best breastfeeding positions for improving sore nipples.

Chapter 23

My Breasts Are Huge!

In This Chapter

➤ The difference between breast fullness and engorgement

➤ Preventing breast engorgement

➤ What to expect with breast engorgement

➤ Comfort measures for breast engorgement

➤ Alternative feeding methods during engorgement

Perhaps you've heard a few stories about breastfeeding that equate to a fisherman's big fish story. These rather graphic stories usually center on the size of a woman's breasts during breastfeeding. My sister-in-law tells me that with her first baby her breasts were the size of cantaloupes. I found that hard to believe. I asked myself how someone so petite and wearing only a size 34B bra could grow melons on her chest.

When her second baby was born, I saw those melons and I believed. She had grown them on the front of her chest! I couldn't believe I was seeing such engorgement for the first time in my professional career. I feared that they would explode.

You may be quite concerned or afraid about this happening to you. Understanding what contributes to breast engorgement and ways to prevent it should set your mind at ease. You'll also want to know how to manage it in case it happens to you.

What's Happened Here?

For the first week after delivery the amount or volume of colostrum increases to a mature milk supply as a result of hormone stimulation. With an increase in milk volume, your breasts will typically become full. Sometimes you feel that the amount of milk in your breasts makes you quite full! It is absolutely normal for this fullness in your breasts to occur. It usually diminishes within 48 to 72 hours as your baby empties your breasts frequently. The amount of milk that you produce adjusts to meet your baby's appetite.

Engorgement results when your baby does not empty all the milk from your breasts for one reason or another. Breasts that become engorged typically feel hot, hard, and very swollen. Engorgement is defined as moderate to severe swelling and the distention of the breasts in the early days of lactation.

Lactation Lingo

Engorgement is the enlargement and significant swelling of the breasts in the early days of breastfeeding. It can occur from an increased blood supply as well as an increase in milk production. Engorged breasts feel hot and hard and appear very swollen.

Getting Bigger

When you experience breast fullness it is only temporary swelling and results in mild discomfort. It will last two to three days while your production of breast milk increases. You also experience an increase in your blood flow to the breasts resulting from your baby's suckling. This makes you glow and feel a bit flushed while breastfeeding.

You'll know that you have breast fullness when the following has happened:

➤ Fullness starts in two to three days with your baby's suckling.

➤ You notice some mild swelling in your breasts.

➤ Your breasts remain soft enough for your baby to latch onto easily.

Nursing Mom's Notes

You should notice breast fullness about two to three days after you start breastfeeding. This tells you that your milk production has increased. Your breasts will have a mild swelling and remain soft enough for your baby to latch on for a feeding.

Your breast fullness will last for about 72 hours at the most. Your breasts will appear a bit swollen but you should be able to gently compress your breast tissue. Your general swelling results from the increase in the amount of milk your breasts produce. During breast fullness your baby will be able to suckle comfortably. Your baby should be able to grasp the nipple and areolar tissue in its mouth without any difficulty.

Your breast fullness should not become breast engorgement if you breastfeed your baby every one to three hours. You may need to wake your baby at three hours if it's still sleepy. It is essential for your baby to be awakened and to suckle your breast. Your baby should also empty your milk from your breast with each breastfeeding. This also keeps breast fullness from becoming breast engorgement.

Hot and Heavy

Breast engorgement is also temporary. You do not typically experience this condition. It is a pathological condition that can be prevented.

You'll know that you have breast engorgement if the following happens:

➤ You develop large, swollen breasts in three to seven days with your baby's suckling.

➤ You experience moderate to severe swelling in both of your breasts.

➤ The skin on your breasts becomes hot to your touch.

➤ The skin on your breasts becomes tight and shiny.

➤ Your breasts are tender and painful to touch.

➤ Your body temperature increases greater than 98.6°F.

When you shorten your feedings, or don't feed frequently enough, your breasts can become engorged with milk. If your baby doesn't empty the milk you produce with each feeding, you can become engorged with milk. Typically, here's what happens:

1. Your areola becomes full with milk and stretches out your nipple.

2. Your baby cannot grasp your swollen areola in its mouth.

3. Your milk sinuses are not "milked" and thus are not emptied.

4. The pressure from your full milk sinuses then backs up your milk ducts.

5. Your milk ducts become swollen and full of milk.

6. Residual milk in your ducts causes pressure on your alveoli or milk-producing sacs.

7. This increased and unrelieved pressure diminishes your milk supply.

Breast Beware

Shortened and infrequent feedings cause breast fullness to turn into breast engorgement. A sleepy baby must be awakened every three hours to breastfeed. Your breasts must be emptied with every breastfeeding.

You can see then how breast engorgement happens. The swelling can get worse if you don't act quickly to relieve it. Your body's response to the increased ductal pressure and milk stasis results in hot, red, and tender skin.

You can also get breast engorgement if you decide to quit breastfeeding and bring it to a complete halt. I've heard it referred to as "cold-turkey." You must gradually reduce the stimulation and removal of any breast milk that you started to produce in the first place. A sudden cessation of an established body process can result in infection and disease. For more about stopping your breastfeeding, refer to Chapter 30, "Weaning Your Baby."

Once you have breastfeeding weeks or months underway, varying degrees of engorgement can result from a missed feeding. When you don't empty the breast milk from your breast for some reason, the same chain of events can result. When your baby first sleeps a long stretch during the night, you usually end up with a missed feeding. You may wake up from a solid, restful sleep to find your breasts super firm and ready to empty. This circumstance is easy to remedy with lots of breastfeeding or the use of a breast pump to empty you breast milk. You'll also see engorgement result when you skip your usual feeding time or can't manage to express your milk for five or more hours.

LactFact

Engorgement is often associated with the onset of lactation. It is pathological, not physiological, in nature. Pathological means that it has been caused by a certain condition or under certain circumstances. Physiological means that is a normal life function for any plant, animal, or human being.

Engorgement can also occur once milk production has been established. If a breastfeeding is missed, skipped, or prolonged the milk sinuses, ducts, and alveoli will expand with milk. When a baby first sleeps for a lengthy time period, a mother experiences engorgement. Any mother that suddenly quits breastfeeding will also experience engorgement.

An Ounce of Prevention

An ounce of prevention here is well worth the pound of cure! In other words, prevention of engorgement in the first place will save you the pain and misery that engorgement can bring you. When your baby does not empty all of your milk produced during a breastfeeding, breast milk retention results. Swelling starts in your milk sinuses and ducts. Your body responds and you know the rest of the story.

What I want most is for you to prevent yourself from developing breast engorgement, period. You need to be observant and mindful of your breast-feeding techniques. I want you to be on the look-out for any sign that your breast fullness is headed for the engorgement territory. There are some common pitfalls that tired, exhausted mothers get themselves into. Make sure that your spouse or partner understands the basics of breastfeeding to help you through in the beginning.

By following these measures you should prevent breast engorgement from making you a target:

➤ *Supplements* of water or baby formula must not be used for three to four weeks, unless your physician specifically orders it.

➤ Every 24-hour period you should breastfeed 8 to 12 times. You must practice this for at least your first 10 to 14 days after childbirth.

➤ Express your breast milk with a medical-grade piston breast pump if you miss any feedings or your baby won't breastfeed.

➤ Should you decide to wean, it must be gradual.

Can I Still Breastfeed?

Your baby will continue to breastfeed when you experience breast fullness. Your baby will be able to grasp the areola in its mouth. Suckling will be effective and efficient. Your breasts should be emptied following each breastfeeding.

Lactation Lingo

To **supplement** means to fill in, add to, or supply when a deficiency is present. Offering expressed breast milk, baby formula, or water to a baby along with breastfeeding are all examples of supplementation.

Nursing Mom's Notes

Eight to 12 breastfeeding sessions every 24 hours should reduce or prevent any engorgement. Follow this pattern for your first 14 days of breastfeeding. If you can't make eight for any reason, use a medical-grade electric piston breast pump to express your breast milk and meet your minimum.

Breast engorgement, on the other hand, causes the opposite scenario. Your baby will not be able to grasp your areola in its mouth. Your baby can only grasp your nipple. Unable to compress your milk sinuses, your baby will not get milk. There's food in your pantry but your baby just can't get to it. Obviously this makes for a very frustrated and fretful baby.

To breastfeed while engorged you must help to express your breast milk before a feeding. You can manually express milk from your areola with your thumb and fore-fingers. You might find, though, that a medical-grade piston breast pump can be adjusted to a minimum vacuum and will apply intermittent suction similar to your baby. This will help to soften your areola and start the flow of milk.

Remember the consequences if you don't relieve engorgement through breastfeeding, manual expression, or the use of an electric piston breast pump. The retention of milk in your breasts will have negative results. Your milk production will diminish and eventually stop.

Lactation Lingo

Ligaments are strong fibrous tis-sue bands connecting the bones of the body. Coopers' ligaments are triangularly-shaped ligaments that lie under the breast tissue.

Breast Beware

Use of an electric breast pump to relieve engorgement with sustained vacuum and high pressures will cause further breast-tissue and nipple damage. Your electric breast pump used for engorgement must have an intermittent suction release and a minimum vacuum setting.

Now Try This

There's no denying that engorgement can be a very miserable experience for you. And who wants to be miserable when you're celebrating the birth of your new baby? You can expect some of these symptoms with engorgement:

➤ Hard, firm breasts

➤ Reddened skin

➤ Tight, shiny skin

➤ Low-grade fever

➤ Nipple trauma

Your breast engorgement may last about three to seven days, depending on the severity of your condition. During this time you should wear a properly-fitted bra 24 hours a day. Yes, you should sleep in it. I highly recommend an all-cotton bra that offers breathability and that absorbs moisture. You must support your enlarged breast tissue without causing more pain and undue stress from stretched *ligaments*.

Expect to use at least one of the following techniques along with plenty of breastfeeding to help empty your milk during engorgement:

➤ **A medical-grade electric piston breast pump.** This is a must if your baby is not breastfeeding well enough to soften at least one of your breasts.

➤ **Hand expression.** This will help to soften your areola and help your baby to latch on.

➤ **Massage, massage, massage.** This will help start the flow of milk, stimulate let-down, and encourage the flow of milk along the ducts and out through your nipple.

You should expect any comfort measures to help but not necessarily relieve your engorgement entirely. Cold packs applied to your breasts after breastfeeding will help to reduce the blood flow in the affected area. A cold source will also feel very good to you.

You might try any of these cold sources for relief:

➤ Reusable ice packs

➤ Bag of crushed ice

➤ Bag of frozen vegetables

➤ Unused disposable diaper soaked in water, shaped, and frozen

➤ Chilled cabbage leaves

Try to place a dry washcloth or kitchen towel against your breast when using ice packs or crushed ice to prevent skin irritation.

Warm packs may not be a great source of relief and can actually aggravate your swelling. Severe engorgement may only feel better when you lie flat on your back. This helps shift the weight of your breasts and distributes the fluid a little better.

LactFact

Cabbage leaves have been reported to relieve engorgement and offer pain relief. For many years, cabbage has been used in Europe to treat swelling and edema on the body. Chopped-up leaves are applied as a poultice to the afflicted body part and wrapped with a towel. To treat engorgement, refrigerated cabbage (Brassica oleracea) leaves are applied around the breast with the nipple exposed. They are left in place for about 20 minutes. Whether it's the coolness or a component in the cabbage has yet to be determined, but the results are positive. Symptoms of engorgement have been relieved in as quickly as two hours!

Your Feeding Plan

It is best for you to breastfeed your baby as much as possible during the engorgement period. Your baby is the best source of stimulation and suckling for your breasts. You can push, pull, and squeeze all you like, but your baby can usually do it better.

Getting your baby to grasp and latch on to your engorged breast will be your biggest challenge. Try some of these techniques before breastfeeding your baby:

➤ Hand express breast milk from your areola. Your milk sinuses may be very full. This will help to soften your breasts for your baby to attach.

➤ Use your hands and massage your breasts. Do this before and throughout your breastfeeding session.

➤ Try some relaxation techniques including breathing deeply, playing soft music, and breastfeeding in a darkened room.

➤ Take a warm shower to help you relax. Try to empty the breast with hand expression.

➤ Bathe your breast in a bowl of warm water before the start of breastfeeding.

➤ Apply a source of warmth to your breast for two to five minutes. A moist towel, a washcloth, or a disposable diaper soaked in warm water should help.

➤ Use a medical-grade piston breast pump to soften your areola, draw out your nipple, and start the flow of milk.

Remember once your baby is positioned and latched on to your breast, let your baby breastfeed until completely satisfied. Your baby will release from your breast. Try the following after breastfeeding your baby:

1. Apply a cold compress to your breast. It will help to reduce the swelling in your breast. It will also feel good.

2. Consider taking a mild pain reliever such as acetaminophen or ibuprofen. Both will help with swelling and offer mild pain relief.

Nursing Mom's Notes

Mild analgesics can be taken immediately before breastfeeding or after a breastfeeding session is finished. Ibuprofen, acetaminophen, and codeine will not peak in the breast milk for about 30 minutes.

If your baby does not latch on to your breast because of the swelling from your engorgement, you will need assistance with breastfeeding. This means you will have to express your milk every two to three hours. Hand expression is possible but you won't get the vacuum source. You will get the best results using a medical-grade piston breast pump. Engorgement is a medical condition that you must treat with the use of medical equipment. Until your baby does latch on to your breast, you will need to express your milk after your attempt at breastfeeding.

You have been misinformed if any health care professional advises you not to express your milk with a breast pump during engorgement. Such a health care professional does not understand the pathology and appropriate management of engorgement. He or she may indicate that you will cause too much milk to produce. This is not the case. Overproduction of breast milk will not happen during the engorgement period. Your production has actually stopped along the assembly line. You will only pump long enough to make your breasts comfortable. You will remove the milk that your baby cannot or will not. This type of pumping will not produce an oversupply of breast milk.

If your baby will not latch on to your breast and feed, you should consider the use of alternative feeding methods to give your baby any expressed breast milk. You should try not to use a bottle with an artificial teat. This may allow your baby to develop a preference to bottle-feeding and will not encourage breastfeeding. Consider these feeding alternatives for giving expressed breast milk during this time:

➤ Finger feeding

➤ Eyedropper

➤ Supplemental device

You should start to see an improvement in your engorgement within three to seven days. Breastfeeding should get easier once you get past your big hurdles. It's best that you not face this situation alone. Get some professional lactation help as soon as possible to get you back up and breastfeeding.

The Least You Need to Know

➤ It is typical to experience breast fullness when breast milk production increases. It is not typical to experience breast engorgement.

➤ Engorgement results from infrequent and ineffective breastfeeding.

➤ Avoid supplements of water and baby formula, unless ordered by your physician or health care provider.

➤ You should use a medical-grade piston breast pump with minimum vacuum and intermittent suction, with engorgement. You should use it before or following each breastfeeding attempt.

➤ Cold therapies can relieve engorgement better than heat sources can.

➤ Consider alternative feeding methods when providing your baby with expressed breast milk.

Chapter 24

Unique Nipples

In This Chapter

➤ Variations in breast nipples

➤ Nipple preparations for breastfeeding

➤ Testing yourself for nipple variations

➤ Use of products for nipple correction

➤ Breastfeeding with your unique nipples

Just like feet and hands, breasts and nipples can come in all shapes and sizes. Every living being is designed with variations. That's what makes us unique.

You may have taken a look at your breasts and nipples and declared, "There's no way that this will work in a baby's mouth!" Well, you'd be surprised about what Mother Nature has already planned for. Breastfeeding with what you've got is very possible, especially if you have some variations to your nipple shape and size.

What's Happened Here?

It is helpful during your pregnancy to determine what type of breast nipple you have. This way you won't be surprised or concerned when the time comes to start breast-feeding. The nipples of most women can be classified as the following types:

➤ Everted   ➤ Dimpled

➤ Flat   ➤ Inverted

Nipple variations.

NIPPLE VARIATIONS

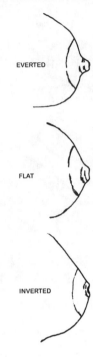

EVERTED

FLAT

INVERTED

A nipple that flattens or pulls inward when compressed is being drawn inward by adhesions. These adhesions are bands of tissue that keep a steady tension within your nipple tissue. These adhesions are a unique design in your body's anatomy. Don't be alarmed, though, because a flatness or inversion may not present a problem to you with breastfeeding. The influence of your hormones during pregnancy can often help to soften or loosen these adhesions. But some corrective action can be taken if you choose before you deliver as well as once you begin your breastfeeding.

Your health care provider really should examine you during your prenatal visits for any variations in your breasts, areolas, and nipples. This exam of your breasts and nipples should take place during the third trimester of your pregnancy. Your health care provider can take this opportunity to discuss and answer your prenatal breastfeeding concerns. If you have flat or *inverted* nipples, your provider will make any recommendations to you for prenatal preparation. Your health care provider may also refer you to a lactation professional for further evaluation and instruction.

Lactation Lingo

An **inverted** nipple is one that folds completely inward within the breast tissue.

If you haven't been fortunate to have a breast exam during your prenatal visit, you can try to check for yourself. This quick test for nipple type should take only a few minutes:

1. Stand in front of a mirror with your breasts exposed. Exposure to the air may be enough to tell if your nipples protrude or evert.

2. Squeeze gently about one inch behind your nipple with your thumb and forefinger. This represents the location where your baby will grasp your areola with its gums.

3. Determine if your nipple everts, flattens, dimples, or inverts.

4. If your nipple appears flat, gently pull it outward to see how it will respond when your baby grasps it in its mouth.

5. Repeat this check with your other nipple.

If you find that your nipples do not extend outward or cannot be pulled outward, it may be best that you take some corrective action.

Once you determine the results of your test, an attempt can be made to correct any nipples that are flat, dimpled, or inverted before your delivery. You may approach your health care provider or lactation professional for further assistance with any corrective action you choose to pursue.

You could also choose to do nothing and wait it out. See what your baby will do once latched on to your breast. I've seen some nipples that were totally inverted become totally everted just from a baby's suckling.

Can I Still Breastfeed?

Keep in mind that oftentimes the case of nipple flatness, dimpling, and inversion will correct itself from the beginning to the end of your pregnancy. Hormones, especially relaxin, can play an important role in softening ligaments, *adhesions,* and skin elasticity. This natural relaxation of the nipple tissue helps with first-time breastfeeding.

Breast Beware

You shouldn't twist, pull, roll, or squeeze your nipples to correct flattened, dimpled, or inverted nipples.

Nursing Mom's Notes

You can perform your nipple test after you step out of the shower in the morning.

Lactation Lingo

An **adhesion** is a band of tissue that keeps a steady tension between or within the body.

The degree or severity of a true nipple inversion may not affect your baby's ability to breastfeed effectively. Your baby may be able to grasp your areola and easily draw your inverted nipple far back into its mouth. Nipple inversion often gets a whole lot better with a second or third baby that you may have. Don't think that flat, dimpled, or inverted nipples will impair or prevent you from breastfeeding. And don't let someone tell you that you won't be able to breastfeed, either.

Your health care provider should carefully examine your nipples if they are flat or inverted. This is a type of nipple that is nonprotractile. In other words, it doesn't protrude outward from its base. Your doctor will want to follow your progress with this nipple type. Your pediatrician or family physician will also want to follow your infant's weight gain and ability to latch on to your breast.

The biggest breastfeeding challenge that you may face is latch-on to your breast. The other possible problem with flat, dimpled, or inverted nipples is that you may experience some soreness if your nipple isn't drawn far enough into your baby's mouth. Keep in mind that once you stimulate your milk supply, any fullness or engorgement may stretch and flatten the best of anyone's nipples. When flattening occurs, you may be so preoccupied with getting your baby to latch on that positioning gets totally forgotten. This can result in nipple soreness.

Breast Beware

You may experience some soreness with flat, dimpled, or inverted nipples if your nipple isn't drawn far enough into your baby's mouth while breastfeeding.

Breast Shells

You can try to correct your flat, dimpled, or inverted nipples by wearing breast shells. A breast shell is a plastic, dome-shaped cup that can separate into two pieces. It has holes for aeration. When placed over your breast, the back of the shell applies gentle pressure to your areola. Your nipple is pushed through a center opening about the size of a nickel. It is held in place while wearing a bra.

Try the Ameda® breast shell to correct flat or inverted nipples.

(Source: Hollister, Inc.)

You should wear breast shells during your last trimester of pregnancy. It is contraindicated to wear them if you are at risk for preterm labor or have experienced any uterine contractions. The stimulation from the shell's pressure may cause the release of oxytocin and cause subsequent contractions. You should begin by wearing a shell for one to two hours during the day. Gradually you can increase your wearing time to all day. You should not wear them while sleeping at night.

You can also wear your breast shells before feeding your baby. Put them in place about a half an hour before breastfeeding. If you collect any milk in the cup, you can save it as long as it's less than an hour old. You should wash your shells with hot, soapy water after each feeding.

Nursing Mom's Notes

You should begin by wearing a shell for one to two hours during the day. Gradually increase your wearing time to all day. Take them out at night before you sleep.

LactFact

Exercises to help separate adhesions causing retraction or inversion are called Hoffman's exercises. These exercises may only be effective for treating dimpled or inverted nipples if you repeat them several times each day. By placing your index fingers on either side of your nipple and gently pulling outward, your nipple is stretched and everted for a few minutes. By using these exercises just before a breastfeeding, your baby can help to stretch the nipple even further and for a longer period of time.

Expect This

It's not how your nipple looks on the outside that counts. Looks may be deceiving. It's what happens on the inside of your baby's mouth during breastfeeding. As long as you position your baby's mouth well around your areola, the force from suction often draws your nipple outward. You may even see flattened, dimpled, or inverted nipples begin to stand out between feedings.

Your nipple typically stretches or elongates to twice its resting length when it's being suckled. Oftentimes with a good latch-on to your breast your baby can apply a significant amount of suction to decrease the degree of any nipple inversion.

When using a breast pump, particular attention should be given to the breast shield or cup that is applied to your breast and nipple. Your nipple needs to have room to be drawn down into the nipple tunnel. The flare of a breast shield needs to be the correct size for you. An adequate amount of pressure must be applied to your milk sinuses for a milking action to occur.

The overall measurement of an average breast shield has an outer diameter of 68 to 82 millimeters. The depth of the flare in an average breast shield is 35 to 40 millimeters. The breast shield diameter and flare must cover your areola to properly milk the sinuses. The diameter of the center opening is an important feature if you have large nipples. Trying to fit a big nipple in a small hole will bring you ineffective results.

Breast Beware

Don't use a breast shield for pumping that is too small for your nipple. This will cause a rubbing or chafing that can eventually lead to nipple soreness.

The HygieniKit® breast shield, for use with any Ameda® breast pump.

(Source: Hollister, Inc.)

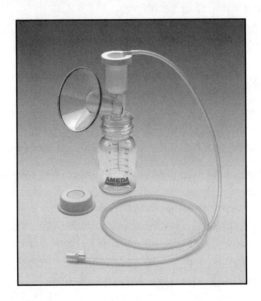

Getting yourself sized with the correct breast shield may be next to impossible. The breast pump industry does not have standard measurements or size ranges to help with your selection. Neither does the lactation field in general. We are lacking measurements and data for nipple, areola, and breast sizes to help establish guidelines for proper fit.

I have thrown together a basic comparison of breast shield measurements on the market today. My rather crude chart should help you with sizing yourself until further data can be gathered. If you have large breasts and large or elongated nipples, you may find the PersonalFit breast shield by Medela appropriate for your needs.

Breast Shield Dimensions

Brand	Flange Diameter	Nipple Tunnel
HygieniKit by Ameda®	78mm	25mm
Breastshield by Medial®	77mm	24mm
PersonalFit by Medela®	87mm	27mm and 30mm
Extra Large Glass by Medela®	40mm	

Your Feeding Plan

When you start your breastfeeding experience, you'll be able to see what kind of successes or challenges your baby has with your nipples. Practicing the basic latch-on techniques that you've learned about so far will help immensely if you have a nipple variation. I have taken each of the nipple varieties and pointed out some of the feeding scenarios that you may encounter.

Large, Elongated Nipples

If you are among the women with nipples that are very large and very long, consider yourself anatomically lucky. The advantage of having an elongated nipple is that it makes for easier breastfeeding. It will stand out at attention without giving you any grief. Lactation consultants tell some mothers that they have "great nipples for breastfeeding."

Sometimes, though, with a small or premature baby, this size of nipple may make for a challenging start to breastfeeding. A small baby may gag or not be able to open wide enough with attempts to latch on. In some instances, your baby may slide to the tip of an elongated nipple, causing eventual nipple soreness.

You need to evaluate your position frequently while breastfeeding. In most cases with elongated nipples, your baby's growth eventually enables a better latch-on to your breast. And oftentimes your baby learns to open wider to pull the nipple and areolar tissue farther back into its mouth.

Flat Nipples

Mothers with flat nipples can try to "exercise" them before use. I'll bet you never knew that exercises for the nipple existed. Well, now you do! A nipple exercise is a tissue-stretching routine that may help to break up any adhesions causing your nipple to invert. It is recommended that you also stretch your nipple before breastfeeding, to help

Nursing Mom's Notes

Place a cold washcloth over your flattened nipple before a breastfeeding. It should react to the chill and stand out better.

elongate the nipple prior to feeding. Additionally, your nipple will stretch from your baby's suckling during your feeding.

You can also help to shape your nipple just before feeding. This works with a flat nipple to help make it protrude better. Place a cold cloth over your nipple to make it react to the chill. The cold might cause it to stand out better.

Inverted Nipples

It is especially important with inverted nipples that after you finish breastfeeding you air-dry your skin before it folds back inward. You can do this by placing your index fingers on either side of your nipple and gently pulling backward. This should expose the nipple tissue to air. It is especially important to air-dry this kind of nipple to prevent any case of nipple soreness.

You can always rely on a breast pump to come to your rescue. Just about any breast pump will do since all you need is some suction. Place the flange of the collection kit or a hand breast pump over your nipple and areola. Apply some vacuum or suction with several cycles to gently draw out your nipple. After a few minutes, you can stop using your pump and bring your baby to your breast to latch on.

Supernumerary Nipples

Supernumerary nipples are accessory nipples or glandular tissue located anywhere along a line between your clavicle and your groin. This line is called the nipple line. An accessory nipple may have an areola and a functional mammary gland. That means that this nipple is capable of producing and releasing breast milk in response to hormonal stimulation.

LactFact

The case of the supernumerary nipple is often an interesting, not to mention funny, discovery. Most women are unaware that they have an "extra" nipple until they begin lactating. A supernumerary nipple is an accessory nipple that can be located anywhere along the nipple line between the clavicle and the groin. It often appears as a skin mole. An accessory nipple will leak or spray breast milk with letdown. Women who report getting soaked from the underside of their breast may discover an extra nipple if they take a look underneath with a hand mirror.

The Least You Need to Know

➤ Variations in breast nipples include flat, dimpled, and inverted nipples. Pregnancy has a way of correcting some nipple variations.

➤ Unique nipples will not impair or prevent you from breastfeeding.

➤ Breastfeeding with flat, dimpled, or inverted nipples may result in soreness if your baby does not draw your nipple far enough into its mouth.

➤ You can wear breast shells before and after pregnancy to help correct flat and inverted nipples.

➤ You can use a breast pump to help draw out flat and inverted nipples before breastfeeding. It's very important to use a breast shield that fits your breast correctly.

Chapter 25

Breast Infection

In This Chapter

➤ Identifying a breast infection

➤ Contributing factors

➤ Taking care of yourself

➤ Getting help from your health care provider

➤ Remedies and medications for getting better

It's a fact of life. Just when you least expect it, you can get sick. Where you got it, nobody knows. But a bug of some sort gets you and makes you feel miserable.

There's a chance that the breastfeeding bug can bite you, a new mother. And it can happen at a very inopportune time. If you're tired, run down, or short on sleep, a breast infection can set in. Understanding the circumstances surrounding a breast infection might help keep you from getting bitten in the first place.

Why Did This Happen?

One of the questions you'll undoubtedly ask yourself is what you have and how you got it in the first place. You may be beside yourself about the circumstances at hand. You've worked so hard to improve your skills. Learning the skill of breastfeeding and certainly the frequency of feedings can make it a challenge for any new mother to stay rested and healthy.

You should know about a few types of infections that you might see with breastfeeding. Some require attention by a health care provider, while others are minor and may only take some simple measures to correct. The infections often seen with breastfeeding include the following:

➤ Nipple bleb

➤ Plugged duct

➤ Mastitis

➤ Yeast infection

I will explain each of these conditions to give you a better idea about what's happened. It may help you identify the circumstances that brought on the condition. In some cases there may not be an explanation for the condition itself.

Nipple Bleb

I want you to know about this condition because it probably happens more often than clinicians get told about. It's a very minor condition with a simple resolution. A nipple bleb is nothing more than a glorified pimple at the tip of your nipple. How you got it may be a question no one can answer.

Breast Beware

You may have a small amount of blood from a nipple bleb when it opens and drains. It is not harmful to your baby if swallowed while breastfeeding.

Remember that a pimple is a pore that's stopped up with oil from your skin, along with some dead skin cells. A nipple bleb appears as a pimple at the end of your nipple. It may be filled with oil, dead skin cells, and residual breast milk.

If residual breast milk remains in your nipple pore and is not emptied, it forms a collection of milk debris. This results in the bleb that you see on the end of your nipple. It is a plug in your nipple pore. You may only realize that you have this bleb if you feel a soreness or tenderness at the tip of your nipple. You may have to use a mirror to see this bleb.

Plugged Ducts

I'll come right out now and say that you will not be able to see a plugged milk duct. You will only be able to feel it. A plugged duct is similar to a nipple bleb. Instead of the nipple pore, you get the accumulation of oil, dead skin cells, and residual breast milk in your milk ducts. This "plug" causes your milk duct to react with swelling and a mild irritation.

Oftentimes you can have a very sore area of your breast. It may also feel lumpy. This area may be small or large depending on the size of the duct and the area of your breast that's affected. The surface of your skin may be reddened over the area where the plugged duct is located. This area may also feel warm if you touch it.

You may experience a plugged duct at any time during your breastfeeding. It may be in the first weeks or months of your breastfeeding. It usually results from an ineffective emptying of your breast where residual milk is retained in your breast. This may happen if you switch your baby to your other breast when your first breast wasn't emptied completely.

It may also happen as a result of a missed feeding or taking a long pause between your feedings. A very tight bra or a bra with an underwire can impair your flow of milk and help to cause a plugged duct. A limited amount of fluid consumption as well as some dehydration may also make you susceptible to developing plugged ducts.

Mastitis

This type of breast infection is seen in about one fourth of breastfeeding mothers. It is often experienced in the first weeks and months of breastfeeding. It may result from a plugged milk duct.

You'll know that you have *mastitis* when you feel like your body has been pulled inside out. You'll feel like the flu has set in. Your arms and shoulders will ache and you may develop fever and chills. A headache may result and you may get some nausea and vomiting. Some moms have said they feel like they've been run over by a truck.

This kind of infection usually involves one of your breasts. Your breast may become reddened, swollen, and very sore in the affected area. A crack in your nipple may have invited a bacterium to infect this particular area of your breast. A plugged milk duct that didn't improve may have progressed into mastitis. Wearing too tight of a bra, stress, or exhaustion may put you in a position to develop this type of infection.

Lactation Lingo

Mastitis is an infection in the breast tissue that produces tenderness, redness, and heat. It also produces flu-like symptoms of fever and muscle weakness.

Yeast Infection

This is a fungal infection of the nipples or breast, caused by yeast. This type of yeast can cause nipple thrush as well as ductal candidosis. The culprit is oftentimes the *Candida albicans* fungus. If the source of yeast fungus is in your baby's mouth, it can spread quite easily to your nipples. It can also develop further into an infection of the mammary ducts. This is known as ductal candidosis.

Nipple thrush can develop several weeks or months after breastfeeding has been started. Your breastfeeding proceeds without any complaints until your nipples suddenly begin to redden and become tender. Sometimes your skin may flake and the skin on and around your nipples may itch. A rash may develop and your nipples may begin to burn.

Your baby may have gotten a yeast infection while delivering through your birth canal. Some women can have a mild yeast infection during pregnancy and not know it. You may have received an antibiotic during your labor, or you may have gotten an antibiotic through your intravenous fluid after a cesarean delivery. Antibiotics can cause an overgrowth of yeast in your body. Some women can be yeast carriers and may have experienced a yeast infection prior to pregnancy.

These are all possible causes for developing a yeast infection of the breast or nipple. A fungal infection of the breast or nipple can be very frustrating for you while breastfeeding. It will be important for you to recognize it and seek appropriate treatment before your condition worsens, and before it's progressed too far for you to resolve.

Breast Beware

Doctors often use antibiotics following cesarean section delivery and for any vaginal or uterine infection. Antibiotics often kill off good bacteria. This can contribute to an overgrowth of "normal" yeast in the body and cause a yeast infection.

Can I Still Breastfeed?

Your biggest concern with continuation of breastfeeding is whether you will transmit any infection to your baby. The answer to your question is that an infection of the breast probably will not affect your baby because it is not an infection of the breast milk.

Nursing Mom's Notes

Make sure that you get plenty of rest if you feel yourself getting run down. Eat a well-balanced diet and drink plenty of fluids. This can help ward off an infection.

It's important to understand that an infection of the breast or the nipple will probably only affect you. The exception to this is a yeast infection. If your baby passed the fungus to you then the probability is high that you will continue to pass the infection back and forth to each other. This will continue until the both of you are treated.

The overall answer about whether you can still breastfeed is "yes." Even with a yeast infection, breastfeeding can continue. In many cases it is essential that you continue to breastfeed with any breast infection, to help improve the underlying cause for the infection in the first place. If ineffective or infrequent emptying of the breast was the probable cause for your infection, then breastfeeding, and lots of it, can only improve your circumstances.

Your biggest challenge with continuing to breastfeed with a breast infection will be to bear with any symptoms associated with it. The flu-like symptoms of mastitis can be downright challenging to anyone, let alone to a new mother. Any pain associated with a nipple or ductal yeast infection would make any breastfeeding mother ask if she should remain loyal to breastfeeding.

If your health care provider tells you or suggests that you cannot breastfeed with any breast infection, you'll probably want to get a second opinion. If you stop your breastfeeding suddenly, your condition could worsen and become more difficult to treat. Any health care provider who tells you to stop breastfeeding with an infection may be misinforming you. Ask another provider or follow up with your lactation professional.

Breast Beware

Stopping "cold turkey" once breastfeeding is established is a sure way of getting a breast infection. If you are told to "just stop" breastfeeding, the person providing this misinformation is responsible for any infection you develop.

If you are unfortunate enough to get a breast infection while breastfeeding, don't stop breastfeeding until you have all the information in hand. Please use the information that I have provided to help any health care provider understand the circumstances surrounding breast infections and breastfeeding. You can continue to breastfeed as well as seek appropriate treatment for some of these infections.

Remedies

There are some measures you can take to help remedy these ailments. While some remedies you can use at home, you might need to seek further evaluation from your health care provider or lactation professional for other remedies.

Deleting Blebs

A nipple bleb may be quite sore and somewhat painful with your breastfeeding. After all, it is a clogged pore in your nipple that's similar to a pimple. You may see a white spot on the end of your nipple that's similar in appearance to a whitehead.

If you can see your nipple pore swollen with a white substance, you may want to try to open it. Try the following steps to do this:

1. Use a warm washcloth or some source of warm, moist heat.
2. Apply it to your affected nipple about 15 minutes before you expect to breastfeed. This should help to open and loosen the pore.
3. You can try to open the plug with a sterile needle.
4. A slight amount of bleeding may result once opened, but it will not cause any harm to your baby if swallowed.

Unplugging Blocked Milk Ducts

A plugged milk duct may happen for a variety of reasons. Mothers with these circumstances might expect to experience them more often:

- ➤ High milk volume
- ➤ Breastfeeding multiples
- ➤ Tightly fitted bra
- ➤ Dehydration
- ➤ Stress and fatigue
- ➤ Consuming supplements or multivitamins

If you experience one or more of these, you may be prone to developing plugged milk ducts. It may take you two or three days to improve your flow of breast milk and to relieve the symptoms of plugged milk ducts. It's important to attempt to correct and improve the circumstances so that it doesn't develop into mastitis.

Expect the area of your breast where the plugged duct is located to be sore, reddened, and generally uncomfortable. You will want to use gentle massage and to apply some moist heat over your breast area. You might have some slight discomfort or localized pain that results before and during your breastfeeding.

Curing Mastitis

Getting quick and appropriate treatment for mastitis helps for this breast infection to be short-lived. It may be for only 24 hours that you experience the worst of your symptoms. You'll want to get prompt and proper attention toward your circumstances. If you can identify the cause of your infection, you may reduce your chance of having a reoccurrence.

Nursing Mom's Notes

The symptoms of mastitis usually last 24 to 48 hours. Take care of yourself just as you would with the flu. Confine yourself to bed for rest and sleep. Breastfeed your baby in bed. Drink hot and cold liquids, and eat to satisfy your appetite.

You can definitely expect flu-like symptoms with your mastitis. You may experience any of the following:

- ➤ Fever
- ➤ Chills
- ➤ Headache
- ➤ Aches
- ➤ Nausea
- ➤ Vomiting

This breast infection usually involves one breast, but may include both of your breasts in some cases. The infected area of your breast may be reddened and inflamed as a result of your infection. You will not feel good and should expect it to take 24 to 48 hours to start seeing your condition improve.

Expect a visit to your health care provider to diagnose this infection. It can't be treated over the telephone. Your physician or health care provider may want to treat this breast infection with an antibiotic. Antibiotics are usually prescribed for this type of breast infection, but may not be absolutely necessary. Some infections caused by a virus are not treatable with any medication. Time will take its course and symptoms will improve. Many women have experienced mastitis and had their condition improve without taking a prescribed antibiotic. The concern here is that antibiotics can lead to a yeast infection, the number-one breast infection on your list to avoid.

Treating Yeast Infections

A yeast infection of your breast may involve the surface of your nipple skin, your milk ducts, or both. You can expect many health care providers to be rather skeptical about whether a yeast infection of the breast even exists. Lactation professionals are the ones who have documented many mothers' symptoms of probable fungal infections of the mammary gland. The challenge has been to prove the existence of yeast in these mothers' milk ducts.

LactFact

Candida albicans is the yeast that causes candidiasis, or a yeast infection, of the nipples, the areola, or the milk ducts. When it occurs orally it is referred to as Monilia, or thrush. This yeast normally lives in the stomach, intestines, genitals, and urinary tract. It also occurs naturally on the skin. Antibiotics can trigger an overgrowth of the body's yeast. Treatment for yeast overgrowth includes an antifungal cream, exposure to air and sunlight, as well as washing and boiling any undergarments or breastfeeding products that come in contact with the breast or breast milk.

A yeast infection can probably be diagnosed based on your symptoms alone. An infected nipple may appear bright red or mildly pink, with flaking skin and some mild swelling. You may experience some stinging, itching, or burning that continues between each of your breastfeedings. Changes in your baby's position at the breast will not improve the discomfort that you feel.

Pain in your milk ducts will be the symptom that you experience when your yeast infection develops within the ducts of your breasts. This pain often occurs with each breastfeeding. You may feel a pain that will shoot through your breast and cause a burning sensation with the letdown of your breast milk. Some women describe the pain feeling like shards of glass in their breast. It's very important to have your health care provider evaluate any persistent breast pain that you may experience. Sometimes a breast infection can be a fungal infection also combined with a bacterial infection.

You and your baby should both be treated if a yeast infection is identified. Many times the course of action for an itchy or reddened nipple is an antifungal cream. This will kill the fungus responsible for your infection. An antifungal is often available over-the-counter in many pharmacies and drugstores. Your health care provider should tell you how often and how long you should use the antifungal cream. You should spread the cream over the affected area of your nipple and areola. Some women prefer to wipe it off before breastfeeding.

If your infection is located inside your milk ducts, the best course of treatment is an antifungal medication in a pill form. This is often the fastest and most effective treatment for a ductal yeast infection. An infection within the mammary gland may be best treated with an oral medication. That's why your health care provider may prescribe an oral medication for you.

The medication of choice to treat a fungal infection in the milk ducts is an "Azole," such as clotrimazole, miconazole, or ketoconazole. Treatment typically lasts 14 to 28 days. The dosage amount is probably not enough to treat your baby, too. Therefore, your baby must be treated separately.

Gentian violet has also been long used as a fungicide to treat yeast infections. It comes from the root of the *Gentiana lutea* plant. It is not a prescription medication and is available over the counter. You can paint this purple solution on your nipple and areola. You typically use it once a day for about three to seven days. It stains whatever it comes in contact with, so plan to wear an old bra and some dark clothing.

Nursing Mom's Notes

Gentian violet is a fungicide available over the counter and is inexpensive. It will stain anything and everything it contacts. Wear some dark or old clothing if you use this antifungal for your yeast infection.

Your Feeding Plan

It will be very important to continue to breastfeed your baby if you experience any of these breast infections. The key to a quick recovery will be to increase the frequency and length of your feeding sessions.

You may want to try these steps for breastfeeding with a nipple bleb or plugged milk duct:

1. Take off or stop wearing your bra, especially if it's too tight or an underwire.
2. Plan to breastfeed about every two hours. Allow your baby to feed from the breast that's got the plug or bleb.

3. Use a warm, wet washcloth and hold it against your breast about 15 minutes before you breastfeed. Massage your breast thoroughly before as well as during your breastfeeding.

4. Drink more liquids such as water, juice, and milk. You should urinate more frequently with pale yellow urine after you do this.

5. Try to use different breastfeeding positions so that your baby empties your affected breast. This will enable better emptying of breast milk through the milk duct and gland.

6. Get some rest. You may not be getting an adequate amount of rest and sleep. You should probably kick back and turn your notch down a few paces.

Your feeding plan with a breast infection like mastitis requires frequent breastfeeding, and possibly the use of a piston breast pump to improve the emptying of your breasts. You'll want to follow a few of the suggested steps to improve from a bout of mastitis:

1. Get your rest and sleep in bed. You should plan for at least 48 hours of bedtime. You will breastfeed in bed during this time. Use the side-lying position and the football hold for breastfeeding.

2. You will need to breastfeed at least every two hours. Do not just stop breastfeeding your baby if you are advised to do so. Your breastfeeding should be as long as it takes for your breasts to feel empty. Remember to take your time.

3. Use a warm, moist washcloth held to your breasts for about 15 minutes, before you breastfeed. Massage your breasts well, before and during a breastfeeding. This will help to stimulate a good emptying of breast milk.

4. Consider the use of a medical-grade piston breast pump to follow each breastfeeding. This will ensure that you have adequately emptied your breasts with each feeding.

5. Drink many fluids to increase the amount of urine that you pass. Fluids are especially important if you've had a high fever or have become dehydrated.

6. Contact your health care provider if your symptoms don't improve within 24 hours. Thoroughly discuss any need for an antibiotic. Your physician may recommend a fever reducer and mild analgesic for your symptoms.

In many cases where you have a yeast infection of your breast, any pain that you experience may preclude you from wanting to breastfeed. You may find that the only comfortable approach is to express your breast milk using a medical-grade piston breast pump. This enables you to maintain a good stimulation and a thorough emptying of your breasts while you and your baby get treatment for this fungal infection.

You may want to follow this course of action for breastfeeding with a fungal infection:

1. Get plenty of rest and sleep. You'll be able to improve your condition when you have the right amount of rest.

2. You should eat a well-balanced diet. When you don't consume the proper amounts of nutrients you increase your risk for infection. Reduce your consumption of sugars.

3. Wear an all-cotton bra and launder it in hot water. You may add some bleach or vinegar to the rinse water. This will help to kill the yeast spores and keep the fungus from residing in your undergarments.

4. Use reusable breast pads of cotton and change them whenever they become damp or wet. Launder them in hot water and add bleach or vinegar to the rinse water.

5. If you are using bottles with artificial teats or nipples to feed your baby, they must be washed thoroughly and boiled daily to prevent the fungus from spreading. Consider throwing away any teats, latex nipples, or pacifiers that may be the source of contamination.

6. Seek appropriate treatment from your health care provider or lactation professional. Both you and your baby need to be treated to prevent the fungus from being passed back and forth to each other.

The Least You Need to Know

➤ You will be able to continue breastfeeding with any breast infection.

➤ Plugged milk ducts and mastitis may result from incomplete and infrequent emptying of milk from your breasts.

➤ Rest, sleep, and plenty of fluids are self-care measures you can take with any infection.

➤ Using a medical-grade piston breast pump will increase your frequency and effectiveness of breast milk expression.

➤ Both you and your baby need treatment to keep a yeast infection from being passed back and forth.

Chapter 26

Baby Says No

In This Chapter

➤ Reasons your baby won't breastfeed

➤ Reducing your baby's chance for breast refusal

➤ Alternative feeding options

➤ Feeding breast milk without breastfeeding

Everyone would probably agree that the most disappointing experience with breast-feeding is when a baby won't suckle from the mother's breast. They just don't, won't, or refuse to breastfeed under any circumstances. No matter what we do, it just does not seem to work.

In a private practice setting as a lactation consultant, I have been challenged with the parents who come for help to get their babies to breastfeed. While everyone's circumstances are different, there are some factors that may contribute to a baby's refusal to breastfeed. I'll point out to you what may cause your baby to refuse to breastfeed as well as the choices you can make to help get your baby back on the track to breast-feeding.

What's Happened Here?

The first question parents will ask is what has caused their baby not to breastfeed. You know by now that it's instinctual for a baby to suckle, and that most babies will breastfeed. Identifying the exact reason that a baby refuses to breastfeed may be diffi-cult to pinpoint, but there are some factors that help a baby say "no."

Milk from a Bottle

It seems that just about any baby who gets several feedings from a bottle in the first few days after birth will prefer this feeding method over time. It may be a matter of *imprinting,* which means allowing a pattern or figure to be repeatedly available over time. Whether it's breast milk or baby formula in the bottle, a baby who learns to suck from a bottle seems to prefer that method over time.

I've explained in the first chapters how a baby learns the skill of breastfeeding. The baby coordinates its jaws, the muscles of its mouth, and its tongue to stimulate and remove milk from the breast. When feeding from a bottle, it doesn't take much to get the liquid out. With the help of gravity and some suction, a baby can easily empty the contents from a bottle.

Lactation Lingo

Imprinting means to fix or impress permanently, as on the mind.

Parents may tell me that when they gave their breastfeeding baby a bottle, it was sucked right down. Well, that's right. A breastfeeding baby given liquid from a bottle doesn't have to follow through the steps of latch-on, stimulation, milk production, and milk removal. The contents in the bottle have already been prepared and there's simply no food prep to do. The stimulation and compression of the milk sinuses doesn't have to happen. All that a baby needs to do is suck and swallow.

So, a baby who's given bottle feedings in the first days of breastfeeding will probably take to this easier method of feeding. And that method is usually bottle-feeding whether it's breast milk or baby formula. If this action is repeated, then it becomes learned. Again, it can become an imprinted method. With an artificial nipple supported in its mouth, a baby simply applies suction and controls the flow of milk with its tongue. Now if you try to get your baby to latch on to your breast and use its tongue to suckle, the confusion sets in. This is what's referred to as nipple confusion.

Breast Beware

Offering a pacifier to a baby in the first weeks of breastfeeding may cause nipple confusion. A baby misses a nutritive breastfeeding when sucking on a pacifier. A baby should be imprinted with suckling from the breast to ensure frequent feedings and to avoid nipple confusion.

Pacifiers

Giving a pacifier to a baby is very much like offering a baby a rubber nipple from a bottle. The only thing a baby can do with a pacifier is to support it in its mouth and just suck on it. It's the activity of sucking then that pacifies or helps to calm a baby.

The results of sucking on a pacifier, then, will not yield a food source. A baby can only suck on a pacifier and can't use its tongue to stroke and suckle like it does to the breast. If your baby learns only to suck, it may prefer not to follow through with the suckling activity necessary for breastfeeding. The preference may be to just suck and the results may be a refusal to breastfeed.

LactFact

A cleft lip is a fissure or a split defect in the skin that develops during pregnancy. It may be surgically repaired in the first month after birth. The breast can actually fill in the gap, enabling the baby to suckle quite well. A cleft palate is an opening in the roof of the mouth. This defect may involve the soft or hard palate inside the mouth. This, too, develops during pregnancy. The possibility of breastfeeding with a cleft lip or palate depends on the type and size of the opening. The baby may need a device that seals off its nose from the mouth to create negative pressure for breastfeeding.

Mouth's Design

There could possibly be some differences in the design or shape of your baby's mouth. These differences alone can contribute significantly to whether or not your baby is even able to breastfeed.

The following anatomical features may contribute to a baby's inability or refusal to breastfeed:

➤ Arch in the mouth

➤ Tight frenulum

➤ Cleft palate

➤ Cleft lip

It will be extremely essential to identify any of these differences in your baby's oral cavity to determine if they cause your baby to refuse breastfeeding.

Nursing Mom's Notes

The white patches from thrush can be found on your baby's tongue, gums, or mucus membranes inside the mouth. The white patch may cover the tongue in a thin film. You won't be able to wipe it away.

Thrush

A yeast infection that affects the mucus membranes is known as thrush. The *Candida albicans* fungus can cause it. Your baby can contract it if you have a vaginal yeast infection at the time of your baby's birth. Your baby can also get it from your nipples or milk ducts if you have a breast or nipple yeast infection.

With thrush, your baby may have a diaper rash that's bright red around its buttocks or genitals. Your baby may also have white patches on the mucus membranes of its mouth, gums, or tongue. Look inside your baby's mouth. These ulcerations inside the mouth may make your baby refuse to breastfeed or pull off from the breast. The discomfort inside the mouth quite possibly makes breastfeeding uncomfortable.

The telltale sign of oral thrush—the white patch on the baby's tongue.

(Source: Beth Mark)

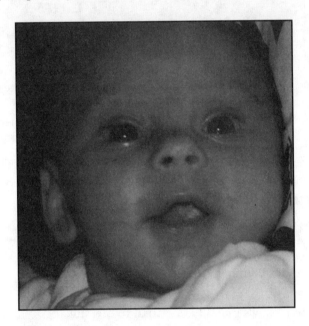

Can I Still Breastfeed?

Obviously the answer to this question about still breastfeeding is, "Well, yes, if my baby would just breastfeed." Breastfeeding will need to take on another form until you can find the reason for your baby's inability or refusal to suckle. You'll need to express your breast milk and offer it to your baby. You'll also need to try to find any reason why your baby may not be breastfeeding and try to resolve it.

Sometimes a baby will start to breastfeed and then suddenly pull off or stop. The baby's cruising right along and then stops dead in its tracks. It may pull off of your breast in a screaming fit or just let go after a good latch-on. This may happen for any of the following reasons:

➤ Full stomach

➤ Gas bubble

➤ A cold

➤ Teething

➤ Sudden, forceful letdown

➤ Different taste

➤ Perfume or soap scent

Nursing Mom's Notes

You might try using a vaporizer or saline drops in your baby's nose to help loosen any congestion from a cold. Babies breathe best through their noses and they like to smell the breast during a feeding.

When a baby has a full stomach, whether from enough food or an air bubble, it's not unusual to respond by pulling off the breast and stopping during a feeding. If your baby needs to pass a bowel movement, it's very likely that your baby will need to focus on the task at hand. Having a bowel movement can help to improve anyone's appetite!

If your baby has a cold, the nose may be stopped up from the swollen membranes or thick secretions. A baby has to be able to breathe through its nose. When the mouth is fastened securely to your breast and its nasal airway is blocked, it can't draw air in readily. It's like going under water and having to surface for a gasp of air. When air won't come in through your nose easily, the only other possibility is through the mouth.

Nursing Mom's Notes

If you have a large flow of milk with letdown, try the lying-down position to breastfeed your baby. You might also try laying flat on your back for breastfeeding. The clutch or football position will also "sit" your baby up to the breast and help with swallowing large amounts of milk.

If your baby has an ear infection, the activity of suckling may pull on the inner-ear canal. This can be quite painful, especially if it is swollen and inflamed. Teething may begin as early as four to six months. The gums may be sore and uncomfortable while breastfeeding. Any other discomfort associated with suckling can cause your baby to be irritable or to refuse to breastfeed.

A sudden flow or gush of milk from your breast can cause your baby to gasp or choke. A large flow of milk is hard to control, so your baby's only choice is to pull away from your breast to breathe. It may not be a refusal to breastfeed but just a temporary adjustment to your flow rate of milk.

Although I don't believe that what you eat causes gas in your baby's stomach or digestive system, it may affect the taste of your milk. Some spices or flavors in your diet may change the usual taste of your milk. Since the overall flavor of your breast milk is sweet, a bitter or sour taste may really disappoint your baby. In other words, what your baby expects in a meal may not be there. The objection comes in the form of refusal or complaining about the breastfeeding. The scent from a soap, lotion, or perfume that you may use could also turn your baby off from breastfeeding. Since smelling your food is an important feature of the dining experience, this could be a real turnoff and decrease the appetite of your baby.

Breast Beware

Disappointment and tears may result if your baby refuses to breastfeed. Find someone to talk to and one who offers support during this challenging time. Consider a consultation with a lactation professional for further evaluation.

When Baby Says No

There are a few basic things to expect when your baby says "no" to breastfeeding. It's possible that the refusal may be temporary or permanent. You should be patient and stick with it long enough to decide whether it's temporary or permanent.

It's probable that there will be some disappointment from you, especially if you had your heart set on breastfeeding. The other disappointment comes from the fact that you may never find out the reason for your baby's refusal to breastfeed. Some of the possibilities for refusing to breastfeed that I pointed out may not be a cause at all. You may say that you followed all the steps to get off to a good start and you still ended up with a baby who says "no" to breastfeeding. I'd have to admit that I would be pretty disappointed, too.

You might expect these things to happen if your baby refuses to breastfeed, whether it's a temporary or permanent refusal:

1. You can try on your own to identify any factors that may have caused your baby to stop breastfeeding. If it is early in your breastfeeding experience, you should try to change any causative factors that you can. If your breastfeeding experience has already been well-established, it may be just a temporary circumstance that's caused your baby to suddenly stop. Teething and introduction of solid foods may be two likely factors.

2. If you can't resolve matters by yourself, you should expect to seek some professional help. This is especially important if you want to try to resume breastfeeding. There may be some techniques and circumstances that an expert in the field of lactation can help you with.

3. Babies with nipple confusion or a preference to bottle-feeding don't change their pattern overnight. You'll need to be patient.

4. You'll need support and understanding from your spouse or partner during this challenging time. You shouldn't have to face this all on your own. Your support system can listen and offer any advise to you at this time.

5. Your maternal instinct may be to blame yourself. You may ask what it was that you did to cause this to happen. You might wonder if you had done something differently whether you'd be faced with this now. Well, there's no need to do this. You should only look forward and try to resolve or make the best of your circumstances.

6. You will probably want to throw in the towel and possibly quit breastfeeding. After all, if your baby does not want to suckle from your breast, you may ask if there's any point to continue. Be certain that you discuss it with your baby's health care provider as well as with your lactation professional before making a decision to quit. You need to have all the facts in hand, as well as professional advice, to make this decision. Many women who have quit on their own often regret not making an informed decision.

Your Feeding Plan

It's a fact that if your baby doesn't want to breastfeed, you will have to resort to another feeding method. But you shouldn't abandon all hope and resign to failure. I've seen and have been told some amazing stories. There have been many babies who have made a complete turnaround and picked up breastfeeding after a temporary refusal or after having been started with bottle-feeding.

This is especially true of premature babies whose only introduction to feeding was from a bottle. Let's face it, if the hospital personnel in the nursery will only use a bottle to give your baby your breast milk, we'll have to live with it. With a little coaxing, patience, and persistence I have seen a premature baby latch on to the breast like it's been breastfeeding from the start. Babies mature over time and this may enable them to learn to suckle quite easily.

Make Your Own Milk

You can definitely choose to express your breast milk and feed it to your baby if your baby won't suckle your breast. If you choose to do this, you'll need to use a medical-grade piston breast pump. This will be your best source of stimulation to your breast. It will also be an efficient means of emptying milk from your breast effectively.

You'll need to express your breast milk at least every two to three hours or as often as your baby has been breastfeeding. This is the frequency that your breast needs stimulation. If you drop below this number, you may risk a decrease in your milk supply. If this happens you may need to consider baby formula to fill in and meet your baby's nourishment.

Remember, when pumping to express breast milk and maintain your milk supply, it's best to use a collection kit that stimulates both breasts. By pumping both of your breasts at the same time, you get a great source of stimulation and help to keep up your milk supply.

By Bottle

After your consideration of cup or finger feeding, you might consider feeding your baby by bottle. Yes, I'll admit I explained at the start of this chapter that bottle-feeding is a factor that may contribute to breast refusal. Under these circumstances, however, you may not have a choice when it comes to your feeding method. If a baby won't breastfeed, one must resort to some means of providing food to a baby.

Nursing Mom's Notes

You can express your breast milk and feed your baby with a bottle if you are not comfortable with cup or finger feeding. Try to use an artificial nipple or teat with a long shaft. Keep offering your baby the opportunity to suckle from your breast.

I have had several clients use the Avent feeding system with their babies and reported good results. The silicone teat or nipple has a long shaft that can be pulled deep into the baby's mouth. This stretchable nipple seems to enable a baby to transition back into breastfeeding with some persistence and patience from the mother.

You may also find that an orthodontic nipple is beneficial to use for bottle-feeding a baby who won't breastfeed. It may help to fit the shape of the mouth but may not keep as much air out of your baby's tummy. You should burp your baby often, as bottle-feeding enables your baby to swallow more air with the feeding.

Feeding Gadgets

Feeding devices are available to use in combination with breastfeeding. These may help your baby to latch on to your breast and assist with feeding. They can help to complement breastfeeding and offer you an alternative in the meantime. The idea behind a feeding gadget is to entice your baby to your breast for a feeding. Once latched on, a reward of breast milk can be offered to satisfy your baby.

Probably the best-known gadget in the lactation arena is the supplementer, such as the Supplemental Nursing System by Medela. This is a device with a container to hold breast milk or baby formula that enables your baby to consume liquid while suckling at the breast. The container is worn around your neck and the small tubing can be taped to your nipple. It works once your baby is latched-on to your breast so that suckling can be rewarded with breast milk. The tubing of the supplementer can also be secured to your finger and used for finger feeding. Once suckling begins, your baby's feeding is complemented with liquid.

Your feeding can also include use of a nipple shield. If your baby has problems getting latched on to your breast, a thin, flexible silicone shield can be placed over your nipple and areola. This can help your baby secure your nipple in its mouth for a breastfeeding. When using a nipple shield, caution must be taken to follow your baby's weight gain. Some babies don't stimulate the breast or empty the milk very well when feeding with a nipple shield. You will want to slowly remove the shield when your baby seems to latch on better with breastfeeding.

Use of an eyedropper or syringe-and-tubing combination is another alternative device for giving your baby breast milk. Some lactation consultants working with helping your baby to breastfeed may suggest this. The advantage is that you can continue to offer your breast milk while trying to reestablish suckling at your breast.

Feeding devices can be cumbersome as well as time consuming for a parent feeding a baby so frequently. It's important for you to make a decision based on what you can do comfortably. You know the amount of patience you have, especially being challenged with a baby who refuses to breastfeed. Decide on a workable plan and know that you can alter it as your circumstances permit as well as change.

Nursing Mom's Notes

Cup feeding enables a baby to sip the liquid rather than to suck it. Nipple confusion is less likely to occur because sipping is different from sucking. Even premature babies can be taught to feed from a cup before they begin to breastfeed.

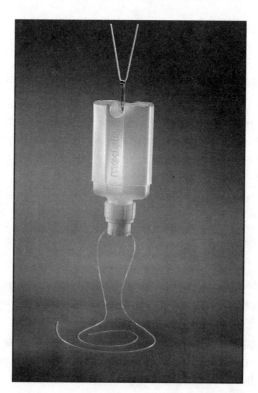

The very popular Supplemental Nursing System™ by Medela®.

(Source: Medela, Inc.)

The Ameda® baby cup for alternative feeding.

(Source: Hollister, Inc.)

The Least You Need to Know

➤ Some babies will take preference to bottle-feeding if it is used repeatedly after birth, and then will not learn breastfeeding.

➤ Allowing a baby to suck on a pacifier during the first weeks of breastfeeding can cause it to refuse to breastfeed. Using a pacifier at this time prevents frequent and nourishing breastfeeding.

➤ The shape of a baby's mouth, an ear infection, or a mouth infection are reasons why a baby may not breastfeed.

➤ You can choose to express your breast milk and give it to your baby with a bottle. If you satisfy your baby with breast milk, you may resume breastfeeding with some patience and time.

➤ Several devices are available to help you breastfeed and give breast milk at the same time. A supplementer enables you to give breast milk while your baby suckles at your breast.

➤ A baby's refusal to breastfeed can be an emotional and disappointing experience for you. Choose what you can handle comfortably and within reason. Find someone who will offer support and allow you to ventilate.

Part 7

Glad You Asked!

No doubt you have some burning questions about breastfeeding. Is it possible for a woman who hasn't been pregnant to actually produce milk? If you stop breastfeeding, can you start up again?

With your baby dependent on you for nourishment, it's important that you watch what you put in your body. Be cautious about any medications or supplements. Anyone with questions about consuming alcohol and smoking should definitely read on.

A few tips and suggestions for a manageable wardrobe are found in this part. Places to go and people to meet are a must once you've mastered the art of breast-feeding.

At any time during your breastfeeding, the need or desire to wean may arise. Circumstances may come up suddenly or you may just decide you want out. It's important that you know your possibilities around weaning. Read on for more information and points to consider.

Chapter 27

Adoptive Nursing

In This Chapter

➤ Breastfeeding your adopted baby

➤ A look at relactation

➤ What to expect with adoptive nursing

➤ Preparations and supplies

➤ Stimulating your milk supply

The practice of breastfeeding an adopted baby has probably been around for years. Sometimes it wasn't a matter of only adoption but of survival. When a mother did not survive childbirth and her baby did, someone had to feed her baby. For many years, the only means of feeding was from the breast of another woman.

In this day and age, we rarely see a mother who dies from complications of childbirth. Our modern health care system offers many screening tests that can help predict any complications of pregnancy. What we do have today are many babies in need of loving, supportive families. When a baby joins a family through adoption, maternal instinct may inspire any mother to want to breastfeed her new baby. So if you've heard about it or wondered if it's possible, read on.

Adoption Basics

Generally speaking, breastfeeding an adopted baby involves the *induction* of breast milk production. This means that someone literally starts from scratch. Lactation can be caused or started with the stimulation of the breasts through the use of herbs or medications, as well as the actual suckling of a baby at the breast.

The literature speaks of women who were able to breastfeed a baby during times of war, famine, and natural disaster. Literally, a woman would pick up an infant or child whose mother had died and put it to her breast. Whether she had breastfed before or never in her life, the breast was stimulated to produce a substance that sustained an infant with its nutritional value.

In situations where extreme stress or desperation prevails, you may see the power of mind over matter. The repeated stimulus to your breasts can result in a breast secretion capable of nourishing an infant. And the added stimulation of an herb or medication can complement the process.

Lactation Lingo

Induction means to produce or cause something to happen or to begin. Induced lactation means to start the production or secretion of breast milk.

LactFact

Cross nursing involves the breastfeeding by a lactating woman of a baby who is not her own. Many cultures outside of Western society practice this. It can sometimes be referred to as surrogate nursing. Cross nursing is similar to adoptive nursing but is usually a temporary circumstance. The baby's mother in situations such as childcare may arrange for cross nursing. A mother who cross nurses will continue breastfeeding her own child in addition to another baby. Cross nursing has been used to stimulate a mother preparing to breast-feed her adoptive baby. The stimuli from an established breastfeeding baby can be an excellent primer for induced lactation.

When we look at breastfeeding an adopted baby, the principles are the same. You welcome a new baby into your arms and become responsible for nourishing and nurturing your baby. You want to give your baby all the love you can possibly provide. What better way than through breastfeeding.

Sometimes, breastfeeding an adopted baby may involve *relactation*. Relactation involves the stimulation of lactation in a woman who did not initially breastfeed after birth. It may also include a mother who resumes breastfeeding after it has been discontinued. By simply reintroducing the stimulus to her breasts and emptying any breast milk that's produced, a mother can resume some form of a milk supply.

A woman does not have to be pregnant or have nursed before to produce breast milk. This is truly an amazing situation. Simply by stimulating the right hormones, a woman is capable of producing breast milk. Remember that the mammary gland is a modified sweat gland. The power of the human brain is such that enough stimuli from the brain can cause some incredible feats by the human body.

Regarding the basics of breastfeeding an adopted baby, the focus should not be on milk production but rather on the relationship that you establish with your baby. The power of human bonding can prevail in a situation where a human baby needs love, shelter, and food.

Lactation Lingo

Relactation is the process of stimulating milk production in a woman who did not initially breastfeed after birth. It can also apply to resuming lactation after it has been discontinued for a certain period of time.

To-Do List

Before you set out to breastfeed an adopted baby it would be best to learn as much about it as you can. More and more mothers who adopt babies want to try to breastfeed them. As with any new task or skill, it's especially important to know what you are up against.

You may find it extremely helpful to contact a health care professional who's supportive of breastfeeding an adopted baby. A lactation professional may offer you a referral to other mothers who have breastfed their adopted babies as well assist you with your preparations. A La Leche League leader may also have some contact information for an adoptive mother.

Nursing Mom's Notes

The focus of breastfeeding an adopted baby is the relationship that you develop and establish. Suckling at the breast can provide the love, shelter, and trust that a baby needs.

You should also talk to your pediatrician or family physician about breastfeeding your adopted baby. This may be met with much speculation from your physician. You physician will consider the health and well-being of your baby, but may not agree with your decision. You could choose to find a physician who is supportive of your decision.

It's important to understand that many adoptive mothers need to supplement their milk supply while they breastfeed their adopted baby. Supplementation may be baby formula. In some cases, a mother may contact a human milk bank for a milk supply for her baby. You can offer it to your baby through a supplementation device at your breast or through finger feeding. See Appendix C, "Resources," for manufacturers of supplementation feeding devices.

In some circumstances, a mother may make arrangements with another breastfeeding mother for a milk supply. I will have to caution you about this. There is a possibility that an infectious disease may be present in this donated milk. Human milk can transmit viruses such as HIV and hepatitis. Don't risk the chance of transmitting any virus to your baby. Strongly consider a milk supply through a human milk bank where donations are screened as in a blood bank practice as well as pasteurized.

Be sure to discuss with your spouse or partner about your decision to breastfeed your adopted baby. You'll not only need support but also input about the feeding choice for your new baby. Make sure that you address all concerns and questions to ensure a positive experience for everyone involved.

It is also extremely important to understand that adoption proceedings may not go as you had planned. I have had several clients consult with me about breastfeeding an adopted baby only to see it end in an emotional nightmare after weeks and months of preparation. So be realistic and upfront with all adoption procedures.

Breast Beware

Don't risk the chance of acquiring a virus such as HIV or hepatitis with a breast milk donation from a friend, acquaintance, or relative. Human breast milk donors should be thoroughly screened and donor breast milk should be properly pasteurized.

Getting Started

Preparing to breastfeed your adopted baby involves some supplies and some effort on your part. There may or may not be an advantage to stimulating your milk supply before your baby arrives. Some lactation consultants and adoptive mothers have differences of opinion. I cannot tell you one preparation works over another.

You should consider these points in your preparation strategy:

Nursing Mom's Notes

Contact a lactation professional or a La Leche League leader who can support and advise you on your decision to breastfeed your adopted baby. He or she may also help you make contact with another adoptive mother who breastfeeds.

➤ Contact a health care professional about adoptive nursing.

➤ Read up on any information about adoptive nursing.

➤ Talk with a mother who has breastfed her adopted baby.

➤ Locate a supplier of medical-grade piston breast pumps.

➤ Begin nipple and breast stimulation with hand massage.

➤ Locate a supplier with a feeding supplementer.

You may want to try to stimulate your milk supply before your new baby is due to arrive. This may only result in stimulating and signaling your mammary gland in preparation of milk secretion. In other words, you may or may not develop colostrum as a result of your stimulation efforts. If you choose to use breast stimulation, you should begin about 8 to 10 weeks before your new baby's due date. You should use a medical-grade piston pump for the best stimulation. A single-pumping accessory kit where you switch between breasts should suffice.

You'll want to start for 5 to 10 minutes of pumping each day for six to eight times throughout your day. Pump each of your breasts. It's possible that you may start to collect a clear or yellowish substance from the stimulation. This is the early milk, or colostrum, that's produced by your breasts. This is a good sign that stimulation is appropriate. Don't worry if you don't see anything, either. You may not get any drops of milk until you actually begin to breastfeed your new baby.

If nothing results from your pumping efforts, you shouldn't feel that it hasn't been worthwhile. Everyone's degree of response can vary; don't be discouraged or doubtful with these early weeks of preparation. Your focus should remain on bonding and establishing a trust between you and your new baby. There's no better way to develop a bond between you and your baby than through suckling at your breast.

The herb called *fenugreek* can also be used in your preparation for a milk supply. It is a galactogogue. It acts to stimulate the breast cells in your mammary gland. Fenugreek is available in the form of capsules, tea, and tinctures. Some mothers report the best results come from a tincture while others say the capsules are most effective.

Breast Beware

Adoption proceedings may not go as planned. All of your preparation, including the stimulation of your milk supply, may come to a sudden halt at any time. This may result in a great deal of disappointment and emotional upset for you.

Lactation Lingo

Fenugreek is an herbal galactogogue. It is a substance capable of stimulating the production of breast milk. You can consume it in the form of a tea, a capsule, or a tincture.

You can choose to take fenugreek in the following ways:

1. You can steep fenugreek seeds into a tea. Allow it to steep for 20 minutes to get the strongest tea. Drink this two to three times each day.

2. You should take two to three capsules of fenugreek three times each day.

3. Add 10 to 15 drops of fenugreek tincture to a hot liquid such as water or an herbal tea. Drink this at least two times each day.

Successful breastfeeding of a newborn baby begins at birth. This includes your adopted baby, too. If possible, you should plan to be present at the time of your baby's delivery. Allow your baby to suckle at your breast as soon as possible after birth. Discuss with any hospital or birth-center personnel, including the lactation consultant, your intentions to breastfeed your adopted baby. Be aware that policies and procedures regarding adoption may not permit you to breastfeed right away. You may have to begin by addressing the legal issues and documents.

Nursing Mom's Notes

The only type of breast pump to use for inducing your milk supply is a medical-grade piston breast pump. Other breast pumps will not give you the source of effective stimulation and vacuum.

A feeding *supplementer* enables you to give breast milk or baby formula to your baby while suckling at your breast. A supplementation device is a container with feeding tubes for used with breastfeeding or finger feeding. Many mothers have used this with adopted babies to coax their babies to their breast for feeding. It may take you several tries to get the hang of using this type of feeding device, so be patient. Your reward of breastfeeding your adopted baby is to make it feel like your own.

Lactation Lingo

A **supplementer**, such as the Supplemental Nursing System by Medela, enables you to give your adopted baby breast milk or baby formula while suckling at your breast. You can also use it to finger feed your baby.

Most adoptive mothers find that they have to supplement with baby formula or donor breast milk. Some adoptive mothers who have successfully breastfed an adoptive baby may claim that their milk supply was plentiful. Don't make expectations based on these anecdotals as it may discourage you. Talk to your baby's health care provider and ask about recommendations for supplementation. Keep in mind that donor breast milk may be an expensive option. If your baby has medical necessity for it, you may find that health insurance will cover the expenses. Otherwise, make plans to pick up the tab for whichever nutritional supplement you choose.

The Least You Need to Know

➤ Breastfeeding your adoptive baby is entirely possible.

➤ Most adoptive mothers need to supplement their milk supply with donor breast milk or baby formula.

➤ Relactation involves the stimulation of your milk supply if lactation wasn't established after giving birth.

➤ You can help induce your milk supply by stimulating your breasts with a medical-grade piston breast pump several weeks before your adopted baby's due date.

➤ A supplementation device enables your baby to suckle at your breast while getting breast milk or baby formula.

Mmm.. chocolate!

Mmm.... chocolate milk!

Chapter 28

Eat, Drink, and Breastfeed

In This Chapter

➤ What you should eat

➤ What you should drink

➤ Food and drinks to consume in moderation

➤ Taking medications

There's no doubt that you will question what you should be eating and drinking as you breastfeed. After all, pregnancy has primed you for some sound nutritional eating habits. You will provide the nutritional source for your baby through your own breast milk. So, it is important to focus on what comes in through your mouth, in order to balance the right components in your breast milk.

Keeping yourself nourished while breastfeeding is not hard at all. You'll be glad to know that there aren't any hard and fast rules about what to eat and what to drink during your breastfeeding. You'll follow the basic daily food allowances that you used during your pregnancy. And you'll even add your favorite sweets to your food plan, only in moderation! This chapter will take a look at the eats and the drinks that should be making their way down your hatch.

What's to Eat?

The U.S. Department of Agriculture has put together a wonderful food plan for everyone, advising on the right foods to eat. It's called the food pyramid. It's a great plan that works for everyone, including you, the breastfeeding mother. It's divided into the following five groups:

➤ Bread, cereals, pasta, and rice

➤ Fruits

➤ Veggies

➤ Meat, fish, poultry, eggs, and nuts

➤ Milk, yogurt, and cheese

It has recommendations for the number of servings that you should consume each day as you eat. Realize that these are suggested guidelines. You may have some days, depending on your metabolism, that you can't quite meet your quota. And you may have some days that you exceed the recommendations, especially if your appetite is ravenous.

As a breastfeeding mother, you will want to consume an additional 500 to 700 calories with your diet each day. That makes a total of about 2,000 to 2,200 calories for daily intake. It's quite easy to consume these additional calories. If this sounds like a lot to you, you shouldn't worry. These are the calories needed to manufacture breast milk. These are the calories that your breastfeeding baby will consume.

A balanced and nutritional diet is needed to fuel your energy requirements. After all, you are manufacturing breast milk in addition to taking care of yourself and your baby. Eating from the recommended food groups will put you on track to face the energy demands of being a new parent.

Nursing Mom's Notes

You'll want to consume between 2,000 and 2,200 calories each day while breastfeeding. That's an additional 200 to 300 calories on top of what you've eaten during pregnancy. These are calories that your baby will consume in breast milk!

The Breadbox

Breads and cereals, pasta, and rice are great sources of complex *carbohydrates*. These foods add the "spark" to your sparkplug so that you can keep on ticking. These foods are also a great source of fiber. The number of recommended servings from this food group during your lactation is 9 to 11. That's a lot of carbos!

Some examples from this food group include …

➤ Bagel

➤ Muffin

Lactation Lingo

A **carbohydrate** is a substance such as sugar, starch, or cellulose that's composed of carbon, hydrogen, and oxygen. It is a fabulous fuel for your body.

➤ Waffle

➤ Bread

➤ Cereal

➤ Pasta

➤ Rice

➤ Tortilla

Try to eat at least two servings with your breakfast in the morning and one or two servings for a mid-morning snack. Two servings at lunchtime get you half of your daily recommended intake. A snack in the afternoon and a couple of servings with your supper tops you out at nine. You'd be surprised how something from the bread-box keeps you mentally and physically fit.

The Fresh Fruit and Veggie Stand

It may be that vegetables aren't your favorite and may not sound too appetizing. But the fact is, they provide a great source of minerals, vitamins, some fiber, and carbohydrates that are essential for your body to function. Variety is your key to consuming what is required.

You'll want to look at getting three to five servings as a breastfeeding mother. Your veggies can be cooked, but you'll get more bang for your buck if you eat them raw. When you boil or steam vegetables ever so lightly, the minerals and vitamins end up in the cooking water.

If you've been told to avoid vegetables such as broccoli, brussels sprouts, cauliflower, or onions while breastfeeding, I'm going to tell you differently. Rumor has it that these "gassy" vegetables will give your baby gas and cause the horrific crying called colic. This is just not so. There isn't any scientific evidence that shows that these foods cause problems in breastfed babies. So you'll just have to gobble up your veggies.

Fruits are plentiful when it comes to the vitamin content, especially the citrus kind. Carbohydrates and fiber abound in a wide variety of fruits that you can consume. The recommended daily intake while you breastfeed is two to four servings. You can add fruits to just about any dish that you prepare, to help satisfy a sweet tooth.

Breast Beware

There is no scientific evidence that shows that broccoli, onions, brussels sprouts, or garlic cause gas in your breastfeeding baby. They may produce flatulence in your bowels, but not in your baby's. You may eat what you like, but don't overdo it.

You can combine fruits and veggies with just about any bread, cereal, or grain. You might consider any of these snack combinations to meet your daily quota:

➤ Bagel with jam or jelly

➤ Celery and peanut butter

➤ Dried fruit mix

➤ Apple slices

➤ Raw veggies and dip

➤ Fruit salad

➤ Fruit juice popsicles

These snacks are nutritional and quick to prepare. If help is available with food preparation, ask someone to fix you fruit and veggie snacks.

Proteins

If you recall anything from science class about amino acids, these are the building blocks for cells in your body. Amino acids are a group of nitrogenous organic compounds, which are the foundation of many proteins. Protein is an essential nutrient and not one to omit from your food plan.

It's recommended that breastfeeding mothers consume three to four servings of protein each day. Now, this isn't very much when you take a closer look. A one-ounce serving at lunch and a three-ounce serving at supper meet your need for the day. You should eat a variety from the protein group such as meats, fish, beans and peas, eggs, and nuts. Again, be creative about combining proteins with other daily food groups.

LactFact

Calcium is an essential mineral for bone density and strength. A loss of calcium from the bones makes them brittle and prone to fractures. Osteoporosis is a debilitating disease that affects thousands of women. Consuming inadequate amounts of calcium during the childbearing years causes this. During pregnancy and lactation, you should consume 1,200 to 1,500 milligrams of calcium daily. Studies show that the average woman takes one serving of calcium daily. That's milk over cereal at breakfast!

The Dairy Barn

Milk, yogurt, and cheeses are dairy products that some of you may crave. They are essential for breastfeeding mothers because of the source of calcium, vitamin D, and phosphorus they provide. Body parts like our teeth and bones, as well as our heart and muscles, require these minerals in order to function properly.

During lactation you should strive to consume at least four servings from the dairy barn each day. Dairy products are an excellent source of calcium. Breastfeeding mothers need at least 1,200 to 1,500 milligrams of calcium intake every day. This helps to keep an adequate supply in your body to prevent the debilitating disease called osteoporosis in your later years.

Some of you may say that you can't or won't "do" milk products because of taste or lactose intolerance. You can get calcium from several food sources other than milk and cheese. Look for calcium-fortified foods like orange juice, bread, and cereals to consume. These foods also contain calcium:

➤ Salmon

➤ Sardines

➤ Turnip greens

➤ Bok choy

➤ Kale

➤ Broccoli

➤ Oranges

➤ Almonds

It's also important to point out that if you have a strong family history of allergies, some traces of dairy products in your breast milk may be bothersome to your baby. Your baby may react to traces of cow's milk, eggs, fish, wheat, and citrus foods. You should only do something about this if your baby shows any signs of reaction. You may have to make changes to your food consumption accordingly.

Breast Beware

Your prenatal vitamin will provide you one serving of calcium when taken daily. Switch to a calcium supplement when you deplete your prenatal vitamin supply. Be sure to add three more servings of calcium-rich foods each day.

What's to Drink?

It's very important that you supply your body with plenty of fluids while you breastfeed. Remember that breast milk is made up of 87 percent water. You should drink to satisfy or quench your thirst.

A good habit to develop is to drink fluids each time that you breastfeed. That means that in the first weeks you will get 8 to 12 servings of liquids each day. Why is that?

Because that's how often you should be breastfeeding. Plenty of fluids help to remove waste products and toxins from your body.

Your fluids can include any of the following:

➤ Water

➤ Fruit juice

➤ Milk

➤ Vegetable juice

➤ Soup

When you are drinking enough fluid, the urine that you pass will be pale yellow to clear. If it appears dark yellow and concentrated, it's a sign you should drink more.

Nursing Mom's Notes

Fresh fruits and vegetables provide an excellent source of water and natural fiber. This will help keep your bowels moving regularly.

Water

Besides being an important component of breast milk, the cells in your body need water, too. The cells in your baby's body also need this water. And there's no better source than a mother's milk.

Just like your baby, water helps to regulate your bowels by keeping fluid in them. Your baby passes a soft, runny-liquid stool while breastfeeding. This is the tell-tale sign of a breastfeeding baby! Fluid in your bowel keeps you from being constipated. Being well hydrated keeps any swelling in your hands, ankles, and feet at a minimum. And frequent passing of urine helps minimize your chances of a urinary tract infection.

Strive to drink about eight glasses of water each day. Fresh fruits and vegetables are also a great source of water. That's what they're mostly made of. Eating fruits and raw veggies will help you consume these food groups!

Milk and Juice

Fruit juices are adequate sources of liquid, but you'll have to be careful about the quantity you consume. Many contain large quantities of sugar in the form of fructose or corn syrup. You may want to limit your intake of these sugary concentrations.

You don't have to drink lots of milk to make lots of breast milk. I'm not sure where that old wives' tale got started. Milk can be quite a good source of fluid to consume, especially since it delivers a powerful concentration of calcium and phosphorus. You may want to combine milk in a soup, pudding, or a milk shake. This works well if you aren't that fond of milk by itself and need to hide it in a food that you do like.

Coffee, Tea, or Soda?

Consumers drink these three liquids in massive quantities every day. And the truth is, they are not good for your health. Caffeine is a stimulant and I'll admit that I rely on a jump-start every morning. It zaps your brain to keep it alert and functioning when you need it most.

Tea, cola sodas, and coffee all contain caffeine. You'll do best while breastfeeding if you can limit your caffeine consumption to 200 milligrams or less. That's about two eight-ounce cups of coffee or soda, or three cups of tea. The longer your tea steeps, the greater the concentration of caffeine. Coffee, teas, and sodas act as a *diuretic,* which actually dehydrates you. So, all in all, you want to minimize your caffeine intake or just "decaf" yourself altogether!

Lactation Lingo

A **diuretic** is a substance that increases the flow of urine. This can flush essential nutrients such as calcium, potassium, and sodium out of the body before they are used.

Consume These Foods in Moderation

There are some foods that are necessary in our food intake but that should be consumed in moderation. These are foods containing fats, oils, and sweets. These foods can be bad for you if you just plain eat too much and too many of them. Your body needs fat, but only a very small amount.

There's good fat and there's bad fat. The same goes for sugar. You should consume no more than four servings of fat each day. This amounts to just a few teaspoon and tablespoon quantities. Breastfeeding may burn up the calories, but overindulging in a vat of oil doesn't help.

Breast Beware

Caffeine is a central nervous system stimulant. It will increase your heart rate and metabolism, and may interfere with your sleep. It can cause nervousness and anxiety. Caffeine is a diuretic, and it is also an addictive drug.

Sweet Things

Some of us have a real craving when it comes to sweets. Mine just so happens to be chocolate. Is there anyone else out there? I was bound and determined to breastfeed and eat my chocolate. The happy medium for me was to combine my cravings in small quantities with foods that were good for me, such as a milk shake with an added tablespoon of chocolate. Or maybe a half-cup serving of chocolate ice cream, or some trail mix with chocolate candies added.

You can eat desserts and sweets while breastfeeding as long as you don't overdo it. Take a small sliver of cheesecake and add some spoonfuls of fresh fruit. Eat a couple of cookies with a glass of milk. It will satisfy your craving and satisfy your serving of fruit or dairy in the meantime. Don't deny yourself all your sweets; just remember to eat them in moderation.

LactFact

Excessive nicotine in the body can interfere with the letdown reflex during breastfeeding. This usually results in a low milk supply. Babies of mothers who smoke while breastfeeding show less weight gain than babies of nonsmokers. Breast milk does help to provide respiratory protection to babies whose mothers do smoke.

Nursing Mom's Notes

You should take any medication just after breastfeeding or pumping. The medication should peak and begin to be excreted before your next feeding. Drink plenty of water, as many drugs will dehydrate you.

Alcohol

A hand always goes up in class asking about a glass of wine while breastfeeding. I love to answer this one. I'll cut to the chase and say that an occasional alcoholic beverage should not be a problem. Regular or excessive consumption of alcohol *is* a problem, though. Any breastfeeding mother who regularly drinks alcohol does pose a threat to her baby.

Some studies have shown that a baby may consume less breast milk or refuse to breastfeed if its mother has consumed alcohol. It may be the smell; it could be the taste. Alcohol can interfere with your letdown, minimizing or preventing your release of breast milk.

Timing is important here. You could consume an alcoholic beverage just after you have finished breastfeeding or expressing milk from your breasts. If your feedings are two to three hours apart, alcohol can peak in your bloodstream and be excreted between feedings. Remember that food in your stomach helps to absorb alcohol. Also remember to replenish your fluids, as alcohol will dehydrate you.

If You Take Medications

You'll probably find that guidelines about which medications are compatible with breastfeeding are very hard to come by. No one wants to be responsible for addressing this hot topic. There are some things to consider, but generally speaking, many medications are compatible to a certain degree with breastfeeding. Any medication that you take will reach your breast milk in some quantity. The active amount of the medication that you take, however, is usually not enough to cause harm to your breastfeeding baby.

There are a few points to take into consideration before taking a medication:

➤ How old is your baby?

➤ What is your medical necessity for the medication?

➤ How long will you need the medication?

➤ How quickly is the medication eliminated from your body?

➤ What is the timing of the feeding with the dosage?

➤ How is the medication taken?

You'll probably get different advice from your health care providers and your pharmacist. They take into consideration the safety and well-being of your infant. Many physicians use the advice from the manufacturer's package insert. And the *Physician's Desk Reference (PDR)* is usually written to protect the manufacturer from liability. In other words, statements usually read that you should not take medications if you are pregnant or nursing.

So, what's a breastfeeding mother to do? Generally, if a mother needs one of the following medications, it is usually compatible with breastfeeding:

➤ Analgesics

➤ Antibiotics

➤ Anticonvulsants

➤ Antihistamines

➤ Antihypertensives

➤ Bronchodilators

The timing and action of the medication are of primary importance. The active ingredient will likely peak in your bloodstream and pass into your breast milk if you are in the process of breastfeeding as well as milk expression. That's when you make most of your milk. Remember that the breast itself is not a reservoir of breast milk. It's an organ that secretes a substance when it is actively stimulated.

If you can take the medication after your breastfeeding or pumping and it is eliminated readily from your system, then this is the medication of choice. How often and how much should be considered; medications that are not compatible with breastfeeding should obviously be avoided.

The Least You Need to Know

➤ Your food plan should include breads and pasta, fruits, vegetables, meats, and dairy products while breastfeeding.

➤ It is essential that you consume 1,200 to 1,500 milligrams of calcium each day.

➤ Drink eight glasses of water every day.

➤ Only consume coffee, tea, and sodas in small quantities. You could also eliminate them from your food plan.

➤ You can eat sweets and fats in moderate amounts.

➤ There are several medications that are generally safe to take while breast-feeding.

Stepping Out

One of the best things about breastfeeding is the incredible portability that it offers when you need to pick up and go. The fact that you carry your baby's essential food source in your body, without having to pack or prepare, store, heat anything up, or cool anything down, is amazingly convenient. No need to hunt around in your frig or even think about what to prepare. Your fast-food restaurant is open day or night, ready to serve.

As a new parent, you'll certainly want to show and share with everyone your new baby. And there's nothing better than to step out for a little outing with your new baby. Think of it as a field trip. There will be a few things you'll want to bring along. And you'll certainly need to be dressed for the occasion. In this chapter, I'll help you to get organized and to look at your wardrobe; I'll also offer up some advice about getting out and about with your breastfeeding baby.

Location, Location, Location

Anywhere you want to be, you can breastfeed! I'm serious. You see people everywhere, everyday, stuffing all sorts of food items in their mouths. People driving down the road with their two hands around a big burger. So what's all the fuss about a baby wanting to eat a meal wherever and whenever hunger strikes?

Well, it's where the baby gets its food that sends people squawking. It just so happens that baby food comes from a mother's breast and not from a paper wrapper or a styrofoam carton. And there are plenty of people who will make a big stink about where and when that breast serves up a meal.

Nursing Mom's Notes

You should be able to breastfeed anywhere that allows babies and children. If food and drink are not allowed, you can respond that breast milk is a contained liquid.

One of the biggest challenges that you are up against when you step out with your breastfeeding baby is the general public: neighbors, shoppers, and even friends and family. If nobody wore a stitch of clothing, a woman's breasts would be exposed all of the time. We wouldn't need to keep ourselves covered and to be careful about breastfeeding under cover. But this just isn't the case in today's environment.

You'll probably need to approach breastfeeding in public with some discretion. That is, being prudent or cautious about your location and your surroundings so as not to ruffle too many feathers. You'll have a chance to find a few great locations as well as to develop a routine for breastfeeding that's easy for you.

Private Performance

The first place to practice and get comfortable with your breastfeeding is in the privacy of your own home. You'll breastfeed with the greatest of ease without someone staring and glaring at you. You might try in front of a mirror to see what others will see you do.

You should try breastfeeding in a relative's home for another private location. It gives you a chance to feel more at ease with a few more people around. You could step into an empty room to get your baby latched on and pull a light blanket over your shoulder. Then you can walk in and join in a conversation or watch a television show. Take the opportunity to answer any questions about your breastfeeding. Many people, including relatives, feel uncomfortable about breastfeeding because they just don't know much about it. Offering a few answers will help to boost your confidence and to put someone else at ease.

Another private place to breastfeed is in your vehicle. I would always climb in the back seat and offer up a warm meal. Lock your car doors for more security. If it's hot outside, you might run the air conditioner. If snowflakes are flying, then snuggle your baby up under your coat and make sure the engine is not running. You might park away from other cars for the most privacy.

Several shopping areas and department stores have a private lounge for you to sit down and breast-feed. This may be a welcome relief to put up your feet and park your stroller. You can use the bath-room facilities to take care of yourself and then re-sume your shopping. I've had clients tell me that several airports also have a "family" room where privacy for breastfeeding is available. You may want to check these places out.

A semi-private place that welcomes breastfeeding is the movie theater. What a great way to treat your-self and cuddle your baby at the same time. Make a date with your spouse or partner and bring your baby along. I would take advantage of an after-noon matinee and get out of the house.

Public Performance

Breastfeeding in public requires a little more cre-ativity on your part. So as not to create a spectacle of yourself, you'll want to find a place where the throngs and multitudes of people are minimal. Most public locations that allow babies and chil-dren should permit breastfeeding on the premises. It's best if you turn your back to the crowd when getting your baby to latch on. Then pull a blanket or sweater over your shoulder and relax. You don't have to cover up if you don't want to. Most peo-ple will only see that you are cradling a baby in your arms.

Breast Beware

Do not breastfeed your baby while operating a motor vehicle. If you are a passenger in a mov-ing vehicle, you should not breastfeed. Your motor vehicle should be parked where breast-feeding can take place safely.

Nursing Mom's Notes

If you attend a meeting or join a group of co-workers, let them know in advance if you plan to bring your breastfeeding baby. Forewarned is forearmed, and you may avoid an embarrassing or inappropriate scene.

If you venture out to a restaurant for a meal, ask that you be seated in an area where your back faces the crowd. A booth or a table in a remote corner works well. There shouldn't be a problem with breastfeeding your baby in a restaurant location where everyone else is feeding, too!

A park or recreation area can be public but usually offers up an area that's remote and quiet. Your job is to find that location. You'll be able to enjoy what nature has to offer when you can relax and breastfeed.

Casual Wear

The clothing you'll wear when you are breastfeeding should be simple. You'll want something that's comfortable and easy to wear. Laundering your wardrobe should be as easy as you can make it on yourself as a new mother.

Many breastfeeding mothers find that a blouse or shirt that buttons up the front can be quite convenient for breastfeeding. This may be a leftover from your pregnancy attire or an extra-large ladies' size. You might also ask your spouse or partner for a loaner from his closet.

Breast Beware

Underwire bras do not provide a comfortable fit for breastfeeding mothers. The wire can constrict and pinch, possibly leading to plugged ducts and a restricted milk flow. Mothers with recurrent mastitis improve after they go wireless.

Casual wear is usually comfortable to wear. Garments made of cotton tend to be cool in the warmer months, and warmer when it's cool. Cotton also absorbs moisture, and moisture is something that all breastfeeding mothers experience! A shirt that can pull up from your waist offers convenient access to your breasts.

Try to wear light-colored or patterned clothes that will hide any breast milk that you leak. Garments with stretch fabric like Lycra offer a wealth of comfort and a bit of support to breastfeeding mothers. I found that stretch shorts and aerobic tights under a large T-shirt worked well for my wardrobe.

Your casual wear should include a supportive bra. A cotton bra will be more comfortable than one made with a synthetic material. Read the label and look for the cotton content of the fabric. Any bra with Lycra or Spandex will give you added support from it's elastic component. The bra cups should be cotton and easy to open for breastfeeding.

Dress Ups

Getting dressed up to step out can make you feel like a whole new person. The trick to getting the right outfit is finding a two-piece combination. A blouse-and-skirt or blouse-and-slacks combination may be your winning ticket. You can access from the waist and remain discreet about your breastfeeding.

Once you're all dolled up and heading out for an afternoon or evening, you'll want to take along some extra items. This is in case you leak milk or your baby spits up on your snazzy outfit. Pack some extra breast pads, either disposable or reusable, in your purse or tote bag. You might consider a clean bra if your outing will be several hours. Take a lightweight sweater that can take off the chill or cover up a noticeable mishap.

If you're dressed up to go out without your breastfeeding baby, you might have to plan for milk expression while you're away. Plan to express your breast milk at the times your baby usually feeds. A small, portable hand pump can be tucked into your purse or tote. You could also plan to hand express your milk into a cup, a sink, or a toilet if necessary.

Specialty Attire

Many maternity and specialty stores carry garments specifically designed for breast-feeding mothers. You may have a garment from pregnancy that also gives you breast-feeding access. The designs available today include buttons, overlapping seams, and snaps that allow the garment to open at or near the breast.

LactFact

There are several clothing manufacturers that design and carry garments made especially for breastfeeding. These may be available at department stores, maternity stores, and through mail-order catalogs. Some pattern companies have designs available for you to sew your own breastfeeding attire. Try these companies for breastfeeding apparel:

➤ Japanese Weekend
  1-800-808-0555; www.japaneseweekend.com

➤ Laura's Closet
  1-888-766-0303; www.laurascloset.com

➤ Motherhood Maternity
  1-800-466-6223; www.motherhood.com

➤ Motherwear
  1-800-950-2500; www.motherwear.com

And for sewing patterns:

➤ Elizabeth Lee Designs
  1-800-449-3350; www.elizabethlee.com

You might try looking in your department store's maternity section for these specialty garments. And if you don't see it, you should ask. Sometimes the garment is designed so well that you don't notice that it's for breastfeeding. Some mail-order catalogs offer a vast array of seasonal garments including bathing suits with access for breastfeeding. One mail-order company specializes in women's sizes beyond 1X. I would recommend that you take some measurements to help with your selection of the right size. Many companies exchange garments that are not worn or soiled with breast milk. If you can sew, there are also patterns available to whip up these specialty garments. Look in Appendix C, "Resources," for additional clothing resources.

The Least You Need to Know

➤ Private locations for breastfeeding include your home, a relative's home, and your own vehicle.

➤ You can breastfeed in a public location wherever babies and children are allowed.

➤ Take along some clean breast pads, another bra, and a sweater when venturing out.

➤ Clothing that opens easily above your waist is your best choice for breastfeeding.

Is this it...
Are we through?

Chapter 30

Weaning Your Baby

In This Chapter

➤ What exactly is weaning?

➤ Reasons why you may choose to wean

➤ Taking a safe approach

➤ What to expect while you wean

There's no doubt that every breastfeeding mother will ask or be asked about when to bring this whole thing to a halt. Seems like you just got over any hurdles of getting started and someone starts talking about when you're going to quit. How long should I continue breastfeeding? Now that I've gotten up and running, is there an expected end or a final destination for me?

Weaning may be a mother's decision, her baby may lead it, or it may be a joint effort between a mother and her baby. For whatever reason, you may find yourself in a position to end the hours, days, or months of breastfeeding your baby. We'll take a look in this chapter at the various defining aspects of weaning as well as the safest approach to whittling down your supply of breast milk.

Choosing to Wean

First and foremost, let's take a look at the definition of *weaning*. It means to gradually take away, to detach, or to alienate from an activity or source. This usually happens by replacing the source or activity with a substitute, slowly and gradually over time. Weaning from the breast means that the sole nutrition of breast milk begins to be replaced with a complementary food. A complementary food may be liquid or solids. This food may eventually become the sole source of nutrition for a baby. Anytime that you introduce something other than breast milk into a baby's diet, weaning begins.

The recommendation for exclusive breastfeeding through a baby's first year is a great goal for most mothers to reach. However, when the desire to breastfeed is no longer mutual for one reason or another, the choice to wean may arise. A mother should consult her baby's doctor, her spouse or partner, or a lactation professional to help with any decision to wean from breastfeeding.

Breastfeeding provides your baby with comfort and security. Yes, it's nutritional, but it also satisfies your baby's emotional and psychological needs. That's important to consider when making the choice to wean. A mom can choose to partially wean to continue giving her baby the nutritional as well as psychological and emotional benefits. The majority of nutrition may be replaced with another source, but suckling at the breast will continue to provide the comfort and love your baby needs.

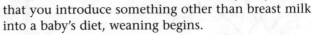

Lactation Lingo

To **wean** means to gradually take away, to detach, or to alienate from an activity or source. This usually happens by replacing the source or activity with a substitute, slowly and gradually over time. Weaning from the breast means that the sole nutrition of breast milk is replaced with a complementary food.

Mom's Choice

Your choice to wean your baby from the breast may be for a variety of reasons. Yes, it may be you, and you alone, who wants to stop things altogether. You've had enough and you just want life to be the way it was before baby. You may decide that you can't breastfeed or express breast milk with your return to work. There may be circumstances where nipple soreness, fatigue, or a breast infection influences your decision to wean.

Weaning may be a socially or culturally driven activity. The practice or norm of weaning can be dictated by what everyone else is doing. If your best friend tells you that she weaned her baby from breastfeeding at four months of age, you may be influenced to do the same. Health care providers may also strongly influence the early weaning of breastfeeding babies. It seems like the moment something goes wrong or appears different, the suggestion to stop breastfeeding comes from every direction. In the United States, weaning usually takes place within the first year for many babies.

Probably the biggest influence to stop breastfeeding is the demands of work combined with the demands of home. You just can't seem to do it all. You feel an incredible burden to meet everyone's needs and give 110 percent effort in the meantime. Every time you turn around somebody wants something from you. Your baby doesn't understand the pressures and circumstances of life in the big world. All your baby sees and hears is the sweet smile and reassuring voice of you, its mommy. Studies show that the demands of work and time schedules drive many women to choose to wean from breastfeeding. When life becomes hectic, not to mention overwhelming, controlled and scheduled feedings seem like a solution.

LactFact

Weaning in the United States usually takes place within the first year of life. The age at weaning in cultures outside of the United States is between two and three years. Feeding schedules adopted from baby formula feeding have been associated with early weaning. The pressure from friends, family, and health care professionals may also contribute to early weaning in some circumstances. Western society tells mothers of breastfeeding toddlers that it's an unacceptable or perverse activity.

Baby's Choice

Many babies will show a readiness to sample other food sources between six and eight months of age. This means solid foods as well as other liquid sources. A new feeding experience means that your baby can use its tongue and can practice chewing even if teeth haven't popped through it's gums. The baby's digestive system is also at a point of maturing enough to begin digesting something other than breast milk.

Breast milk can be the sole source of nutrition throughout your baby's first year. But when the readiness for solids appears or when you desire to

Nursing Mom's Notes

Babies prefer the taste of breast milk to other foods and liquids. Mash a ripe banana with some of your breast milk and see if your baby doesn't gobble it up.

introduce solids, you can start around your baby's sixth month of age to make a transition to the combination of breast milk and solid foods.

Some babies show a readiness to wean to a cup between seven and nine months of age. They actually begin to reach for things they can hold and handle. After all, they spend a lot of time watching mom and dad put things in their mouths and want to try it, too. Your baby may become disinterested in suckling from your breast because the desire to explore new feeding experiences is so great.

Breast Beware

Fruit juice provides vitamin C as well as carbohydrates and calories, but it shouldn't be used exclusively. Breast milk is an important source of protein and calcium and should be continued at least through your baby's first birthday.

So, it may be that your baby is asking for an expansion of its food horizons and the process of weaning begins. It doesn't mean that you take your baby from the breast but rather that you expand your baby's diet to include solid foods, liquids, and breast milk. Some mothers offer fruit juices at the start of weaning, which are okay, but aren't to be used in excess. Fruit juice provides vitamin C as well as carbohydrates and calories, but you shouldn't use it exclusively.

Breast milk is an important source of protein and calcium, and should be continued at least through your baby's first birthday. That's why the American Academy of Pediatrics recommends the breastfeeding of a baby through its first year. If you can't or won't provide breast milk, then at least choose to use baby formula through the first year. The importance of a milk source for your baby cannot be understated.

It's an Emergency

Circumstances may arise when you must start the weaning process because your condition warrants sudden weaning. You may have a sudden illness or an emergency beyond your control. After discussing with your baby's doctor, you make the decision to stop your breastfeeding. This may be very difficult for you and your baby to handle.

Breast Beware

Severe engorgement will result if abrupt weaning occurs during the first six weeks of breastfeeding. The mammary glands will remain partially functional for about one month following cases of sudden weaning.

With breastfeeding already established, your breasts will continue to function and to make milk as programmed. The sudden cessation of emptying milk from your breasts will probably result in engorgement. It may be severe if you are in the first four to six weeks of breastfeeding. You will need to gradually empty the milk from your breasts when they become full. You or someone else can do this with a breast pump or manual expression.

Mothers experiencing abrupt weaning can get a *milk fever*. This is similar to flu-like symptoms of fever, chills, aches, and overall weakness. It probably results from the resorption of breast milk into your body. After all, if your milk isn't emptied or expressed, it has to go somewhere. And that somewhere ends up being through your filter system, the lymphatics. Your symptoms of fever, aches, and chills will last about three to four days. They'll probably combine with any other symptoms of illness that you're experiencing.

Safe Weaning

Once the decision has been made, it's time to start your weaning process. You'll need to replace each feeding with another food source. This source will depend on your baby's age and developmental stage at weaning. You may choose between solids and liquids from a bottle or cup. This food source can be any stored breast milk you have on hand, baby formula, or solids.

> **Lactation Lingo**
>
> **Milk fever** is a syndrome of fever, muscular weakness, and pain associated with engorgement of the breasts or the sudden cessation of breastfeeding.

> **LactFact**
>
> Solid foods are usually introduced between six and eight months of age. Babies born prematurely should be at least six months old based on their due date. It's helpful to prepare quick and easy solids for your baby. You might try some of these: cut-up apples, pears, oranges, and bananas; strips of toast; cheese strips or cubes; crackers; a hard-boiled or scrambled egg; yogurt.

Consider the following steps with your weaning process:

1. Start with a morning feeding and offer expressed breast milk, solids, juice, or baby formula. You may choose a bottle, a cup, or a spoon to feed with.

2. Be patient and take your time. That's why a morning feeding may be best. After all, you are introducing a new skill to learn, and breastfeeding wasn't learned overnight.

3. After the feeding you will want to express milk from your breasts to relieve fullness. This should not be a thorough emptying from your breasts. This should be just enough for comfort. Save any milk and offer it with another feeding.

4. Repeat this for two to three days. If your baby has adapted and you have, too, it's time to take away another breastfeeding.

5. Continue with weaning from your morning feeding. Choose the second feeding opposite of your first feeding. For example, if you fed at 8:00 A.M. you should feed at about 2:00 P.M. Follow your second feeding with milk expression, just enough to reduce pressure and provide you with comfort.

6. Continue these two weaning feeds for two or three days. If ready, you will take away a third feeding, let's say opposite the 2:00 P.M. feeding. That makes your third feeding around 8:00 P.M.

You can continue to remove feedings following this pattern until you have completely weaned from breastfeeding. It's up to you how far you want to go and over what amount of time.

If you wish to only wean partially then you can continue with your morning and night breastfeeding. Your body will adjust. Removing just enough milk from your breasts after each weaning feed allows you to safely reduce the amount of milk that you produce. It slowly sends a message that you need a reduction in supply. And without your baby actually suckling at your breast, the stimulation is gradually reduced, too. Mothers who work and who wish to maintain a breastfeeding relationship with their baby often choose partial weaning.

Nursing Mom's Notes

Allow your baby to suckle at your breast when weaning. It provides the comfort and security needed during this time of change. Suckling will probably be brief and provide just enough to satisfy.

You can continue to breastfeed on demand while weaning, to allow your baby the slow and gradual transition to solids and other liquids. These feedings may be short and sweet, especially if your baby needs just a quick snack. Your baby's appetite will begin to be satisfied by the other food sources you offer. Remember that breastfeeding provides comfort and security, and a quick fix may be all that's necessary. If the time spent suckling isn't lengthy and thorough, it won't be enough for significant milk production.

Ups and Downs

Once you start to wean, I can tell you to expect an incredible emotional roller-coaster ride. The hormones associated with breastfeeding will start to bounce around inside your body, including your head. Your emotions will be challenged by everyday encounters.

Remember the hormone prolactin? I know it's been a few chapters since we talked about this one. It's your milk-making hormone, indeed, but it is also responsible for giving you that feeling of inner peace. It's associated with feelings of well-being and relaxation. That's why you fall asleep so readily during and after your breastfeeding.

Breast Beware

Be aware that hormone with-drawal can set in with weaning and may be responsible for any signs or symptoms of depression.

Be aware that hormone withdrawal can set in with weaning and may be responsible for any signs or symptoms of depression. Any mother with a psychiatric disorder needs to be carefully watched as she weans her baby from her breast. That's why mothers diagnosed with postpartum depression go into emotional upheaval when they must stop breastfeeding while taking an antidepressant. This situation may call for a medication that is compatible with breastfeeding to smooth out the hormone roller coaster. Why take away something that may be working quite well between a mother and her baby?

Tears and the ultimate guilt trip are not at all uncommon with weaning. Tears may roll down your cheeks as you question what you are really doing here. Is this right for me? Will my baby hate me for doing this? Why am I trying to do so much? You'll feel torn about making the decision and ask if there is another solution.

Your baby can make the choice to wean. I remember all too well the morning my baby girl sat up in bed and flipped my nipple with her finger. I asked if she wanted to nurse. She sat like a baby monkey, big grin on her face, and shook her head "no." I can't begin to describe the feeling of disappointment and rejection that I felt. She didn't want me anymore. What did I do to cause this?

There may be feelings of sudden relief with weaning, especially if it's something you wanted in the first place. It's okay to admit this and to celebrate. It all depends on your circumstances. If you experienced painful breastfeeding and can only relieve it through weaning, then that's what is most important.

The circumstances of weaning are unique to every breastfeeding mother and her baby. Whether it happens by choice or by chance, as a parent, you will determine what's best for your physical and mental health and for your baby's as well. The recommendation to breastfeed through your baby's first year of life is exactly that—a recommendation. Make your breastfeeding choices with the information you have in your hands and in your heart.

The Least You Need to Know

➤ You can choose partial or full weaning depending on your circumstances.

➤ Your baby may make the choice to wean from the breast.

➤ In cases of emergency, breastfeeding may stop through abrupt weaning.

➤ It is best for weaning to progress slowly and gradually.

➤ Complementary feedings include expressed breast milk, baby formula, solids, and fruit juices.

➤ Mothers will often experience emotional changes with weaning.

Glossary

acini   The milk-producing cells of the mammary gland.

adhesion   A band of tissue that keeps a steady tension between organs or ligaments within the body.

allergen   Any substance, such as a food or drug, that causes an allergic response. A common allergen among infants is cow's milk protein.

American Academy of Pediatrics   A collective group of physicians who specialize in the medical care of infants and children.

amino acids   A group of nitrogenous-based organic compounds, which are the foundation of many proteins.

analgesic   A drug or pharmaceutical that reduces or relieves pain.

anemia   The deficiency of blood or hemoglobin in the body.

anesthetics   Medications that produce a loss of sensation. General anesthesia puts someone to sleep to block the pain. A spinal, or epidural, anesthesia blocks the pain below the waist.

antibodies   Immunoglobulins that detect and attack bacteria and viruses to help the body resist infection. Exposure to bacteria and viruses causes the formation of immunoglobulins.

areola   The darkened skin around the nipple. It overlies the milk sinuses.

bilirubin   A by-product resulting from the breakdown of excess red blood cells. The excess bilirubin in the blood supply causes jaundice.

bra   A shortened term for brassiere, a woman's undergarment that supports the breasts.

breast shield   The plastic or glass component of a milk-collection assembly. When placed over the breast it enables vacuum to be applied.

Candida albicans   The yeast that causes candidiasis, or yeast infection, of the nipples, areola, or the milk ducts.

carbohydrates   Substances such as sugar, starch, or cellulose that are composed of carbon, hydrogen, and oxygen. They are a fabulous fuel for your body.

cesarean or **C-section**   The delivery of a baby through a surgical incision made in the mother's abdomen and uterus.

colic   A term for a baby's extreme, unexplained irritability that continues day after day.

colostrum   The thick, yellowish fluid in the breast that's the first breast milk. It has highly concentrated proteins, immunoglobulins, vitamins, and minerals.

dehydration   The loss or removal of water.

diabetes   A disease marked by excess sugar in the bloodstream because the pancreas fails to produce insulin.

diarrhea   An excessive and frequent looseness of the bowel.

discreet   Judicious or prudent; exercising caution with any action or speech.

diuretic   A substance that increases the flow of urine. This can flush essential nutrients such as calcium, potassium, and sodium out of the body before they are used.

Docosahexaenoic acid or **DHA**   The primary fatty acid found in brain matter and the retina of the eye.

donor milk   Human milk from a human milk bank, in which the milk is pasteurized and the volunteer donor mother is screened.

doula   An individual who surrounds, interacts with, and aids the mother at any time within the period that includes pregnancy, birth, and lactation.

Durable Medical Equipment or **DME**   Equipment that is appropriate for home use and is manufactured mainly to treat the injured or ill.

emollient   A soothing agent or medicine. Breast milk contains milk fats and proteins that act as emollients when applied to the breast.

engorgement   A moderate to severe swelling and distention of the breasts in the early days of lactation. It is pathologic, not physiologic, in nature.

EOB   An explanation of benefits.

fenugreek   An herbal galactogogue. It is a substance capable of stimulating the production of milk. It can be consumed in the form of a tea, a capsule, or a tincture.

foremilk   The first milk obtained at the start of suckling or the onset of milk expression. It contains less fat than hind milk.

frenulum   The thick band of tissue that attaches the tongue to the floor of the mouth. Tongue-tie refers to a short or very tight frenulum that restricts the thrust of the tongue beyond the gum.

full time   A 40-hour workweek of employment.

galactagogue   A material or action that stimulates the production of milk within the breast.

hind milk   The milk released from the breast near the end of a breastfeeding. The fat content may be two to three times the concentration found in foremilk and helps to satisfy the appetite.

hormone   A substance, secreted by certain glands, which passes into the blood and stimulates the action of various organs.

human milk bank   A service that screens and processes donated human milk. Physicians prescribe donor milk for recipients, usually infants.

immunization   The introduction of a viral strain or substance into the body that stimulates it to form antibodies.

immunoglobulins   Proteins produced by the body and passed from mother to baby during pregnancy. The five types are IgA, IgD, IgE, IgG, and IgM. IgA is the primary immunoglobulin in colostrum and breast milk.

imprint   To fix or impress permanently, as on the mind.

induce   To produce or cause something to happen or to begin.

induced lactation   The process by which a nonpregnant mother is stimulated to lactate.

inpatient   An assignment of patient status for hospitalized persons who are recipients of bed and room service.

inverted nipple   A nipple that folds completely inward within the breast tissue.

irritation   Heat and redness in the skin caused by friction.

jaundice   A yellowish skin color in newborns caused by the breakdown of excess red blood cells. A yellow color appears on the skin because a newborn's liver cannot process the bilirubin very quickly.

job-share   The sharing of a job or position between at least two people.

lactation   The time period during which a mother secretes milk from her breast for her infant.

lactose   The predominant carbohydrate in breast milk. It is the combination of glucose and galactose.

lascivious   Loose or lustful.

latch-on   The act of fastening on to something securely.

legislation   The act of making or enacting laws.

letdown   The milk-ejection reflex, or MER.

lewd   Obscene or indecent.

ligaments   Strong, fibrous tissue bands connecting the bones of the body. Coopers' ligaments are triangularly-shaped ligaments that lie under the breast tissue.

lipase   An enzyme that breaks down fat.

lymph   A watery, alkaline fluid contained in the tissues and the organs of the body.

mamma   A child's name for mother. It also means milk-secreting gland.

mammae   The Latin term for breasts meaning milk-secreting organs.

mastitis   An infection in the breast tissue that produces tenderness, redness, and heat. It also produces flu-like symptoms of fever and muscle weakness.

mature milk   Breast milk commonly produced in the second or third week of breastfeeding. It contains little or no colostrum and contains high amounts of lactose, fat, and vitamins.

mechanical   Produced or operated by machine. Mechanical expression means expressing or removing breast milk using a breast pump.

meconium   A newborn baby's first bowel movement, a thick greenish-black substance.

medically necessary   Appropriate and necessary for the symptoms, the diagnosis, or the direct care and treatment of a medical condition.

MER   Milk-ejection reflex. It's also called letdown because of the release of milk.

milk fever   A syndrome of fever, muscular weakness, and pain associated with engorgement of the breasts or sudden cessation of breastfeeding.

milk sinuses   Small reservoirs in the milk ducts that lie under the areola of the breast.

milk's in   Refers to the feeling that a mother gets when the quantity of her milk has increased following delivery.

Montgomery glands   Small oil glands in the areola of the breast. They become more prominent during pregnancy. They secrete a fluid that lubricates the nipple, and may number between 20 and 24.

necrotizing enterocolitis or **NEC**   An inflammation of the intestinal tract that may cause the tissue to die. Premature infants are at great risk for this disease if they do not ingest human milk.

nipple   A pigmented protuberance of the breast containing 10 to 20 nipple pores through which breast milk flows.

nutritive suckling   A breastfeeding that is nourishing or promotes growth.

outpatient   An assignment of patient status for persons cared for in a clinic, a room, or an area of the hospital where the stay is quite brief.

oxytocin   A hormone secreted by your brain that stimulates the release of breast milk.

palate   The roof of the mouth. The hard palate lies at the front of the mouth behind the gum line. The soft palate lies behind the hard palate and extends to the throat.

pasteurization   The process of heating milk to destroy organisms and substances that produce illness.

phytochemicals   Chemicals derived from a plant source.

premature infant   A baby born before 37 weeks gestational age, regardless of its birth weight.

prolactin   A hormone that stimulates the mammary gland to produce and secrete milk. The term describes its action, meaning to support or stimulate lactation.

puberty   The earliest age at which an individual is capable of reproduction.

reflex   The automatic action of the motor nerves under a stimulus from the sensory nerves.

relactation   The process of stimulating milk production in a woman who did not initially breastfeed after birth. It can also apply to resuming lactation after it has been discontinued.

rooming in   Keeping a baby in the room at all times while in a hospital or birth center.

rudimentary   Not fully developed.

SMB   An acronym for Sister Maja's Broestpump.

Special Supplemental Nutrition Program for Women, Infants, and Children
A popular government-subsidized program known as WIC. It was established in 1974 and is administered by the Food and Nutrition Service of the United States Department of Agriculture.

suckling   The act of pulling milk from the mother's breast using the lips, jaws, and tongue.

Sudden Infant Death Syndrome or **SIDS**   Also known as crib death, it is the sudden, unexplained death of a baby that happens while the baby is napping or sleeping.

supplement   To fill in, add to, or supply when a deficiency is present. Baby formula is an example of a nutritional supplement.

supply and demand   A term used for breast milk production where the more milk that is emptied from the breast, the more milk the breast supplies.

support   To bear the weight of, to sustain, to encourage, to advocate or maintain.

third-party administrator   The person or group licensed to perform policy administrative services and pay claims on behalf of an insurance company.

trauma   A wound or bodily injury with a lasting effect caused by a violent force or severe pressure.

wean   To gradually take away, to detach, or to alienate from an activity. Weaning from the breast means that the sole nutrition of breast milk is replaced with a supplemental food.

wet nurse   A woman hired to suckle one or several infants with her breast milk.

Further Readings

Duke, James A. *The Green Pharmacy.* Emmaus, Pennsylvania: Rodale Press, 1997.

Frantz, Kittie. *Breastfeeding Product Guide.* Sunland, California: Geddes Productions, 1994.

Huggins, Kathleen, and Linda Ziedrich. *The Nursing Mother's Guide to Weaning.* Boston: The Harvard Common Press, 1994.

Lawrence, Ruth A., and Robert M. Lawrence. *Breastfeeding: A Guide for the Medical Profession, Fifth Edition.* St. Louis: Mosby, Inc., 1999.

Riordan, Jan, and Kathleen G. Auerbach. *Breastfeeding and Human Lactation, Second Edition.* Boston: Jones and Bartlett Publishers, Inc., 1998.

Stuart-Macadam, Patricia, and Katherine A. Dettwyler. *Breastfeeding: Biocultural Perspectives.* Hawthorne, New York: Walter de Gruyter, Inc., 1995.

Yalom, Marilyn. *A History of the Breast.* New York: Alfred A. Knopf, Inc., 1997.

Resources

Agencies and Organizations

You may find useful breastfeeding information and support from these agencies and organizations.

American Academy of Pediatrics
141 Northwest Point Boulevard
Elk Grove Village, IL 60009-0927
1-800-433-9016
www.aap.org

Baby-Friendly USA
8 Jan Sebastian Way #22
Sandwich, MA 02563
508-888-8044

Best Start Social Marketing
3500 E Fletcher Avenue, #519
Tampa, FL 33613
813-971-2119
www.beststartinc.org

**Consumer Product Safety
Commission**
1-800-638-2772
www.cpsc.gov

Depression After Delivery, Inc.
P.O. Box 1282
Morrisville, PA 19067
1-800-944-4773
www.behavenet.com/dadinc

Doulas of North America
13513 N Grove Drive
Alpine, UT 84004
801-756-7331
www.dona.com

Health Canada
Ottawa, ON K1A 0K9
613-954-5995
www.hc-sc.gc.ca

**Healthy Mothers, Healthy Babies
Coalition**
121 N Washington Street, #300
Alexandria, VA 22314
703-836-6110
www.hmhb.org

Human Milk Banking Association of North America
1719 E 19th Avenue
Denver, CO 80218
303-869-1888

INFACT Canada
6 Trinity Square
Toronto, ON M5G 1B1
416-595-9819
www.infactcanada.ca

International Lactation Consultant Association
4101 Lake Boone Trail #201
Raleigh, NC 27607
919-787-5181
www.ilca.org

La Leche League
1400 N Meacham Road
Schaumburg, IL 60173
1-800-LA-LECHE
www.lalecheleague.org

Mothers of SuperTwins
P.O. Box 951
Brentwood, NY 11717
631-859-1110
www.mostonline.org

National Organization of Mothers of Twins Clubs
P.O. Box 23188
Albuquerque, NM 87192
1-800-234-2276
www.nomotc.org

Nursing Mothers Counsel
P.O. Box 5063
Palo Alto, CA 94303
650-599-3669
www.nursingmothers.org

Women, Infants, and Children (WIC)
www.nal.usda.gov/fncs

Manufacturers

The following manufacturers can help you locate a reseller of their breast pumps, breastfeeding products, and apparel.

Ameda
2000 Hollister Drive
Libertyville, IL 60048
1-800-323-4060
www.hollister.com

Quality, comfortable, and effective breastfeeding products.

Avent America, Incorporated
475 Supreme Drive
Bensenville, IL 60106
1-800-542-8368
www.aventamerica.com

Manual breast pump and infant feeding accessories.

Bravado! Designs, Incorporated
1159 Dundas Street East, #140
Toronto, ON M4M 3N9
1-800-590-7802
www.bravadodesigns.com

Fashionable nursing bras with comfort and style, maternity underwear and breast pads.

Care Wear
2902-A Colorado Avenue
Santa Monica, CA 90404
1-800-793-2229

Nursing apparel.

Fancee Free Manufacturing Company Incorporated
6609 Olive Boulevard
St. Louis, MO 63130
1-800-325-5088

Nursing bras ranging from 32A to 50J. Best support bra on the market for larger sizes.

C. J. Grenier, Limited
4835 Colonial Avenue
Montreal, QC H2T 1W4
1-800-561-2502
www.cjgrenier.com

Fashionable maternity and nursing bras.

Hollister Incorporated
2000 Hollister Drive
Libertyville, IL 60048
1-800-323-4060
www.hollister.com

Quality breast pumps and breastfeeding accessories.

Japanese Weekend
222 Dore Street
San Francisco, CA 94103
1-800-808-0555
www.japaneseweekend.com

Contemporary nursing apparel.

Lact-Aid International, Inc.
P.O. Box 1066
Athens, TN 37371
423-744-9090
www.lact-aid.com

Supplementation feeding device.

Lansinoh Laboratories
333 North Fairfax #400
Alexandria, VA 22314
1-800-292-4794
www.lansinoh.com

Ultra-purified lanolin.

Leading Lady Companies
24050 Commerce Park
Beachwood, OH 44121
1-800-321-4804
www.leadinglady.com

Nursing bras and sleepwear.

Martek Biosciences Corporation
6480 Dobbin Road
Columbia, MD 21045
1-800-522-5512
www.martekbio.com

DHA supplement for pregnancy and lactation.

Laura's Closet, Incorporated
1602 Buckingham Road
Stoughton, WI 53589
1-888-766-0303
www.laurascloset.com

Fabulous nursingwear for all occasions.

Medela Incorporated
1101 Corporate Drive
McHenry, IL 60050
1-800-435-8316
www.medela.com

Quality breast pumps, nursing bras, supplementation devices, and breast-feeding accessories.

Parenting Concepts
P.O. Box 1437
Lake Arrowhead, CA 92352
1-800-727-3683
www.parentingconcepts.com

Baby slings and parenting things.

Information and E-Commerce

Breastfeeding.com
www.breastfeeding.com

The number-one Web site for breast-feeding information, support, and attitude!

Mommies & Poppies
www.mommies-poppies.com

Your complete breastfeeding resource with breast pumps, nursing bras, baby slings, and accessories at discounted prices!

Promotion of Mother's Milk, Inc.
www.ProMoM.org

A nonprofit organization striving for public awareness and acceptance of breastfeeding.

Index

F

R